COLONIAL AUSTRALIA BEFORE 1850

Brian Fletcher

PhD, MA, DipEd,
University of Sydney

NELSON

To Stephen, Martin, Geoffrey,
Nigel and Angela

First published in Australia 1976
Reprinted 1977, 1980, 1981, 1983, 1986, 1989 (twice)

Thomas Nelson Australia
480 La Trobe Street
Melbourne Victoria 3000
and in Sydney, Brisbane and Adelaide

Associate companies in London, Toronto and California

ISBN 0 17 004986 8

Printed in Singapore by Kyodo-Shing Loong Industries Pte. Ltd.

Foreword

The purpose of this book is to survey the principal features of Australian history before the mid-nineteenth century. New South Wales as the oldest, largest and most important colony necessarily occupies substantial space, but the focus is on the continent as a whole and attention has been paid to the other settlements. Within this framework an attempt has been made to analyse the formative influences operating at various stages and to examine the main trends of development in political, economic and social life. Parts of the book are based on primary research and throughout use has been made of recent writings published as well as unpublished.

My thanks are due to Dr H. King, Dr J. Waldersee and my wife, each of whom read and made valuable comments on my manuscript.

Brian Fletcher
University of Sydney

Contents

vii

Illustrations

Tables

Acknowledgements

Grateful acknowledgement for permission to reproduce the following illustrations is made to: the Mitchell Library, Sydney, for 'Black-eyed Sue and Sweet Poll of Plymouth', 'A View of Sydney on Norfolk Island', 'South West View of Hobart Town, Van Diemen's Land', 'Bay Whaling', 'A Government Gaol Gang', 'Samuel Terry, the Wealthy Convict', 'Emigrants at Dinner', and 'The Squatter's First Home'; the National Library for 'Victoria Square, Port Essington'; the British Museum for 'The Flourishing State of the Swan River Thing'; the La Trobe Collection, State Library of Victoria, for 'Collins Street, Melbourne', 'The Kapunda Copper Mine' and 'Klemzig'; and to the Dixson Galleries, Sydney, for Watling's 'A Direct North View of Sydney Cove'. The maps showing advantages of Northern Australian settlement and the squatting districts of New South Wales are taken from *British Parliamentary Papers, Papers Relating to Australia* (Irish University Press, 1969), Vol. 9, p. 605 and Vol. 7, p. 412, respectively. Our thanks to Henry Ross, cartographer, for the maps of Australia and the voyages of exploration.

one: **Discovery**

The Aboriginals and Prehistory

The first Australian settlers were not the convicts and their gaolers who were transported to Botany Bay in 1788 but the Aboriginals who had arrived possibly as much as 50 000 years earlier. The land to which they came was different to the one later occupied by the whites. Changes in the world's climate arising from the Ice Age had altered the rainfall belts, bringing water to parts of Australia that are currently desert and vegetation where little now exists. The interior, far from being barren, contained rivers and lakes together with palm groves and grassy plains on which grazed large creatures resembling the kangaroo, the wombat and the emu. Besides influencing the flora and fauna the Ice Age also affected the oceans, freezing vast quantities of water in great ice sheets and reducing sea levels by some 75 metres. Land which is now submerged was exposed. Northern Australia was joined to Papua New Guinea and the whole continent was linked to Asia by islands interspersed with only short stretches of water. In the south Bass Strait was non-existent, Tasmania and Kangaroo Island forming part of the mainland.

The absence of sea barriers helps explain how the Aboriginals who possessed only primitive boats were able to reach Australia. They appear to have come from south-east Asia in three successive groups. Although some anthropologists believe it impossible to say why they migrated, others consider that they were driven out of their homelands by an influx of people fleeing the severe cold that spread from the north. The first to arrive were the Negritos, a

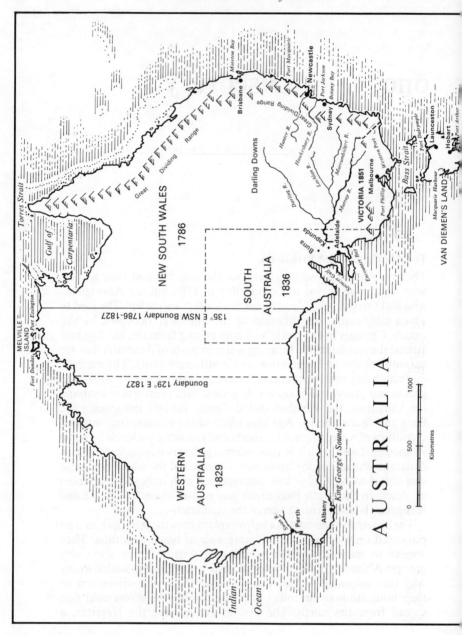

pygmy people with dark skins, curly hair and broad noses. They were mostly killed, absorbed, or driven south by the second wave of migrants, the Murrayians, who were related to the Ainu of Japan. The third group, the Carpentarians, whose racial links were with the Vedda of Japan and the hill people of Deccan and Malaya, settled exclusively in tropical regions.

Following their arrival and the passing of the Ice Age the climate became warmer, the rainfall belts receded and the interior of Australia turned into desert, or semi-desert. The huge creatures which had once found a home there gradually died out, although the fact that they also became extinct in the wetter conditions of Tasmania suggests that the coming of man, as well as climatic changes, helped to kill them off. Some 8 000 years ago Papua New Guinea was separated from Australia, and the island chain which had previously formed the bridge with Asia was submerged. About 3 000 years earlier Tasmania had become an island. According to some authorities the Negritos had already moved into this region and were now able to survive in safety. Another possibility is that the native inhabitants of Tasmania were descended from the original Negroids of Melanesia and arrived by sea.

Australia was now less accessible and received no more migrants from Asia. Potential colonisers such as the Hindus, the Chinese and the Muslims, who moved across the mainland of Asia, established themselves no further south than Timor and Macassar. While the religious beliefs of the Hindus deterred them from making the sea voyages that might have brought them to Australia, the Muslims at first lacked the ships and naval skills needed for long voyages and by the time they had improved their techniques the Portuguese had supplanted them. The Chinese proved more venturesome and there has been speculation as to whether they reached Australia. Admittedly, the belief of one Chinese scholar that his countrymen landed in 592 BC and 553 BC to make astronomical observations appears far-fetched. Doubt has also been cast on an argument, based on the discovery of a Chinese statuette near Darwin, for a fifteenth-century visit. This statuette, a representation of Shou Lao, the God of Longevity, is now considered to be of more recent origin than was once thought. Yet despite the lack of precise evidence it remains possible that the Chinese did reach Australia. They were a sea-going people and traded in the east even before the Arabs and the Indians. They undertook voyages of exploration during the fifth century under the eunuch admiral Cheng Ho. Conceivably their vessels touched on the north-west coast of Australia. They were, however, at most temporary visitors who showed no inclination to settle. Much the same held true of voyagers from the Macassar region of the southern Celebes, for whose visits to the northern coast of Australia exists anthropological evidence. From late in the eighteenth century, and probably long before, such people sailed regularly to this region. They came, however, not with any intention of making it their home, but to obtain the trepang, or sea slug, much prized as a delicacy by the Chinese.

Although no other peoples settled in Australia after the arrival of the Carpentarians, therefore, the continent was almost certainly known to Asians long before the Europeans arrived. Quite apart from the Chinese and Macassarese, sailors from other parts of Malaya or Indonesia could have landed on the northern coast. The north-west monsoonal winds which were used by the trepangers could just as easily have brought others and the south-west trade winds could readily have taken them home. Documentary material is lacking, but it seems probable that Asian, rather than European, sailors deserve credit for having discovered Australia. Certainly this region was not isolated to the extent that historians once believed. Anthropological research, although still in its early stages, has already shown that the Arnhem Land natives must have had contact with the Macassarese who influenced their eating and drinking habits as well as their tools, implements and even their language.

Yet although the Aboriginals were exposed to cultural fertilisation by other races, nothing changed the simplicity of their life. Precisely how many Aboriginals inhabited Australia is uncertain. The most commonly accepted figure for the population on the mainland when the first fleet arrived is approximately 300 000, with another 1 200 in Van Diemen's Land. How widely the total had fluctuated over preceding centuries is impossible to say, but it is believed that the 1788 estimate had been exceeded in periods before climatic and natural conditions deteriorated. By quite an early stage the Aboriginals had spread themselves throughout the continent, congregating more heavily in well-watered than in dry regions. Approximately a third lived in what is now Queensland, while others settled along the Murray Valley, or occupied the coastal and river districts of New South Wales and Victoria. Communication was made difficult by the fact that they did not speak in a common tongue. Indeed it has been estimated that 500 languages were used at the beginning of white settlement, some of which differed greatly from others.

The highest unit of organisation was the tribe that contained almost any number of members from as few as thirty to as many as about 500. The tribe occupied a region to which it had a claim based on religious grounds and within this area possessed exclusive hunting rights. It was ruled by a group of elders who were the respected custodians of a complicated lore into whose mysteries the young men were gradually initiated from about the age of twelve. Tribal lore embodied a complex of beliefs about man and the world and was expressed in myths, legends and rituals such as the corroboree. Central to the whole system was the totem, a carving believed to have special powers that operated for the benefit of the tribe.

The tribe rarely assembled and the unit that had most meaning for the individual was the family, or more commonly a small group of families whose members lived and worked together. Work was shared by both sexes and, as was to be expected of a semi-nomadic people, consisted mainly of hunting, foraging and, if they lived near water, of fishing. The Aboriginals knew nothing of agriculture and their only domestic animal was the dingo which they had brought with them from Asia. They led a primitive wandering existence. Their huts were made of mud, branches or bark. They wore little, if any, clothing; their tools were few, simple and, like their other material possessions, easily transportable. Their way of life was not wholly static, but the limited changes which took place before 1788 were slow to occur.

Nonetheless, the achievements of the Aboriginals were considerable. They evolved both a spiritual life and simple but attractive forms of bark and cave painting through which they gave expression to their ideas and creative talents. Although unable to write, they developed a literature which was passed on verbally and which has been favourably compared to the tales and sagas of Europe and Asia. They also had their own music and songs which were accompanied by instruments such as the didgeridoo. Through skill and perseverance they attuned themselves to their surroundings and learned to survive in a land that gave little help to man. Yet although they effectively adapted themselves to their environment, they did little to change it. For the most part they lived upon what their host, the continent of Australia, could provide.

As was to be expected of a land equal in extent to the United States of America, natural conditions varied considerably. The mainland of Australia measured nearly 4 000 kilometres from the tip of Cape York peninsula to Wilson's Promontory and almost 3 200 kilometres across from east to west. Its northern parts were in the tropics, while its southern extremities were lashed by the icy

Antarctic winds. The regions most favoured by nature were mainly located along the coast stretching from the south-east corner of the mainland, then northward along the 'Great Divide'. This belt of highlands, mostly plateaux of between 300 and 600 metres in height, but including ranges of over 1 500 metres, extended the whole length of the continent. By breaking the flow of moisture-laden winds from the Pacific Ocean it precipitated rain along the eastern seaboard in quantities that ranged from monsoons in the north to more moderate falls further south. Vegetation changed with climate and landform, but in general was abundant enough to support a rich and varied fauna.

The highlands which benefited the coastal areas served the interior differently by cutting it off from rain-bearing winds. On the western slopes of what are now New South Wales and Victoria rainfall and temperature were moderate enough to make for dry but not impossible conditions. Life in these parts was more capricious than it was in the east. The rivers, liable to turn into raging torrents in the wet season, became little more than a series of water holes during the hot summers. Good rains could bring abundant wild life and vegetation; drought produced misery. Further west still, stretching from the Darling River to the coast lay an arid and semi-arid zone, most of which had an average annual rainfall of less than 130 millimetres. Here little grew except salt-bush, spinifex and mulga and only the most primitive forms of animal life could be found. At the southern extremities of the west coast equable temperatures and good rainfall produced conditions as favourable as those in the east, but further north the situation deteriorated. Along the north coast itself monsoonal rains brought heavy falls which were quickly over; for the most part conditions were hot, dry and uncomfortable.

Australia, therefore, appeared to have little that might recommend it to would-be colonisers. The most arid of the world's continents, more than half of its total area was desert or semi-desert and part of the rest was barely able to sustain man. It contained an interesting range of vegetation and animal life, but none likely to attract settlers. Nor did its Aboriginal inhabitants possess the qualities, resources and skills that could compensate for the deficiencies in the environment. They led a marginal existence which by the arrival of the first Europeans had taken them barely beyond the attainments of Stone Age man. Asian sailors who touched on the north coast of Australia must have found the Aboriginals a poor advertisement for life there. The stories of impoverished natives and a barren coast which they took back to their homelands may well provide another reason for the failure of Asians to migrate to this region. Certainly the impressions formed by early European explorers helped postpone any idea of a white settlement for over two centuries.

Discovery

The European discovery of Australia was one of the consequences of a growing interest in the Pacific region that dates from the fifteenth century. Geographers of the ancient and mediaeval world had foretold the existence of an ocean in the southern hemisphere and had reasoned that, in order to keep the world in balance, a land mass roughly equal in extent to that of the northern hemisphere must be located there. Despite this speculation, and the belief fostered by the thirteenth-century writings of Marco Polo that south of Java lay a land of riches, no attempt was for long made to investigate the area. Many reasons have been adduced to explain this neglect. Europeans lacked ships, equipment and navigational aids of a kind to make long voyages possible. Their fears of monsters that supposedly inhabited the deep and their belief that no one could cross the equator, so intense was the heat, are supposed to have acted as further deterrents. All this was no doubt true. Yet fear did not prevent later explorers making expeditions into the unknown and there are no reasons for inferring that modern man had more courage than his ancestors. Moreover, many of the technical obstacles to exploration had been overcome by the thirteenth century. Essential navigational instruments such as the compass, the astrolabe and the quadrant had been invented for some 200 years before they were put into general use. What was lacking in the Middle Ages was the incentive to widen men's horizons by exploration overseas. Furthermore, the feudal state which prevailed in much of Europe was not equipped materially or psychologically for the effort involved. Imperial expansion had to await the emergence of the sovereign, independent state with its better mobilisation of resources.

Portugal, Spain, Holland, Britain and France contributed most to the opening of the Pacific, but the last four of these powers were in no position to initiate the process. By the fifteenth century the French and English monarchies had not consolidated their rule and their disunited kingdoms were ill-placed to engage in adventures overseas. England during the latter part of the century was engrossed in the Wars of the Roses and both countries were affected by the aftermath of the Hundred Years' War. Spain was divided into rival kingdoms until the marriage of Ferdinand and Isabella and thereafter a major preoccupation was the conquest of the Moorish kingdom of Granada, which was not completed until 1492. Holland did not exist as an independent nation, the northern provinces which later formed the Dutch republic occupying a subordinate position under the Spanish Hapsburgs. Portugal, in contrast, was a small but centralised and strongly governed kingdom, strategically placed at the south-western tip of Europe. Hemmed in on all sides by Spain, the Portuguese were cut off from involvement in Europe and could only look overseas for new opportunities and wealth.

It was not the desire for gain but hatred of the Muslims that first sent the Portuguese to fresh climes. Starting with the capture in 1415 of Ceuta, a Muslim city at the northern tip of Morocco, they embarked on a series of crusades. Initial inspiration was provided by the energetic King Henry the Navigator who enlisted talented seamen, encouraged ship building and promoted improvements in seamanship. His successors followed his example, providing consistent governmental direction and support, thereby enabling the Portuguese to maintain a lead over other powers. Although missionary zeal continued to influence their activities, economic and commercial considerations played a part. The lure of gold and slaves drew the Portuguese further down the west coast of Africa until in 1487 Bartholomew Diaz rounded the Cape of Good Hope opening the way to the Pacific Ocean.

Meanwhile, the Spanish Crown, having settled its more pressing domestic problems, had begun to heed its small neighbour's attainments. In rounding the Cape the Portuguese would be within reach of the sources of Asian spices. For centuries Muslim merchants had conveyed spices to Alexandria and Beirut, whence Venetian merchants had imported them into Europe. There they were eagerly purchased for use in the manufacture of medicines, drugs and perfumes, and to add flavour to food that would otherwise have been distasteful. The first European power to establish itself in the Indian Ocean could monopolise this lucrative trade. The Portuguese were approaching from the east, but there were those like Christopher Columbus who believed that a quicker route lay to the west. After failing to convince the Portuguese government, Columbus turned to the Spanish court and won the support of Queen Isabella for a venture that promised material gain.

Columbus returned from his voyage in 1493 convinced that he had accomplished his mission. In fact he had reached no further than America and it was not until 1519 that Magellan discovered a way by which the Spanish could sail into the Pacific Ocean around the tip of South America. By then the Portuguese had already defeated the Muslims and established trading posts at Calicut, present-day Kozhikode, on the Malabar coast of India, and in Malacca. Spain was, however, to benefit from her American possessions which provided riches as great as those acquired by the Portuguese. Moreover, Magellan in the course of his voyage discovered and claimed the Philippines which the Spanish settled in 1565. This, together with the fact that her American colonies bordered on the Pacific Ocean, made Spain a Pacific power.

By the early sixteenth century the ocean that washed the shores of Australia was known to Europeans. During the next hundred years no other power was in a position seriously to challenge the Spanish and the Portuguese each of whom, after a period of strife, kept mainly to their own spheres of influence. Nevertheless, some voyages were undertaken in an effort to find out more about the Pacific Ocean and in particular to locate the great land mass known as Terra Australis Incognita that was supposed by geographers to abound in riches. Spanish expeditions led by Mendaña and Quiros discovered the Solomon, the Marquesas and the New Hebrides islands. Quiros's pilot, Torres, sailed along the southern coast of Papua New Guinea after passing through the straits that now bear his name. There are, however, no grounds for believing that he sighted Australia.

But what of the Portuguese whose bases to the north of Australia in the East Indies placed them within striking distance of Australia? Whether this continent was known to Portuguese explorers is a question that historians have long debated. The evidence is inconclusive and considerable work remains to be done before there is any likelihood of the issue being resolved. Much of the present controversy has centred around a series of world maps produced in Northern France between 1540 and 1566. They depict a land mass whose coastline in parts resembles that of Australia and which, although not situated in the correct longitude, is located in the appropriate latitude. Varying sources have been suggested for these maps, but a strong body of opinion believes they were Portuguese. This being so, the question arises as to whether the portrayal of the land mass provides evidence for a Portuguese discovery of Australia. Some writers have answered in the negative, claiming that the land was a mere product of the cartographer's imagination. Others argue that it was a contrivance designed to mislead the Spaniards about that part of the Pacific Ocean. Recent researchers have exposed weaknesses in these arguments and have produced further evidence to support a Portuguese discovery. In 1522 a voyage was made from India at the instigation of the Portuguese authorities by Christovao de Mendonca who could have sighted Australia. Again, in 1529 the Portuguese and Spaniards negotiated a treaty which defined their respective spheres of influence. The line of demarcation was contrived by the Portuguese in such a way as to conceal the area in which Australia west of Melbourne is located. Conceivably they were aware of the existence of land and were anxious to keep this information to themselves.

Such opinions rest on circumstantial evidence and must be viewed merely as hypotheses pointing the way to further enquiry. The one firm conclusion is that the question of which European power first discovered Australia, and when, is more open to doubt than was once supposed. Historians who dismissed claims made for the Portuguese and pronounced in favour of the Dutch appear to have been too hasty in their judgements. The issue, fascinating though it may be, is largely academic. Even if it is eventually resolved in favour of the Portuguese, the fact remains that they themselves did not capitalise upon their finds and their maps gave no guidance to later explorers as to the whereabouts of Australia. The Dutch who are positively known to have sighted this continent did not do so because the Portuguese had shown them where to look. Indeed, they stumbled across it by accident.

By the close of the sixteenth century the Spanish and Portuguese had been joined by other imperially minded powers. The riches of the Americas and the East Indies had attracted France, Britain and Holland. Each of these powers was in process of overcoming the internal obstacles that had stood in the way of overseas expansion. Their activities eventually enabled north-western Europe to supplant the Iberian Peninsula as the main centre of imperialism. Of the three countries the achievements of Britain and Holland were the most noteworthy. The former entered the colonial scene after her Tudor monarchs had replaced instability and dissension by firm and effective rule; the latter after revolting against Hapsburg domination and breaking away from the rest of the Netherlands. Britain and Holland had much in common. Both abandoned the Roman Catholic faith during the Reformation and embraced differing forms of protestantism. Both had an enemy in Spain, the leading Catholic power in Europe and the main driving force behind the Counter-Reformation. Both were small maritime powers and increasingly looked to trade as a source of wealth. Neither had any pretensions to expansion in Europe and were able to avoid the continental involvements which kept the French away from imperial expansion until later.

At first the Portuguese and the Spaniards were too strongly entrenched for others to encroach upon their colonial possessions. In the long run, however, it was impossible to preserve their lead in the face of competition from their more progressive and economically advanced rivals. Spain had too many European commitments and the impetus which the bullion flowing in from her American possessions gave to her backward economy was more than counterbalanced by the ensuing price and wage inflation. A decline set in after the sixteenth century reducing her ability to remain a leading power. As for the Portuguese, their empire was too extended for them to maintain a monopoly over it. To make matters worse, Portugal fell under Spanish rule between 1580 and 1640 and her possessions were attacked by those who, although not her opponents, were the enemies of Spain.

During the seventeenth century Britain and Holland took advantage of these weaknesses. For future Australians the most significant development was the Dutch acquisition of some Portuguese territories in the East Indies. At first the Dutch co-operated with the British and the two traded side by side. After winning their independence from Spain, however, the need for a British alliance disappeared and the Dutch turned against their partner. The Dutch East India Company, which had been formed in 1602, was wealthier than its English counterpart. It was backed by a trade-conscious government whose desire to promote its interests contrasted with the weak support which the Stuart monarchs gave to the English company. Possessing overwhelming strength in the East Indies, the Dutch, under the energetic Jan Pieterszoon Coen, forced the British to retire to India.

Thus was laid the basis for the commercial ascendancy of the Dutch during the seventeenth century. Their achievements, so remarkable for such a small power, resulted partly from the circumstances in which they found themselves after breaking with Spain and the rest of the Netherlands. Confined to a region poor in natural resources, their continued survival depended upon their success as bankers and traders. Unlike the Portuguese, who had come to the Indies partly to save souls and who had been satisfied with modest economic gain, the Dutch arrived in strength, fired less by religious zeal than by a thirst for profit. Not content with the former Portuguese possessions they searched far and wide for riches. More determined and better organised than their predecessors they penetrated further and gained a wider knowledge of the Pacific region.

Amongst the territories to attract the Dutch was West New Guinea which had earlier been sighted by the Spanish and which was rumoured to contain gold. Given their interest in this island it was inevitable that eventually they would encounter the north coast of Australia. This first happened in 1606 when Captain William Janszoon, commander of the *Duyfkin*, entered the Gulf of Carpentaria and reached the west coast of Queensland without realising that it was a new land. Later expeditions repaired this oversight and gradually extended knowledge of the northern coast. The west coast of Australia had been discovered in 1616 by Dirk Hartog whose ship, the *Eendracht,* overshot the mark when following a new and quicker course from Holland to Batavia which involved sailing due east for 6 500 kilometres from the Cape of Good Hope then turning north. Once located, the coast was explored by other Dutch skippers *en route* for their base in Java.

These discoveries raised more questions than they answered. The Dutch authorities were intrigued about the land that their sailors had encountered and anxious to determine whether it formed part of the great south land. If not, then was this territory situated elsewhere? It was partly to answer these questions that the services of Abel Tasman were enlisted. Accompanied by his famous pilot and planner, Frans Visscher, Tasman set out from Batavia in August 1642 on an expedition that was also designed to find a shorter route to the trouble-ridden Spanish South American colonies which the Dutch hoped to acquire. The path which Tasman followed took him south of Australia and on 24 November 1642 he encountered an unknown part which he named Van Diemen's Land after his patron, the governor general of the Dutch East Indies. Turning east he reached New Zealand which he explored before sailing to the point at which he became convinced that the west wind track to South America was navigable. He then returned to Batavia by the northern coast of Papua New Guinea. The authorities were not satisfied that he had found the quickest way to South America and in 1644 sent him on a second voyage to test the practicability of a passage along the northern Australian coast. He failed to enter Torres Strait and was obliged to return. The Dutch were not impressed with his achievements, particularly as he had failed to discover anything of commercial value. He was nevertheless an outstanding explorer who established that there

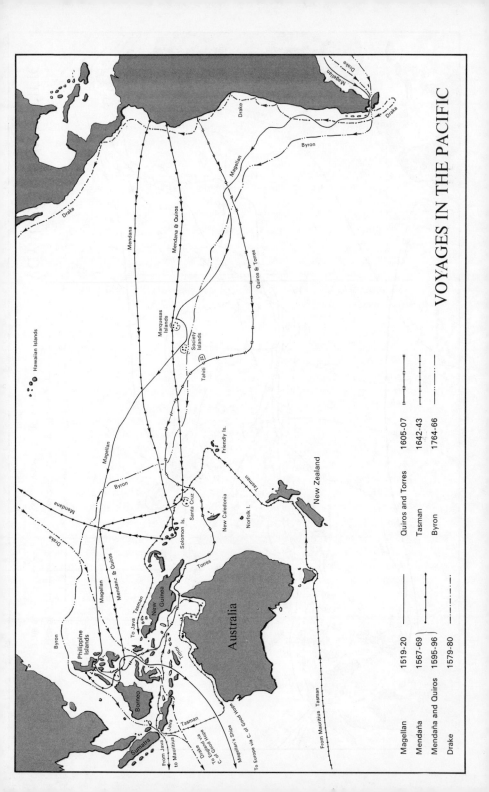

VOYAGES IN THE PACIFIC

Magellan	1519-20	Quiros and Torres	1605-07
Mendaña	1567-69	Tasman	1642-43
Mendaña and Quiros	1595-96	Byron	1764-66
Drake	1579-80		

Hawaiian Islands

Marquesas Islands

Society Islands

Tahiti

Solomon Is.

Santa Cruz

Friendly Is.

New Caledonia

Norfolk I.

New Zealand

Philippine Islands

Borneo

New Guinea

Timor

Torres

Australia

Sumatra

To Java

From Java to Mauritius

Drake via C. of Good Hope

Magellan's Ships To Europe via C. of Good Hope

From Mauritius Tasman

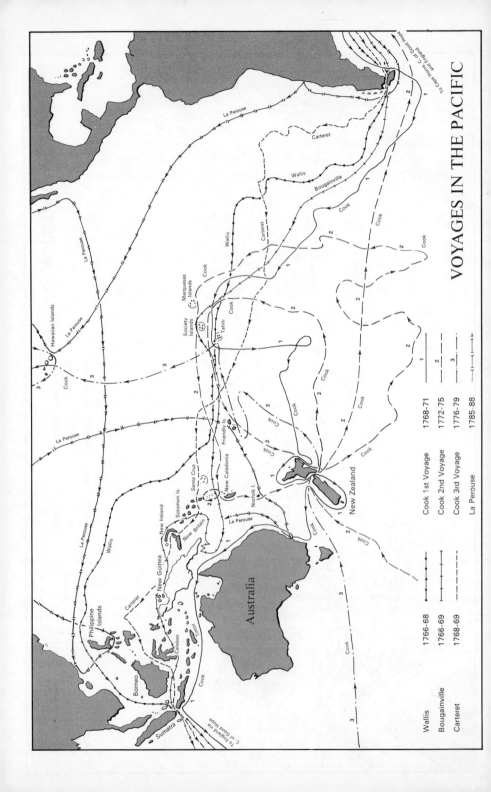

VOYAGES IN THE PACIFIC

was an unbroken coast between Torres Strait and the North West Cape. He charted more of the Australian coast than any previous navigator.

The second half of the seventeenth century saw no further expeditions to the Australian coast. After the initial surge of activity Dutch enterprise withered. They had failed to discover in the land which they had named New Holland anything to warrant further expenditure of energy. They were traders, not colonisers, and the Aboriginals whom they had encountered had no products of commercial value. Nor did the area itself possess any known potential:

> We have not seen one fruit bearing tree, nor anything that man could make use of; there are not mountains, or even hills ... this is the most arid and barren region that could be found anywhere on the earth; the inhabitants too, are the most wretched and poorest creatures I have seen.

This damning appraisal was written by Jan Carstens who visited the northern coast in 1623. Comments on the western coast were no more encouraging and even Tasman's observations, though less bleak, were scarcely of a kind to excite his countrymen.

Yet although nothing of worth had been discovered in New Holland much existed in the surrounding ocean to attract Europeans. Parts of this vast area had still not been traversed and the great south land had not been located. The possibility of riches in the Pacific region continued to lure explorers. Moreover, the seventeenth-century discoveries in mathematics, physics, chemistry and astronomy helped to lay the basis for modern science and a new spirit of enquiry. Educated man began to look afresh at his environment. Amongst the subjects to attract widespread attention was natural history. Botanists and sociologists such as the Swedish professor, Linnaeus, and the French nobleman, Count de Buffon, began the collections and publications that won them international fame. In England the formation of the Royal Society in 1660 reflected the growing preoccupation with natural science, the pursuit of which was one element underlying a heightened interest in the South Seas. Accounts of voyages of exploration were eagerly bought by a public that was fascinated by the native civilisations and by the new species of animal and plant life to be found in the strange world of the Pacific.

Pacific exploration in the eighteenth century had a new emphasis. It was motivated by scientific curiosity as well as the desire for commercial gain and attracted widespread public interest. Further-more, the lead passed to two powers which had not previously played a major role in the area. These were France which, under Louis XIV, dominated Europe and Britain which, by the end of the century, was already undergoing the industrial revolution that was to give her world ascendancy. Before 1763 the French and British were too often at war to pay much heed to the Pacific Ocean. Admittedly, in 1699 the former English buccaneer, William Dampier, who eleven years earlier had become the first Englishman to land on the north-west coast of Australia, sailed in the *Roebuck* on an expedition that would have resulted in the exploration of the east coast of Australia had his original plan been followed. For reasons that are still obscure he altered course and although he made discoveries among the islands near Papua New Guinea he added nothing to knowledge of the mainland. This was the only voyage of significance by either country during the first half of the century. Not until the conclusion of the Seven Years' War did they direct their energies systematically to the Pacific, smouldering enmity providing an additional reason for exploring it. France had lost influence in North America and in India and was anxious to compensate for this. Britain, despite her gains in both regions, was not prepared to allow her rival to obtain the upper hand in the Pacific. Accordingly, both governments took a keen hand in organising expeditions, regarding the matter too seriously for it to be left entirely to private initiative.

The outcome was a sustained burst of voyages that resulted in the Frenchmen, Bougainville, de Surville, and Kerguelen-Tremarec, and the Englishmen, Byron, Wallis, Carteret and Cook, solving within little more than a generation problems that had eluded an answer for over three centuries. By Cook's death in 1779 the main features of the Pacific were clearly established and the myth of the great south land laid to rest. Cook himself played a major part in bringing this about. His three expeditions exceeded in number and duration those of any other explorer and resulted in important discoveries among the Pacific islands. On the way home from his first journey of 1770–1, ostensibly to observe the transit of Venus, but actually designed to discover and annex the south land, he explored and charted the east coast of Australia. Subsequently he demonstrated conclusively that the great south land did not exist. His achievements, like those of his fellow explorers, were a product of courage, resourcefulness, brilliance and high qualities of leader-ship. But they were also made possible by advances in shipbuilding, diet and seamanship which in turn resulted from eighteenth-century developments in science. Of fundamental value was the invention of a satisfactory sea-going chronometer which could keep accurate time and make it possible to estimate longitude facilitating the task of navigation.

The Controversy over the Reasons for Settlement

By 1770, although many important features remained to be clarified, the broad outline of the Australian continent had been established. If its discovery formed part of the wider process of European expansion, its settlement was due exclusively to the British. This was to make it unique among the continents of the new world and does something to explain why its history was less turbulent than that of other parts. The Americas and Africa were to attract a number of European nations, each of which carved off pieces of territory upon whose residents they imposed their own language, religion and customs. The result was to create divisions within the confines of a single land mass. Since each colony served the interests of the mother country artificial borderlines were imposed to separate the colonies. On top of this, European rivalries spread to the colonies bringing war and sometimes changes of ownership. Australia experienced none of these complications. Of the powers that explored the Pacific, the Spanish, Portuguese and Dutch showed no interest in a region that promised neither trade nor strategic gain. The Frenchman de Brosses did urge his government in 1756 to establish an empire in the south seas and suggested that, although the coastal regions of New Holland were unfavourable to settlement, the interior might contain riches. Nothing came of this proposal nor of one which involved sending French colonists to the island of New Britain.

The response of the British government to the discovery of Australia was at first similar to that of other powers. Admittedly, Cook had taken possession of the east coast in the name of King George III, but this was in accordance with a standing instruction to captains to annex territories that might prove useful. His reports on the area, although favourable, contained nothing to make his superiors capitalise upon his efforts. Amongst pamphleteers there was some discussion of the uses to which the new territory might be put, but sixteen years were to elapse before any action was contemplated by the government.

More interest was shown by private individuals, two of whom made proposals for settlement. In 1779 the revolt of the American colonies forced the government to consider an alternative outlet for convicts sentenced to transportation. Amongst those called upon to give evidence before a House of Commons committee of enquiry was the naturalist Joseph Banks who had accompanied Cook on the *Endeavour*. Although averse to a free colony at Botany Bay, Banks observed that the region might suit felons who deserved to suffer hardship. His recommendation aroused no response from official circles and was dropped. The same fate met a plan for the colonisation of Botany Bay by American Loyalists whose support for the Crown during the American War of Independence resulted in their being victimised. This scheme was drawn up in 1783 by James Maria Matra, a former midshipman on the *Endeavour* and later British consul in Morocco. While sympathetic to the Loyalists the government was not prepared to bear the cost of shipping them to an uncertain future some 19 000 kilometres away. At the suggestion of the secretary of state, Lord Sydney, Matra modified his plan to allow for the transportation of convicts to Botany Bay, but the idea was quashed by the Admiralty which considered the settlement too distant and too costly.

By as late as 1785 there was still no indication that the British government would ever take up the option which Cook had opened for it in New South Wales. Events were to produce a change of attitude. During the war of 1775–83 with the American colonies, convicts who had previously been sent there were housed in hulks moored along the River Thames, in the expectation that after the war transportation would be resumed. The unexpected American victory and the colonists' refusal again to become a dumping ground for British outcasts destroyed these hopes. Penal reformers urged the construction of penitentiaries which would reform their criminal inmates and return them to society as respectable citizens. Parliament, however, refused to approve this scheme which it considered costly and uncertain. Existing gaols were intended for prisoners awaiting trial and were not equipped to house convicts who had already been sentenced. In the circumstances it was scarcely possible, without a great deal of additional expenditure, to solve the problem of overcrowding by housing the convicts in Britain. Nor was such a solution considered desirable. Banishment appealed to a governing class which, in the absence of a police force, looked to harsh punishments as a means of eradicating crime. Moreover, there was a strong possibility that convicts who were transported would remain overseas, thus permanently ridding Britain of its criminals. The problem, however, was to find a suitable outlet.

Several possibilities in Africa were considered. All were found unsuitable. Proposals for settlements in Britain's Canadian and West Indian possessions were likewise rejected. This left Botany Bay which had much in its favour. It was believed capable of supporting a gaol and was sufficiently far away to reduce the likelihood of expirees returning. Life was likely to be rigorous: those who were sent there would be suitably punished and others might be deterred from committing crimes. Finally, there were no free persons in the area who might object to the presence of felons.

By July 1786 the British government had decided to establish a settlement at Botany Bay. That penal considerations played an important part in persuading it to act can scarcely be disputed. The statements of those responsible for the decision and the remarks of other informed contemporaries indicate that Pitt's ministers viewed the convict problem seriously and that they saw the new colony as a means of relieving it. But did they have any other motives? This is a question upon which historians have long speculated. As far back as 1888 E.C.K. Gonner, a historian more noted for his work on agrarian than colonial history, suggested that the real reasons for the settlement of New South Wales were commercial and that it was intended to compensate Britain for the loss of her American possessions. More recently, K.M. Dallas, a Tasmanian economic historian, asserted that had the government been mainly interested in the disposal of convicts it would, on grounds of cost and convenience, have selected a more accessible site closer to home. He viewed the decision to despatch the first fleet from an imperial standpoint and argued that convicts were sent to provide the labour force in what was intended to be a naval station similar to those established at the Cape of Good Hope and elsewhere in the late eighteenth and early nineteenth centuries. The settlement was to be a centre for British interests engaged in the Canadian fur trade, in south sea whaling and in the Chinese and South American trade. The evidence for this viewpoint was only slight and historians were mostly unconvinced by Dallas who was justly criticised for paying insufficient heed to the important documentary material that supported the penal interpretation.

The controversy was reopened in 1966 by Geoffrey Blainey who gave it a fresh twist. In the opening part of his widely read book, *The Tyranny of Distance,* he expressed sympathy for Dallas's opinions, but parted company with that historian by arguing that New South Wales was designed to serve two purposes. First, it was intended to be an outlet for convicts and second it was to provide the flax and to a less extent the timber that was needed in England for the manufacture of canvas and the construction of Royal naval vessels. Blainey's views concerning the demand for flax as a motive for the settlement of New South Wales have, however, failed to withstand the criticism of historians such as G.C. Bolton and A.G.L. Shaw who have shown that alternative sources were available. Such writers consider it unlikely that the government would have founded a new colony to raise an article that could readily be obtained elsewhere.

A more persuasive variant of the flax theory was put forward by Alan Frost who argued that the government was anxious to obtain this commodity for use, not in Britain, but by naval squadrons stationed off Bombay and other British ports in India. The first fleet officers believed that it was part of their task to obtain flax and timber. The desire to secure supplies for use in India was uppermost in the mind of the distinguished naval officer and East India Company servant, Sir George Young, FRS, who had supported Matra's schemes and who made two proposals of his own in 1785 for the settlement first of Botany Bay, then of Norfolk Island. Frost admitted, however, that this and the other evidence which he carefully assembled was not entirely conclusive. It opened up strong probabilities but left some areas of doubt. Much the same was true of an article by H.T. Fry who claimed that an important motive behind the settlement of Port Jackson was the need for a naval post which could keep open one of the East India Company's routes to Canton in the event of conflict with France and Holland. In common with his predecessors Fry was able to point to considerations that *could* have influenced the government. What he lacked was the documentary material needed to prove that such factors actually were instrumental in persuading the authorities to act.

This last obstacle has recently been surmounted as a result of further investigations by Alan Frost who has uncovered a letter written by Lord Sydney, secretary of state for home and colonial affairs, to the East India Company on 15 September 1786. This document lends further weight to Frost's view that New South Wales was believed capable of supplying Indian ports with naval stores. More important, it points to an additional reason for settlement, namely the recognition that a base at Botany Bay would be well placed to help protect British interests in India from the French whose activities, as has long been recognised, aroused considerable anxiety. If Britain did not establish herself in eastern

Australia there was always the possibility that some other European power, particularly France, would do so. Such a move, Lord Sydney stressed, 'might be attended with infinite prejudice to the Company's affairs'.

It would appear, therefore, that strategic considerations did influence the decision to colonise Botany Bay. To admit this, however, is not to deny the importance of the convict motive. Lord Sydney's letter stressed this matter and the plans subsequently formulated for the settlement were directed mainly to ensuring that it functioned effectively as a gaol. Admittedly, the government tried to maximise the advantages of its new possession. Phillip was ordered to reserve all the timber that might be useful for naval purposes. Provision was also made for the settlement of time-expired convicts and free migrants on grants of land ranging from 30 acres for a single emancipist to about 120 acres for a married migrant. The inclusion of migrants in this scheme has been seen by the historian Brian Fitzpatrick as a means of providing employment for the increasing numbers who were being impoverished by the industrial revolution. In fact the government had no desire to encourage migration. It recognised, however, that free persons might wish to settle in the antipodes and was merely catering for them in advance. Once in the colony they could serve a useful purpose by raising food, setting an example to the convicts, providing employment and assisting in the running of the settlement. As with most other aspects of the government's plans the provision of grants for migrants was subordinated to those penal purposes which continued to determine the course of policy before 1821.

Colonisation of Norfolk Island and Van Diemen's Land

During this period Norfolk Island and Van Diemen's Land were also colonised. Even before leaving England, Governor Phillip had been instructed 'as soon as circumstances will admit of it, to send a small establishment ... [to Norfolk Island] to secure the same to us, and prevent it being occupied by the subjects of any other European power'. Some six weeks after arriving at Port Jackson he despatched Lieutenant Philip Gidley King and a party of twenty-one officers, marines and convicts to take possession of the island.

Apart from mentioning the desire to keep other powers out, the government made little attempt to explain the occupation of this region and its motives have remained in dispute. K.M. Dallas and Blainey have taken extreme positions, the one claiming that the island was intended as a naval and whaling base, the other that it was designed as a nursery for flax plants that were to be shipped to what he wrongly considered to be the subsidiary settlement on the mainland. Some interest was shown in flax, the existence of which had been reported upon by Captain Cook. This may have provided a reason for settlement, but there was no evidence of a clearly formulated policy to turn the island into a major centre for the industry. The Norfolk Island pine, another supposed attraction, has also been shown to figure less prominently than was once thought. On the other hand, a recent enquiry has suggested fresh motives for the government's action. Three weeks before the first fleet sailed there emerged the prospect of a parliamentary attack on the scheme for settling New South Wales. A penal colony at Botany Bay might be a threat to British shipping because convicts were bound to escape and become pirates. According to historian Ged Martin, by recommending a base at Norfolk Island the government hoped to nullify its critics' case. In fact the opposition made no move, but Pitt's administration recognised that the island might be used to house uncontrollable convicts from the mainland and persisted with its scheme.

No controversy has surrounded the government's motives in settling Van Diemen's Land. That this region was separated from the mainland was not positively known when the first fleet sailed for Botany Bay. As early as 1773, however, Captain Tobias Furneaux, commander of the *Adventure*, formed the impression that a strait might exist. Captain John Hunter reached a similar conclusion while on a voyage to Port Jackson from the Cape of Good Hope in 1789. So too did the Frenchman, d'Entrecasteaux, in 1793 and the master of the *Sydney Cove* which was wrecked on Preservation Island in 1796. The latter reported his belief to Governor Hunter who despatched Surgeon Bass, at first alone then in company with Lieutenant Matthew Flinders, to investigate. By 1799 the two explorers in their leaky, uncomfortable twenty-five ton colonial sloop, the *Norfolk*, had confirmed the existence of Bass Strait and circumnavigated Van Diemen's Land. Although their reports were favourable, Hunter showed no interest in settling the island. Ample resources were available on the mainland and there seemed no point in the governor adding unnecessarily to his responsibilities.

The discovery made by Bass and Flinders had greatly increased the importance both of Van Diemen's Land and of those regions which lay opposite. Bass Strait provided a shorter, safer and cheaper passage for ships sailing from the Indian Ocean to Port

Jackson and beyond. British merchants and whalers stood to benefit and so too did the mainlanders who had been brought substantially closer to the outside world. These advantages might be lost if the island fell into the hands of another power. Such an eventuality seemed to have arisen in 1802 when a French expedition led by the cartographer, Nicholas Baudin, arrived. His presence was approved by the British government which had recently signed the Peace of Amiens with Napoleon and which had received assurances that the mission was purely scientific. Governor King, however, grew suspicious after one of Baudin's officers, while on a visit to Sydney, mentioned the possibility of a French base being established at Storm Bay. There was no substance in this remark, but the governor was not prepared to take a chance and took possession of King Island where the French were anchored. In May 1803, after investigating several sites, he despatched Lieutenant John Bowen and a small party to the Derwent River where on 12 September they set up camp at Risdon Cove. King's intention was to prevent the French gaining possession of the eastern side of the island, but he also sought to provide a base for British sealers and whalers. Similar motives, as well as a desire to find a further outlet for convicts, prompted him in June 1803 to recommend the establishment of a settlement at Port Dalrymple on the mouth of the Tamar River on the northern side of the island. Colonel Paterson was given charge of the expedition, but his departure was delayed and it was not until 5 November 1804 that Port Dalrymple was settled.

Meanwhile, King's actions had been endorsed by his superiors who were equally conscious of the importance of Bass Strait. War had broken out again with France in 1803 and it was evident that Napoleon, who had used the interlude to advance his interests in Europe, was untrustworthy. Baudin might have been honest in his protestations, but there was no telling what actions his government might take. King had safeguarded the southern bounds of Bass Strait, but the northern shores were still unprotected. Accordingly, in April 1803 the experienced and trustworthy David Collins, former judge-advocate of New South Wales and author of the celebrated *Account of the English Colony in New South Wales*, was sent to occupy Port Phillip. The opportunity of becoming the founder of future Victoria was lost on Collins who, acting on the advice of his incompetent surveyor, G.P. Harris, declared Port Phillip unsuited to settlement. He persuaded his old friend and former colleague, Governor King, to appoint him as Lieutenant

Bowen's replacement at the River Derwent where he landed with his small band of troops and convicts on 15 February 1804. Shortly after, he moved the settlement from Risdon Cove to a site on the west side of the Derwent. Here was established Hobart Town which Collins named after the secretary of state to whom he had dedicated the second volume of his book and who had given him the opportunity for command.

Such were the circumstances underlying the establishment of the first settlements in Australia. The key to the whole sequence of events lay in the decision to found a colony at Port Jackson. But for its existence the government would scarcely have sent an expedition to Norfolk Island and would have had no reason to occupy Van Diemen's Land. New South Wales, for its part, had been chosen by the British not in order to extend the empire but for strategic and, above all, penal purposes. Few British colonies began their existence so inauspiciously.

two: **Settlement**

The Convict System

Between 1788 and 1821 New South Wales existed chiefly as an outlet for British convicts. Each year saw felons placed on board the transport vessels and sent on the long, uncomfortable and hazardous voyage to Botany Bay. During the war which lasted from 1793 until 1815 the flow of convicts was small. Men were needed at home to share in the struggle against France and ships could not be spared to transport them. After 1815 the compulsory exodus rose sharply as crime itself expanded in the unsettled conditions of post-war England. By 1821 some 27 658 men and women had been sent to Botany Bay, nearly half in the six years since 1815. The money spent by the British government on maintaining them and paying the salaries of troops and officials was essential to the colony's continued survival.

For over a generation the penal nature of the settlement was the central feature of its existence. The law courts, civil and criminal, were more arbitrary in their proceedings than were those of England and lacked provision for trial by jury. Government was necessarily autocratic in a community whose inhabitants had forfeited their rights as citizens for the duration of their sentences and who needed to be closely disciplined and controlled. Admittedly governors were accountable to the British government. London was, however, far away and the Colonial Office understaffed, overworked and, before 1812 when Earl Bathurst took control, subject to frequent changes of head. Nine different secretaries of state held office between 1788

25

and 1812, some for as little as a few months. Before 1801 they were responsible for home as well as colonial affairs. After that date the Colonial Office was amalgamated with the War Office which greatly increased the burdens of its staff. (See the table of secretaries and under-secretaries on page 190.) In these circumstances the small, insignificant settlement of New South Wales received only limited attention. Much was left to the men on the spot who, as a result, enjoyed considerable scope when exercising their powers.

Before 1821 the settlement was successively ruled by five governors. In addition, there were two periods when control passed to the officer in charge of the New South Wales Corps which had been especially recruited for service in the colony, and which arrived to replace the original marine garrison in 1791. The first era of military rule from December 1792 until September 1795 was a consequence of Governor Phillip's decision to seek medical

Black-eyed Sue and Sweet Poll of Plymouth. The Convicts' Farewell, engraving by Laurie & Whittle 1794, a caricature showing the break-up of criminal associations and harsh social conditions. Sue and Sweet Poll say farewell to their convict lovers. By 1821 almost 28 000 men and women had been sent to Botany Bay.

attention in England for a troublesome hernia. In his absence, which was intended to be temporary, the lieutenant-governor, Major Francis Grose, assumed control. An indulgent and easy-going man who was still suffering the effects of wounds received while fighting in the American War of Independence, he returned home sick in December 1794, leaving the colony under Colonel William Paterson, a brave soldier and competent naturalist and explorer but not a strong administrator. Like Grose he relied heavily on his fellow officers, particularly the young and enthusiastic John Macarthur who had been appointed to a key position in charge of public works. Meanwhile Phillip had resigned owing to continued ill-health and in September 1795 his replacement, Captain John Hunter, arrived after delays caused by the war. Civil authority was restored and the interregnum came to an end. Whereas the first period of rule by the New South Wales Corps was the accidental result of unforeseen circumstances, the second stemmed from the Rum Rebellion of 26 January 1808. Colonel George Johnston, who led the march on Government House which resulted in Bligh's overthrow, governed until the end of the year when his superior, Colonel Joseph Foveaux, arrived from leave in England. Foveaux in turn was replaced in January 1809 by Colonel Paterson, by then lieutenant-governor of the settlement at Launceston in Van Diemen's Land, who reluctantly and after delay returned to the mainland in response to an earlier request by Colonel Johnston.

The rulers of New South Wales did not generally come to power by such means. Normally the secretary of state with responsibility for colonial affairs followed the eighteenth-century practice of appointing whichever suitable nominee had supporters with the strongest claim to patronage. The first four governors were naval officers—a fact which reflected the longstanding involvement of the Admiralty with New South Wales. The advice of this department had been sought when the early plans for settlement were under consideration and it shared in the preparations for the despatch of the first and subsequent fleets. Given this, and the fact that anyone with experience of commanding a ship was likely to have developed the qualities needed to administer a distant and isolated outpost, it was not surprising that governors should at first have been chosen from captains of the Royal Navy. The first, Arthur Phillip, who had a record of distinguished service in the Portuguese and British fleets, was brought out of enforced retirement as a half-pay officer at the instance of his neighbour, George Rose, secretary to the Treasury and a confidante of the prime minister, William Pitt the younger.

Phillip's administrative abilities, resourcefulness, firmness and capacity for withstanding hardship ideally suited him to the task of founding a new colony. Although aloof and uncommunicative, he was a born leader whose inner reserves of character carried him over successive difficulties. Not so his successor, Captain John Hunter, who had accompanied the first fleet as commander of the *Sirius* and spent some time in the colony. He was selected on the recommendation of the commander in chief of the Channel Fleet, Lord Howe, whose judgement on this occasion was no better than it had been in 1787 when he had expressed misgivings about Phillip. Hunter who arrived in September 1795 was an able, experienced seaman whose devotion to duty and desire to please his superiors were amply demonstrated by his work in New South Wales. Already in his mid-fifties, he proved incapable of handling his younger and more active subordinates. He lacked Phillip's sure touch and was overshadowed both by the first governor and by his own replacement, Captain Philip Gidley King, another first fleet officer, who took command in September 1800. King had experience as lieutenant-governor of Norfolk Island and was highly regarded by Arthur Phillip, who had recommended him as his successor. In Admiralty circles he was viewed sceptically, but he found a patron in Sir Joseph Banks whose powerful influence could secure him only a temporary appointment. Not until he had served two years in the colony was he made permanent. Banks was also instrumental in obtaining the governorship for Captain William Bligh whose reputation had been clouded by the mutiny of his crew on the ship *Bounty*. Bligh ruled from 1806 to January 1808 and was the last of the naval rulers. His overthrow, coming as it did at the end of a long series of quarrels between garrison and governor, convinced the authorities that it was preferable to place in command of the colony men whose military background would help them to control whichever regiment was stationed there. The first to benefit from this change was Major-General Lachlan Macquarie, commander of the 73rd regiment, who ruled from 1810 until 1821.

Although governors enjoyed substantial executive and legislative authority, they were unable personally to handle all the details of administration. Even under Phillip, while the settlement was still small, the control of day-to-day affairs was beyond the capacity of one man. Accordingly, provision was made for the appointment of civil officials. A surveyor-general's department was established to handle the task of laying out townships, surveying roads and locating land grants. Surgeons were sent from England to man the hospitals and provide medical care for the convicts. Commissariat officials were despatched to assume responsibility for buying the provisions and clothing needed by those who were maintained by the Crown. A judge-advocate was appointed to preside over the judiciary and subsequently the office of chief justice was created. The men who staffed these and other lower positions, such as store-keepers, superintendents of convicts and overseers of public works, were of varied quality. Some, like David Collins, judge-advocate from 1788 to 1796, were public servants of great integrity. Others, such as Collins's successor, the drunken Richard Atkins, or commissariat officials like James Williamson and David Allan who engaged in 'clandestine commercial speculations', caused much trouble. Yet all in some measure helped place the colony on a secure footing. Without their assistance governors could scarcely have accomplished as much as they did.

The central problem facing successive governors was that of coping with the convicts. In the days when felons had been sent to the American colonies they had been carried by private contractors and upon arrival indentured to settlers. A different system was adopted in New South Wales. The convicts were shipped under contract on privately owned vessels, but the government watched over their wellbeing on the voyage and they became the responsibility of the governor upon arrival. In the absence of private settlers there was at first no alternative to this arrangement. Even after the arrival of private settlers the arrangement persisted because it functioned effectively and enabled the government to retain control over the convicts.

This was made the more necessary by the peculiar role that the government was obliged to play in the economy. No amenities were available when the first colonists arrived and since there was no private labour or capital all the initial spadework had to be performed under government auspices. Before land could be cultivated it had to be cleared of its native bush and tall timbers. Buildings had to be constructed to seat the governor and to house the civil officials, the military garrison and the convicts. Hospitals were needed for the sick and prisons for those who committed crimes after their arrival. Wharves had to be erected for the landing of supplies and storehouses for their safekeeping. Townships had to be laid out, streets and roads prepared so as to facilitate transport and communications. These were continuing and vital tasks whose existence made it essential for governors to have an adequate supply of convict labour at their disposal.

The government was also committed to producing food and raising livestock. All employees of the Crown, whether convict or free, received a weekly ration that included stipulated quantities of meat, flour, peas and groceries. The British authorities took steps to minimise costs where possible. Livestock and seed were despatched with the first and subsequent fleets and governors were at first instructed to employ on the land as many convicts as were required to produce enough food for those maintained by the Crown. This policy was modified after 1803, chiefly because it ran counter to the interests of private settlers whose number was by then considerable. Even before that date opposition from this section of the community and recurrent labour shortages had obliged governors to reduce the area sown. Under Phillip, after a false start in the poor soil of Farm Cove, just over 1 000 acres were planted, principally with wheat and maize, at Rose Hill and Toongabbie in the Parramatta district. Grose and Paterson, acting on the advice of officer farmers like John Macarthur, took much of this land out of production, claiming that government farming was inefficient. Although the gap was never repaired, most years saw some government land under crop. After 1815 Macquarie, who had at first ceased cultivation, was forced to revive government farming to provide employment for the influx of post-war convicts. By 1821 some 600 acres were cropped at Grose Farm, the site of the future University of Sydney, and at Emu Plains on the Nepean River where a variety of crops including tobacco was being grown.

Government stock raising had a less erratic history. There was pressure on governors to build up flocks and herds which were needed to supply meat for the convicts and breeding stock for settlers. After setbacks resulting from the loss of the first consignment of sheep and most of the cattle, gradual expansion occurred. Large areas of grazing land were set aside at Castle Hill and convict herdsmen were employed under supervision to tend the livestock. In addition, to the south-west of Sydney at the Cowpastures on the far side of the Nepean River there grazed untended a large herd of wild cattle, the progeny of those which had strayed in 1788. Discovered in 1795 they eluded all attempts at capture until 1819 by which time they numbered several thousand.

Although the British authorities took positive steps to ensure that the material wellbeing of the convicts was catered for, they showed less concern with other aspects of their existence. Admittedly, some attention was paid to the idea of reform. Governors were permitted to reward prisoners by remitting part of their sentences. Land grants were originally offered only to those of good character and in 1795 a new scheme was introduced under which exceptionally good convicts were entitled to additional acreages. Yet there was no carefully formulated programme aimed at turning convicts into useful citizens. The ideas of penal reformers like Jeremy Bentham had little impact on governmental agencies whose main anxiety was to solve the problem of crime in Britain as cheaply as possible. The deterrent, not the reformative, aspect was uppermost in ministers' minds.

None of the early governors had any specific qualifications for running a gaol. Nevertheless, they did their best to evolve a machinery which combined effective discipline with incentives to good behaviour. Discipline was enforced by a variety of punishments. Convicts found guilty of insolence, laziness, or disobedience might suffer loss of privileges or the lash. Those who broke the law could, in extreme cases and with the approval of the governor, be hanged. Others were sentenced to imprisonment in isolated places where they could not contaminate their fellows. In the very early days one of the small islands off Sydney Cove, then known as Pinchgut and later as Fort Denison, was used for the worst reprobates. After the discovery of the mouth of the Hunter River by fishermen in 1796 a new settlement was established at Newcastle and reserved exclusively for convicts who had committed felonies after reaching the colony. Those with the necessary skills were employed in coalmining, the rest in labouring duties at the township, or in cutting timber, making salt and burning the lime used at Newcastle and elsewhere by the building industry.

Good behaviour was encouraged by a gradation of rewards of which the most prized was an absolute pardon which restored a convict to freedom before his term had expired. Alternatively, governors might issue a conditional pardon which conferred similar rights provided the recipient remained in the colony until his original sentence had elapsed. Less meritorious cases were awarded a ticket of leave which, without affecting their status as convicts, allowed them to work for themselves until their sentences were completed. Of these concessions the second was the commonest particularly under Macquarie who between 1810 and 1820 issued 2 319 tickets of leave compared to 366 absolute and 1 365 conditional pardons.

These inducements and disciplinary measures operated for all convicts whether in government employment or not. It is important to recognise that, although substantial numbers of prisoners were kept in the public service, more were employed privately. From the outset the British authorities made provision for the allocation of convicts to private settlers who were prepared fully to maintain and clothe them. By this means the annual food and clothing bill was reduced and fewer staff were necessary. At first the government was obliged to monopolise the supply of convicts because they were needed to complete essential tasks. As the pioneering work was completed and additional convicts arrived it became possible to allot them to private employers who had also begun to appear on the scene.

The assignment system, as it became known, for long remained an important instrument of penal policy. It placed upon private persons much of the responsibility for disciplining and supporting the convicts. Assigned convicts lived with their masters and sometimes, as in the case of smaller employers, actually shared their houses. Wealthy settlers with large numbers of servants housed them in huts away from the homestead and worked them in gangs similar to those organised by the government. Employers exercised substantial power over their convict workers. They did not have the right to punish them arbitrarily but they were able to bring them before the magistrates who often treated them harshly.

Beginnings of Private Enterprise

Although inhabited mainly by convicts, therefore, New South Wales soon bore little resemblance to a conventional gaol. Its penal inmates, far from being confined within prison walls, lived mainly amongst townspeople or country-folk. A minority were housed at one of the government establishments at Sydney or Parramatta or in the outlying settlements. If a modern parallel is to be sought it is in the open prison or prison farm where convicts enjoy more freedom and make a greater contribution to society than is possible when they are kept in a walled institution. In New South Wales prisoners were even allowed to work for wages in their spare time and they received liquor and tobacco as a reward for special effort.

This softening of the rigours of prison life was less a consequence of the enlightenment of administrators than of the changing circumstances of the settlement. Private enterprise, already foreshadowed in plans drawn up by the government before the first fleet sailed, featured in the life of the colony from as early as 1789. At the end of that year James Ruse and a number of other convicts who had served most of their sentences before arriving received their freedom and were permitted to occupy small grants of land at Parramatta. Each year saw more convicts released from servitude. A small proportion were able to return home either because they had saved the passage money or because they possessed the skills which enabled them to secure berths as crew members of visiting ships. Most were unable to meet these requirements and remained in the colony. Some took advantage of the government's offer of land grants, but more became labourers. Others opened shops, established businesses, entered the professions or set themselves up as skilled tradesmen.

Free migrants were also attracted to the colony after 1793 when the first small, hesitant group stepped ashore from the *Bellona* which had brought them from England. How many arrived before 1821 is impossible to estimate because precise records were not kept. Certainly the flow fluctuated from year to year and remained slight until after 1815 when migration from Britain to the Empire increased. Even so, the number coming to New South Wales formed only a minute proportion of total departures from the United Kingdom. Other colonies were closer and were not tainted by the convict stigma. Yet despite social and geographical disadvantages New South Wales did have much to recommend it. Free land was readily available and in the first two decades the government sometimes paid passages in order to satisfy governors' requests for respectable citizens. Once it became apparent that the colony had an economic as well as a penal potential more and more people were drawn to it.

An informed guess would place the number of migrants by 1821 at around 1 250. Amongst them were men and women who had fallen on hard times and migrated in the hope of bettering themselves. Such people lacked means and so too did the Chelsea Pensioners who arrived after 1815 with only their War Office pensions to support them. By that stage the British authorities had for some time refused to contribute to passages and they also insisted that migrants should have at least £500 capital. Amongst the earliest capitalists to migrate to New South Wales was Gregory Blaxland who came in 1806 to raise sheep. He brought livestock, farming equipment and the sum of £6 000 from the sale of the family estates in Kent. Later he was joined by his brother John and the two men quickly established themselves amongst the leading pioneers of New South Wales. Thereafter, others arrived with increasing frequency bringing capital to invest in the land. They included Richard Brooks, a merchant and former captain of transport vessels, Dr Robert Townson, brother of an officer in the New South Wales Corps, William Campbell, a shipowner and island trader, and Andrew White, son of the first fleet surgeon.

Prominent among the free settlers were members of the civil and military staff. Their main purpose in coming to New South Wales was to perform official duties, but in many cases they established a stake in the community and contributed to its economic and social development. In the late eighteenth and early nineteenth centuries it was customary for officers to expect additional recompense for serving in distant parts. Many of those who volunteered for service in New South Wales did so in the hope of making money. John Macarthur and most of his fellow officers in the New South Wales Corps fell into this category, as did leading members of the civil staff. The British government encouraged their pretensions by giving them permission to own grants of land and engage in farming and grazing. This concession, which was made in 1793, was withdrawn some twenty years later because the officers were believed to have abused it. Nevertheless, for most of the period before 1821 they had the opportunity to acquire landed property.

TABLE 1
Expansion of Population, Agriculture, Sheep and Cattle
Raising in New South Wales to 1820

	Population	Acreage cultivated	Cattle	Sheep	Wool exported (lbs)
1788	933	36	7	29	—
1795	3 388	n.a.	176	832	—
1800	4 936	8 595	1 044	6 124	—
1805	6 900	13 612	4 325	20 617	—
1810	10 452	n.a.	11 267	32 818	167
1815	12 911	19 386	25 239	62 476	32 971
1820	23 939*	31 389	54 103	99 487	99 415

*The muster was wrongly taken in this year and this total is only an approximation.
Source: Historical Records of Australia, Series I, Vols 1–10.

Private settlers engaged principally in the production of grain and meat. These two articles formed the main ingredients of the colonists' diet. The commissariat which was unable to obtain more than a small proportion of its needs from the public farm made substantial purchases from private settlers. It paid between 6d and 1s per lb for meat, up to 10s a bushel for wheat and around 5s for maize. These transactions were much valued by settlers who were paid in Treasury Bills that were negotiable overseas. Free persons could either buy direct from the producer or go to the markets established at each of the principal townships. They bartered goods and services or paid in local currency that was valued below sterling. Whereas commissariat prices were fixed by the governor, on the open market prices depended on the relationship between supply and demand and fluctuated widely, ranging from a few shillings, or even pence in time of plenty, to several pounds when grain and meat were scarce.

By 1821 some half a million acres were owned by private settlers. Of this area 32 273 acres were under crop while the rest was used for running sheep, cattle, horses, goats and swine. Most of the arable land was cropped by the 2 000 or so ex-convict settlers who occupied grants ranging from less than five acres to about 100. Grazing, which required more land and capital, was principally in the hands of some 500 settlers most of whom had come free. Foremost amongst them were the Macarthurs, the Hassalls, the Blaxlands and the Johnstons. They included, however, a number of emancipists whose ability and energy exceeded that of most of their fellows. Samuel Terry amassed 19 000 acres between 1810 and 1821. Richard Fitzgerald, the Hawkesbury storekeeper and settler, acquired 2 442 acres and a number of others owned over 1 000 acres on which they ran large quantities of livestock.

All of the emancipist and most free graziers concentrated on producing meat for local consumption rather than wool for export. The potentialities of New South Wales for the production of fine wool suited to the needs of Yorkshire clothiers had been demonstrated as far back as 1801. Lieutenant John Macarthur, while in England to face charges arising from a duel with his commanding officer, had shown samples of his merino fleeces to Yorkshire clothiers. This wool, shorn from the progeny of merino rams that had been imported from the Cape of Good Hope in 1795 by Captain Waterhouse, was of sufficiently high quality to interest these manufacturers. Their supplies had been cut off by the French occupation of Spain where the merinos originated and they were anxious to find alternative sources. The result of their agitation and Macarthur's advocacy was the appointment of a committee to enquire into the suitability of New South Wales for wool production. The outcome of its deliberations and of governmental discussions which involved Sir Joseph Banks was the decision to grant 5 000 acres of pastoral land in New South Wales to Macarthur against whom charges had been dropped in default of evidence. This area was less than he had requested but it was an important first step and there was the promise of more to come if he succeeded. In June 1805 he returned to the colony accompanied by another prospective woolgrower, Walter Davidson, the nephew of Sir Walter Farquhar, physician to the Prince of Wales and Macarthur's patron. After some difficulties with Governor King who was suspicious of Macarthur, the two men were given grants at the Cowpastures. There, isolated from the rest of the settlers and protected from marauders by the Nepean River, they began their sheep breeding activities. They concentrated on pure merinos, but another leading settler, the Reverend Samuel Marsden, had succeeded in producing high quality wool from crossbred sheep. His activities continued to expand during the first decade of the nineteenth century and for a time his fleeces excelled those of Macarthur.

Colonial wool was eagerly sought in wartime England and prices remained high until after 1815 when, despite a drop, they were still remunerative. Few settlers, however, were prepared to devote time and energy to the slow and costly business of breeding sheep for wool. Meat was safer since it involved none of the risks entailed in sending fleeces on the long, uncertain voyage to London and then waiting months for payment. Nevertheless, the handful of dedicated graziers persisted and their number increased after 1811 when widespread publicity was given to the fact that a recent consignment of moderate quality wool had earned good returns. Marsden, Macarthur and the Blaxlands were joined by men like Hannibal Macarthur who came to the colony to capitalise on the start made by his uncle and William Lawson, a former officer of the New South Wales Corps and pioneer of the Bathurst district who claimed by 1822 to be the third largest breeder in the colony. Exports steadily rose and 175 433 lbs were sent to London in 1821. This was only a minute proportion of total British imports, but a toehold had been gained in the English market and promising possibilities had been opened up.

Meanwhile, enterprising colonists had also spearheaded other developments. New South Wales lay on the route for ships engaged in the China trade and the colony was also accessible to merchants from North America and India. American and British vessels began visiting Sydney as early as 1791 bringing with them merchandise for sale to the colonists. At first the only residents able to buy directly from merchantmen were the civil officials and the officers of the New South Wales Corps whose salaries were paid in sterling, the only currency acceptable to overseas interests. This advantage gave the officers a monopoly over the import trade. Several made substantial amounts of money by retailing goods to other sections of the community at considerable profit. It was not long, however, before others took part in this lucrative activity. The first to breach the monopolistic hold of the officers was Robert Campbell, a merchant whose parent company was in Calcutta. He set up business in Sydney as early as 1798 and undercut the officers by selling goods at lower rates and on more favourable terms. By the time he was established a number of emancipists were also engaging in the retail trade. Some had acquired capital through acting as paid agents for the officer traders with whom they now came to compete. Amongst them was Simeon Lord whose career serves to illustrate how much could be accomplished by an ex-convict with business acumen, enterprise and the ability to work hard. The son of a Yorkshire handloom weaver, Lord was sentenced at Manchester in 1790 for stealing 200 yards of cotton muslin and 100 yards of calico. He arrived at Sydney in August 1791 and was assigned to Lieutenant Rowley of the New South Wales Corps who placed him in charge of his retail business. By 1798 Lord had made enough money to set himself up as a trader and thereafter his activities extended to manufacturing and shipping. He was also employed for a time by the government as the public auctioneer. Other emancipist dealers included Isaac Nichols, Australia's first postmaster, James Larra, a Spanish Jew who ran a highly favoured hotel at Parramatta, Andrew Thompson, a leading figure at the Hawkesbury and a friend of Governor Macquarie, and Samuel Terry whose trading activities made him one of the richest men in the colony.

A further outlet for the energies of such entrepreneurs was provided by the sealing industry. Seals abounded on both sides of Bass Strait and their skins formed one of the colony's earliest exports to England. Sperm whales, whose oil was much prized, also existed in large numbers off the southern coast of Australia. Favourable reports on the prospects of the industry had been made as early as Phillip's day, but it was not until the Spanish had driven the British out of the more attractive South American waters that whalers turned to Australia. New South Wales interests did not play a direct part in the industry because it was impossible to obtain large enough ships locally and too costly to fit them out. Indirectly, however, the community benefited because whalers brought goods for sale and obtained supplies and even crew members from the colony.

The maritime activities of the colonists, which also included trade with near-by Pacific Islands, in turn gave a boost to shipbuilding, one of the earliest industries in New South Wales. The difficulties of land transport necessitated the construction of small packet boats to carry people and goods between Sydney and Parramatta and up the Hawkesbury River to Windsor. Seagoing vessels of a size restricted by law to prevent them infringing the rights of the East India Company were constructed in the yards of the emancipist Henry Kable.

Other industries were founded to meet the needs of the free population. Flour and sawmilling had a lengthy history. In 1812 John Dickson, an engineer, millwright and grazier, brought from England the colony's first steam engine which he used in his grain and timber mills at Sydney, thus giving local industry its first contact with one of the innovations of the industrial revolution. Hand methods of production prevailed in the other secondary industries. James Squire, an emancipist, ran a flourishing brewery at Kissing Point on the Parramatta River near present-day Ryde. Simeon Lord was involved in the manufacture of hats. Others produced pottery, made leather goods from local hides, wove cloth from coarse wool, or turned out bricks for the building industry.

These developments resulted mainly from the initiative of individual colonists. They were, however, made possible and sometimes promoted by governors all of whom favoured the growth of the private sector of the economy. Governor Phillip was forced to depend on public enterprise, but his immediate successors placed substantial numbers of settlers on the land and encouraged farmers and graziers. Governor King took steps to facilitate the spread of an improved system of husbandry modelled on the enlightened practices of the agrarian revolution. He also made a successful attempt to diversify the economy. A friend of Samuel Enderby, head of a major British whaling firm, King was instrumental in persuading the government to allow whaling vessels to bring goods for private sale. Hitherto they had been debarred by the East India Company, but the relaxation of its charter ensured that they no longer had to travel empty to the colony. This gave them a greater inducement to call at Sydney which served King's aim of furthering the development of whaling. King also permitted colonial interests to trade in sandalwood with Pacific islands and encouraged the cedar wood industry on the south coast. He capitalised on the discovery of coal at Newcastle by using convicts in the mines and exporting the products of their labour to the British settlement at the Cape of

Good Hope. The most constructive of the early governors, he has only recently received the recognition he deserves. His successor, William Bligh, did not hold office for long enough to build on these foundations, but he shared King's outlook and his own plans were made abortive by the unsettled conditions between 1808 and 1810.

Macquarie, in contrast, had more than a decade in which to implement his ideas. In common with earlier governors he showed little interest in wool and was sceptical of large pastoralists whose activities, he considered, did little to augment the productive resources of the colony. Nevertheless, he provided them with generous grants and gave substantial acreages to agriculturalists whom he regarded as the backbone of the community. All told he granted some 570 000 acres of Crown land, nearly three times as much as had been disposed of in the twenty years before 1810. Although he did not foster new industries he helped establish the conditions for existing ones to flourish. His extensive public works programme, which was made possible by a surplus of convict labour after 1815, included projects which benefited private interests. He constructed new roads, laid the foundation for new townships at Liverpool and in the Hawkesbury-Nepean districts at Windsor (formerly Green Hills), Richmond, Castlereagh, Pitt Town and Wilberforce. To improve credit facilities and give the currency a sounder footing he sanctioned the establishment of Australia's first bank, the Bank of New South Wales, in 1817.

The Rum Rebellion and Problems of Government

Early New South Wales, then, was by no means a static community. On the contrary it was the scene of bustling activity and enterprise. From insignificant beginnings on the foreshores of Port Jackson, settlement had expanded to encompass the whole of the Cumberland Plain, an area measuring thirty kilometres by sixty. In 1813 the Blue Mountains, which formed a barrier to the west, were crossed by three graziers, Gregory Blaxland, Lieutenant William Lawson, and William Charles Wentworth, who sought pasture for their stock which were starving on the drought-stricken Cumberland Plain. Two years later Macquarie established the township of Bathurst which was linked to the settled regions by a road constructed by William Cox, former New South Wales Corps paymaster and a leading Hawkesbury settler and government building contractor. By 1821 settlers had begun to move across the mountains, not only in a westerly direction, but also north to the Hunter River valley along the trail blazed in 1818 by John Howe, chief constable at the

Hawkesbury and a prominent grazier. To the south Illawarra was already settled by large pastoralists and in the south-west, towards Picton and Goulburn, Charles Throsby, the former Newcastle surgeon, and James and William Macarthur were opening land.

Accompanying this expansion were changes in the structure of the economy. Private enterprise supplanted the government in food production and the basis of the economy was widened as trade and commerce grew, as secondary industry commenced and as a small export trade in wool, sealskins and whale oil emerged. These developments stimulated the growth of Sydney which before 1800 had languished behind Parramatta whose position at the heart of a major farming district had given it temporary supremacy. By 1821, largely as a result of an upsurge in maritime activities, Sydney had been converted from a convict encampment to an attractive township of 12 079 people. It contained wharves and storehouses, a wide range of shops, some small manufactories and, on the high ground, a number of windmills which formed a distinctive feature of the skyline. To add to the beauties of its natural setting were the private gardens and orchards with every variety of fruit tree, the impressive residences of leading citizens and some well-designed public buildings. Amongst these was St James Church, one of several Georgian structures that stand as lasting monuments to Macquarie's vision and the genius of the convict architect Francis Greenway.

If economic life had changed, so too had society which had grown more complex since 1788 when it merely comprised convicts and their gaolers. At the apex was still the governor and his entourage of civil and military officers, while at the base were convicts under sentence. Between these extremes came wealthy merchants and landowners, a mixed group of small to middling property owners and a large number of mostly unskilled labourers. A line of division separated the community socially, though not economically, into those who had arrived free and those who had been transported. In the eyes of leading migrants and officials the ex-convicts were permanently tainted as a result of their once having broken the law. They had offended against the canons of society and could never fully be readmitted to it. For their part the emancipists resented being thus treated. They had paid their debt to society and the better off were no less wealthy than the leading officers and migrants.

The similarity between the wealthy emancipists and migrants was reflected in their style of living. Both owned well-furnished brick or stone houses, kept servants, rode thoroughbred horses, entertained, often on a lavish scale, and observed public events in the same fashion as was done in England. Occasionally there was an opportunity to attend the theatre. As early as 4 June 1789, on the king's birthday, George Farquhar's *The Recruiting Officer* was enacted by eleven convicts in 'a mud hut, fitted for the occasion'. In 1796 Robert Sidaway, an ex-convict, opened a theatre in present-day Bligh Street and on 16 January his manager, John Sparrow, presented Edward Young's *The Revenge*, followed by a farce *The Hotel*. Further plays were performed publicly in 1800 but thereafter the theatre faded for several decades. In the absence of a regular company or an orchestra the colonists were unable publicly to indulge a taste for drama or music. Private houses, however, contained libraries and musical instruments which enabled the more sophisticated to develop cultural interests.

Conditions for the remainder of the community varied widely. Better-off farmers, shopkeepers and traders built simple brick or stone houses and equipped them with locally manufactured furnishings and household articles. Many could afford one or more assigned convicts who assisted in the house or with the business or farm. The mass of the population, however, enjoyed none of these advantages. Life for labourers and small farmers alike was rough and precarious. Their houses were made of bark and bush timber with leaves from the cabbage-tree palm for a roof. Unlined, with no glass in the windows, they had the earth for a floor and contained only rough implements and furnishings. Their pleasures were those of lower-class English society and included gambling and heavy drinking.

Private citizens, no less than convicts, were subject to the control of governors who, in addition to their other duties, faced the difficult task of balancing conflicting interests within a society divided along lines of origin and wealth. Throughout its early history New South Wales contained powerful men who were prepared to exploit the less wealthy and more defenceless sections of the community. On several occasions before 1808 small settlers complained that they were overcharged for every article purchased from local retailers. One of the principal commodities involved was liquor. First sent to the colony by American merchants late in the Phillip period, it was brought thereafter in substantial quantities and sold by local retailers at substantial profits. Historians have tended to exaggerate the ill-consequences of a trade which increased productivity among convict labourers who worked harder for rum than for any other reward. The presence of spirits, however, undermined discipline and caused widespread drunkenness in addition to ruining the many settlers who mortgaged their crops or land to salve their thirst.

Governors regularly issued orders aimed at curbing these and other abuses. Attempts were made to prevent the importation of spirits and to check the illicit stills that operated in isolated localities. A government store was established in 1798 to force down the price of all imported merchandise. Steps were taken to prevent civil and military officers who were extensive retailers from continuing to engage in trade. These and other measures eventually helped alleviate the plight of the less well-off settlers, but at the cost of antagonising those against whom they were directed. The attempts of governors to enforce their orders involved them in conflict with civil and military officials. The latter thwarted the ineffective Hunter and eventually triumphed over his more active and energetic successor, King. The fourth governor, William Bligh, was made of sterner material. Some historians believe that one of the principal reasons for the Rum Rebellion was his success in thwarting the trading activities of the New South Wales Corps. On this interpretation his overthrow was an act of desperation by men who saw their livelihood and power as being seriously threatened.

The Rum Rebellion is one of the more controversial events in early New South Wales history. Some have seen it as a struggle for freedom, others as an example of class conflict. The leading books on the subject have been by biographers whose conclusions have varied according to which of the principal protagonists has formed their subject. George Mackaness, who wrote on Bligh, saw the governor as an honourable man who, although occasionally tactless and unnecessarily forthright, had the welfare of the community and particularly its less wealthy members at heart. M. H. Ellis, the leading authority on John Macarthur, exonerated the New South Wales Corps of many of the charges levelled against it, depicted Bligh as an avaricious, unbalanced tyrant and saw the Rum Rebellion as a justifiable step taken by responsible men who feared for the colonists as much as for themselves. Both interpretations are necessarily one-sided, a shortcoming that marred the stimulating pro-Bligh book entitled *The Rum Rebellion* which was written by H.V. Evatt. Recent historians like A.G.L. Shaw have presented a more balanced view.

An uprising which found men of substance on both sides and in which the lesser colonists played no direct part could scarcely be regarded as a struggle between opposing classes. Indeed the Marxist concept of class conflict serves no useful purpose when applied to the Rum Rebellion. Nor did the uprising stem primarily from Bligh's attempts to control either the officer traders or any other retailers.

Although a man of dominant personality and outspoken views, the governor possessed no greater means of enforcing his measures than had Hunter or King. The only men who could enforce regulations were those against whom they were directed. What does seem to have been at the heart of the conflict was the antagonism of two overbearing, headstrong, abrasive personalities, namely Bligh and John Macarthur. Each saw the other as an obstacle to the fulfilment of his aims. Macarthur had triumphed over earlier rulers and was in no mood to tolerate Bligh's criticism of his wool-growing activities, or the governor's decision to prosecute him for illegally importing a still and for allowing a convict to escape on one of his vessels. Bligh knew how Macarthur had treated his predecessors and was determined to curb a man whom he regarded as dangerous. In the highly charged atmosphere that developed as the court case proceeded, suspicion and fear mounted on both sides driving Macarthur, who was in the more vulnerable position, to the point where he feared for his whole future and perhaps for his life.

In a small-town society like New South Wales gossip spread and rumours quickly magnified. Bligh's brusque manner had already antagonised some of the emancipist dealers, including Simeon Lord, and he had also upset newly arrived settlers, such as the prickly Dr Robert Townson, by refusing them land grants until their claims had been verified in London. Worse, he had affronted the New South Wales Corps by publicly slighting it. When its officers refused to sit on the same bench as the dissolute judge-advocate, Richard Atkins, who was ill-equipped to display impartiality towards John Macarthur, Bligh threatened severe reprisals. Fears were aroused that he might arrest and perhaps order the summary trial of these men. All this provided malleable material upon which Macarthur could work. He eventually convinced the courageous but inoffensive Colonel Johnston that it was his duty to dismiss Bligh. Headed by their commanding officer who left his sick bed especially for the occasion, the Corps descended on Government House and, after arresting Bligh, Colonel Johnston assumed control. The governor's tactless treatment of leading citizens as well as subjective fears and suspicions all played a part in bringing about his overthrow.

For the next two years the New South Wales Corps enjoyed an ascendancy that enabled some officers and their supporters to obtain additional quantities of Crown land, government livestock and convict servants. Yet this second interregnum did not reek of corruption to the extent that was alleged by the pro-Bligh faction. Colonel Johnston had already taken a serious step in leading the mutiny and had no wish to face additional charges. He behaved cautiously and so too did Colonel Foveaux whose administration won rare praise from the normally taciturn Macquarie. Paterson, who succeeded Foveaux, was the weakest of the three administrators and the most susceptible to the influence of his subordinates. He alienated far more land than had either of his two predecessors and was lavish in the assistance which he gave to private settlers. Yet, although his fellow officers benefited, his generosity extended to other sections of the community and he did not try to further his own interests.

In 1810 the New South Wales Corps was recalled after a period of nearly twenty years service that has occasioned much controversy. Some writers believe that the rank and file was composed of the dregs of the army and that it included a high proportion of men taken from the Savoy military prison. M.H. Ellis regards the Corps as the equal of most other British regiments but, as A.G.L. Shaw has pointed out, to say this of a period when the whole army was noted for insubordination and dissoluteness is scarcely to restore the reputation of the Corps. Similar disagreement centres around its role in the colony. While historians such as M.H. Ellis have found much to commend in its pursuits, others, like George Mackaness, view it as bringing little but harm.

More work needs to be done on the composition and background of the Corps before the dispute about its quality can be resolved. From the military standpoint it had functioned effectively and had proved more co-operative than the troublesome marine corps. The decision of the British government to allow the officers land grants also had much to recommend it. Not all acquired farms, but those who did so worked enthusiastically and with exemplary effect. They helped make the colony self-sufficient and were among its best farmers. Some of their number were outstanding stock breeders and imported not only the first merino sheep but also quality cattle and thoroughbred horses. Against this must be balanced the ill-consequences of their trading activities for the rest of the community. Moreover, the fact that they had been allowed to establish an interest in the economy gave them unwarranted power and brought them into conflict with the civil authority whose authority they undermined. The British government should have recalled the Corps long before Bligh was overthrown. Its failure to do so resulted from the pressures of war which made it difficult to spare other troops for service in so unimportant a theatre.

The departure of the New South Wales Corps, and the ensuing

decision to replace the garrison at regular intervals, greatly eased Macquarie's task. Officers of regiments which arrived later engaged in the same malpractices as their predecessors but none stayed long enough to do much damage. The prospects of their dominating the retail trade were reduced as a result of increased competition. More and more goods arrived from overseas causing a glut which contributed to a serious commercial depression that lasted from 1812 to 1814. Financial upsets in Britain and a shortage of cash amongst the agency houses that traded with the colony made the situation worse. Some local merchants were forced out of business and others narrowly escaped ruin. On the other hand, falling prices improved conditions for the lower orders and for the rest of the Macquarie era prices remained more moderate. Liquor circulated in substantial quantities and Macquarie's attempts to control its use accomplished little. The ill effects of the trade were mitigated by a drop in the price of spirits which reduced the likelihood of settlers being ruined through purchasing this commodity.

Besides benefiting from these developments the emancipists gained much from the presence of a governor who believed that, since there was no future for them elsewhere, they should be made welcome in New South Wales. It is wrong to claim that Macquarie opposed migrants and that he sought to turn the colony exclusively into a home for ex-convicts. He appreciated the need for free people, particularly those with capital, and readily provided migrants with extensive grants and other forms of assistance. Emancipists, however, figured more prominently in his plans than in those of any other governor and he was careful, when considering the future of the colony, to ensure that they were adequately catered for. He set aside good areas of farmland around Airds and Appin for their use, readily issued them with grants and tried to ensure that there was an adequate market for their grain. Underlying his policy was the belief that 'the best description of settlers for this country are emancipated convicts'. He praised them for their 'early and laborious habits' and claimed that they were the 'real improvers and cultivators of the soil'. Macquarie's attitude was not shared by contemporaries who had arrived free. Most of these people criticised the small settlers for their lazy, improvident habits and their ignorance of farming. They also rejected the governor's view that once pardoned a convict was entitled to be treated as though he had never broken the law.

Thus far the division between emancipist and free had not created serious problems. Late in the Macquarie period, however, a legal

judgement by Judge Barron Field revealed that, owing to a techni-
cality, the pardons issued by governors did not always restore
emancipists to full citizenship. This defect was later remedied by
the British parliament, but not before it had stirred the emancipists
and made them more sensitive as a group. The antipathy of leading
free settlers and officers was also aroused when Macquarie appointed
ex-convicts such as Simeon Lord and Andrew Thompson, the
wealthy Hawkesbury trader and property owner, to the magistracy
and invited them to dine at Government House, thereby demonstrating that he considered them equal to any colonist. His actions
alienated powerful figures, including the Macarthurs and the
Reverend Samuel Marsden, and formed an important element in
the rift with the ailing Ellis Bent, judge-advocate from 1809 to
1815, and the difficult, opinionated Jeffrey Hart Bent who was
judge of the supreme court from 1814 to 1816. Such conflicts impeded the work of government, particularly when Jeffrey Bent
closed his court rather than admit ex-convict attorneys. Despite
this and the growing misgivings of his superiors who had earlier
been sympathetic, Macquarie continued to favour the emancipists.

Macquarie's beliefs were more commendable than those of his
opponents, but his total disregard for the views of others pointed
to a less attractive side of his character. His stern and narrow
upbringing on the island of Mull in the Inner Hebrides, where his
father had been a tenant farmer, had imbued him with a deep
respect for authority. From observations of his laird, the Duke of
Argyll, he derived a faith in paternalism, while his training in the
army taught him how to command and exact obedience. Nothing
in his background predisposed him to accept the need to compromise
or reason with others. Throughout his career as governor he rode
roughshod over those who disagreed with him, exercised close
control over his staff and accepted no interference with his authority. Such qualities were suited to the task of disciplining convicts,
but they were less appropriate in a man who also had to handle
free persons. Nature and background cast Macquarie for the role
of benevolent despot, not constitutional monarch. His autocratic
behaviour formed another element underlying his worsening relations with migrants and officials. It also aroused the concern of his
superiors, particularly when the complaints of disgruntled colonists
were brought before the attention of parliament. By the time he
returned to London in 1821 the wisdom of concentrating so much
power in the hands of one man had already been questioned by
the expatriate W.C. Wentworth who in 1819 urged the establish-

A View of Sydney on Norfolk Island 1801–4, a watercolour by John Eyre of the colony during the second period of King's administration. Mainland governors used the island as an outlet for convicts, especially those who committed offences after reaching New South Wales, but by 1800 many residents were free and either farmed grants or served as labourers.

ment of representative institutions. As yet this proposal had little support but the demand for political reform was to grow in the next decade.

The Development of Norfolk Island and Van Diemen's Land

Developments in the other Australian settlements had followed a quieter course. By 1821 Norfolk Island had been abandoned for some seven years. Attempts to capitalise on the existence of flax failed because the native species proved unsuitable for manufacturing canvas and other varieties could not be grown. Nor were the spars of the Norfolk Island pines useful for naval purposes. On the other hand, the climate was favourable and the soil more fertile than any initially discovered near Port Jackson. Mainland governors used the island as an outlet for convicts, especially those who committed offences after reaching New South Wales. The population of Norfolk Island by the opening of the nineteenth century had risen to over 1 000. Many residents were by then free and either farmed grants or found employment as labourers.

Despite this progress the government was beginning to doubt

whether the settlement should continue. Now that New South Wales was securely established there was little point in having another outpost which merely duplicated its functions. Supplies had to be sent there at extra cost and the poor harbour facilities had already resulted in the wreck of the *Sirius*. In June 1803 Governor King was ordered to begin transferring the Norfolk Islanders to Port Dalrymple, but the task proved unexpectedly complicated. Although promised compensation the settlers were reluctant to give up their farms. King, who believed that the island offered a valuable source of supplies for whalers and ships engaged in the China trade, made little attempt to hasten their departure. Bligh shared his view and the evacuation was further delayed by the uncertainties that followed the Rum Rebellion. Only after Macquarie arrived was a wholehearted effort made to carry out the government's orders. Shipping was scarce, however, and not until 1814 did the last of the Norfolk Islanders leave.

No such problems confronted the administrators of Van Diemen's Land. Although settled for strategic purposes the island existed mainly to receive convicts who were sent initially from Port Jackson and only later from Britain. Its rulers ranked as lieutenant-governors and were subject to the control of their superiors at Sydney. Despatches had to be sent there instead of directly to London and approval had to be sought in Sydney before expenditure could be incurred or land grants issued. To make matters worse, although a deputy judge-advocate had been sent, no provision was made for a criminal or a civil court and all cases had to be referred to the mainland which caused serious problems and delays. In 1819 circuits of the Supreme Court of New South Wales were held on the island but not until 1824 did the Charter of Justice create a separate legal system.

At first the two settlements at Hobart and Launceston formed distinct administrative entities under David Collins and Colonel Paterson. Both men had experience on the mainland and effectively established their outposts on a secure footing. Paterson, however, was obliged to assume command of New South Wales in 1809 and died *en route* for England in 1810, predeceasing Collins by a few months. At first no permanent replacement was available and for over two years a succession of military officers ruled at Hobart and Launceston. In June 1812 the island was brought under Lieutenant-Colonel Thomas Davey. 'Mad Tom', as he became known, was the most eccentric man to rule an Australian colony. He came with a reputation that was clouded by some dubious financial transactions. Although he committed no such offences while in Van Diemen's Land, his behaviour was at odds with the dignity of his office. His unconventional dress, dissolute habits and easy-going familiarity with his subjects appalled Macquarie who secured his dismissal in 1817. He was replaced in April of that year by Lieutenant-Colonel William Sorrell, former deputy adjutant-general at the Cape of Good Hope who quickly brought order to the colony. His record was so good that Macquarie ignored the fact that, although married with seven children, he was accompanied by Mrs Kent, the wife of a lieutenant who had served with him at the Cape.

Whereas the early rulers of New South Wales were naval officers, the administrators of Van Diemen's Land were drawn from the army. Presumably the government considered that in view of the French threat it was important for them to be experienced soldiers. The civil officials who assisted them were as varied as their counterparts on the mainland. Some were men of integrity and dedication, others were mainly interested in making money. The same was true of the officers of the military garrison, but none was stationed long enough at either settlement to gain a hold similar to that secured at Port Jackson by the New South Wales Corps. No serious clash

South West View of Hobart Town. Van Diemen's Land was recommended to prospective migrants on the basis of its cool climate and meadow-like pasture land which made it more reminiscent of England than the other colonies.

developed between the lieutenant-governors and the military and there was nothing to resemble the Rum Rebellion.

In general, Van Diemen's Land was administered soundly even under Davey whose policies accomplished more than Macquarie conceded. The region was better suited to Englishmen than was the hinterland of Port Jackson. Although only 67 900 square kilometres in area, with a barren plateau in the centre and rugged uplands in the west and south-west, it contained substantial quantities of good land. The climate was cooler than on the mainland and there were no extremes of heat and cold. Because of this and because rain fell evenly over the year, there were none of the floods and droughts that created uncertainties in New South Wales. These conditions, combined with the meadow-like appearance of the pasture land, were no doubt uppermost in the mind of W.C. Wentworth when he recommended the island to prospective migrants as, 'The most truly English country in the world, out of Europe. It is in most respects another England, only with much less refinement, elegance and convenience'.

By 1821 the number of migrants amounted to about 600 men, women and children. Amongst the remaining free persons were the military garrison, 935 former convicts and the 1 400 Norfolk Islanders, mainly emancipists, who had been resettled as a result of the British government's decision to vacate Norfolk Island. Convicts under sentence totalled 3 827 and formed just over 53 per cent of the population. Many were men and women of 'a most vicious description' who proved difficult to control. One of the worst was Michael Howe, self-styled 'Lieutenant Governor of the Woods' who from 1813 led a band of twenty-nine escaped convicts. Davey

TABLE 2
Expansion of Population, Agriculture, Sheep and Cattle
Raising in Van Diemen's Land to 1820

	Population	Acreage cultivated	Cattle	Sheep	Wool exported
1810	1 321	603*	421*	3 573	—
1815	1 933	3 865	8 901	52 890	—
1820	5 468	9 275	28 838	182 468	—

*This total refers only to Port Dalrymple. Details for Hobart are not available.
Sources: J.T. Bigge, *Report of the Commissioner of Enquiry on the State of Agriculture and Trade in the Colony of New South Wales; Historical Records of Australia*, Series III, Vols 1–2.

had only limited success in curbing their activities, but Sorrell sent troops after the bushrangers and broke up the gang with the help of Howe on whose behalf he interceded with Macquarie. False rumours that a pardon was not to be granted prompted Howe again to take to the bush in September 1817 and just over a year later to the relief of the settlers he was caught and killed.

Most of the residents lived in the southern county of Buckinghamshire around Hobart which still betrayed its recent origins. Its buildings were few and 'of the meanest description, seldom exceeding one story in height and being for the most part weatherboarded without, and lathed and plastered within'. Agricultural and pastoral settlement was concentrated on the shores of the Derwent River, North Bay and Pitt Water. From there it stretched northwards for a short distance until the rocky land of the interior was reached. In the northern county of Cornwall the pattern was repeated on a smaller scale. Launceston, named in 1807 after the birthplace of Colonel Paterson, was located about fifty kilometres from the entrance to Port Dalrymple and had fewer natural advantages than Hobart whose harbour was considered superior to that of Sydney. By 1821 the township was 'little more than an inconsiderable village,

Bay whaling. Black whales came close inshore during the breeding season and swam up the bays and estuaries. Unlike the sperm whale, the black whale could be caught from a small boat.

the houses in general being of the humblest description'. It provided an administrative and service centre for convicts and settlers who lived mostly on the banks of the North and South Esk Rivers.

Given that Van Diemen's Land contained fewer people and had been settled later than New South Wales, it was only to be expected that the economy should have been less advanced. Nevertheless more had been achieved by 1821 than the mainlanders accomplished during their first seventeen years. Already nearly half as much wheat was sown as on the Cumberland Plain and the island contained roughly half as many cattle and more sheep than did New South Wales. This is not to imply that the settlers of Van Diemen's Land were harder working than their northern neighbours. The fact that an established colony existed close at hand enabled them to get off to a better start. Livestock could readily be sent from Sydney and the losses on the voyage across Bass Strait were lower than those suffered on the long trip from India or the Cape of Good Hope. Climate and land were well-suited to stock raising and, since there were fewer mouths to feed, farm animals could multiply more rapidly. Arable farming too benefited from the more equable climate. Indeed, the island exported grain and potatoes to the mainland.

Other exports were also developed. In May 1820 a consignment of Macarthur's merinos was sent to the island by Macquarie. Two months later more breeding stock was brought from England, thus enabling a start to be made with wool production. Earlier some of the wealthier colonists had begun to exploit the whaling and sealing resources. Seals abounded off the coast and could easily be obtained. Similarly, the black whale came close inshore at breeding time and swam up the bays and estuaries. The Derwent was often so full of black whales that it became hazardous to sail a boat to Hobart. Whereas catching the sperm whale was beyond the means of local interests, all that was needed to procure black whales was a small rowing boat. After killing the whales they were towed to the nearest bay where an outhouse had been erected and there they could be boiled down. Bay whaling attracted half a dozen local firms and would have aroused even more interest but for the heavy duty imposed in London on oil.

By 1821, therefore, the basis had been laid for an economy no less varied than that of New South Wales. Farming and grazing were the main occupations, but there was also scope for trade and one or two manufacturing industries already existed at Hobart. Van Diemen's Land might be dependent constitutionally on the mainland, but economically it was independent. Indeed, according to the estimate of W.C. Wentworth, the average income of £32 per head was double that of the northern colony. Average figures can be misleading and it is clear that there were wide variations in the standard of living. At the top was a small group of former officers, migrants and emancipists, who owned large properties and engaged in trade or manufacturing. At the bottom were the struggling small farmers and labourers trying hard to eke out a living. Yet this was no different to the situation on the mainland and if many found life difficult few found it impossible.

three: Convicts and Capitalists

The Bigge Enquiries

By 1821 the future of New South Wales and Van Diemen's Land was in doubt because of Earl Bathurst's decision to appoint a commission to enquire into conditions at the two colonies. Originally mooted in April 1817 the idea was not acted upon until September 1818 when, instead of three commissioners, one was appointed. The delay had been caused by the lack of a suitable candidate, but the arrival in London from Trinidad of John Thomas Bigge, chief justice of that island, overcame this obstacle. The thirty-eight-year-old Bigge had practised law since 1806 and was highly recommended by the governor of Trinidad, Sir Ralph Woodward, who was a friend of Bathurst. He was provided with a secretary, his brother-in-law, Thomas Hobbes Scott, who had entered Oxford as an undergraduate after a varied career which included serving as vice consul at Bordeaux and engaging in business as a wine merchant.

The decision to despatch these two men to the antipodes was a result of the secretary of state's determination to familiarise himself with what was going on there. Since 1788 there had been only one enquiry that touched on New South Wales. That was in 1812 when the House of Commons in response to the demands of humanitarians and penal reformers had appointed a Select Committee on Transportation. It issued a brief report and collected evidence that was now out of date. The ending of the wars with France gave Bathurst the opportunity to devote full attention to his imperial responsibilities. An aristocrat of conservative tendencies, who was reputed to wear a pigtail long after others had abandoned the practice, he was a man of great ability. He had once been considered a potential prime minister and although he never occupied that office his talents were equal to it. A full appreciation of his life and work has not yet appeared but it is clear that throughout the years from 1812 until 1827, while he was responsible for the colonies, he took his duties seriously. He improved the administration of his office, introduced Blue Books containing detailed statistical information and appointed commissioners to obtain up-to-date information on several colonial possessions. Day-by-day business was left to his under-secretaries, first Henry Goulburn, who served from August 1812 until December 1821, and then Sir Robert Wilmot who took the name Horton in 1823. Both of these men were parliamentary under-secretaries who occupied seats in the House of Commons where they acted as spokesmen for their departments. After 1825, however, Wilmot Horton was assisted by R. W. Hay, the first permanent under-secretary, who was not a member of parliament but a civil servant. Bathurst allowed these men considerable scope for exercising initiative but he kept himself closely informed as to what was going on and bore ultimate responsibility for the important changes in land and constitutional policy that were introduced during the 1820s. Much of his time was spent on the family estate at Cirencester in Gloucestershire, but whether there or in his office in Downing Street he was constantly preoccupied with the problems of empire.

His appointee, J.T. Bigge, arrived at Port Jackson on 26 September 1819 bearing a commission authorising him to conduct his investigations and order necessary reforms. He was instructed to look into practically every aspect of the colony's affairs and invited to make recommendations on matters ranging from convict discipline to colonial government. Above all he was to determine whether New South Wales was still capable of fulfilling its original purpose. In words that are significant, given the recent controversy as to the reasons for settlement, Lord Bathurst reminded Bigge that the colony had not been founded for territorial or commercial gain. Rather it had been established as a gaol and Bathurst wished to know if it still retained its capabilities as a place of punishment. One of Bigge's tasks was to determine whether the aims of transportation might better be served if convicts were sent only to parts of the mainland that contained no free people. At the same time, he was asked to report on what steps might be taken to advance the interests of New South Wales as a free colony. For over a year the indefatigable commissioner and his secretary toured the countryside interviewing colonists formally as well as informally and collecting documentary evidence. Historians have viewed with mixed feelings the way in which the investigation was conducted. Bigge has been praised as an objective observer whose legal training and judicial background ideally suited him to the task at hand. Others have claimed that the Colonial Office had given him an intimation as to the course of future policy and that this guided his whole approach. He has also been criticised for allowing his findings to be influenced by John Macarthur with whom he established a close and lasting friendship.

Bigge lacked the time to deal exhaustively with the multiplicity of subjects into which he was expected to enquire. He did not always collect enough evidence to sustain his conclusions and he was selective in his choice of witnesses, turning mainly to the wealthier members of migrant society. Some of the charges that have been levelled against him nevertheless fail to withstand close investigation. To claim that he became Macarthur's pawn is to inflate the importance of the owner of Elizabeth Farm. Bigge had an independent mind and the fact that his opinions were similar to those of Macarthur is in itself no proof of the latter's influence. The commissioner, indeed, had made up his mind on the central issue of his enquiry before he met Macarthur. He did not take long to see that the future of the colony lay with large-scale pastoral enterprise. To promote stock raising and especially the wool industry, which he strongly favoured, steps should be taken to make land readily available and encourage migrants with capital. Convicts would also still be sent, but instead of being allowed to congregate around the towns they would be assigned to respectable pastoralists and employed as far away from urban centres as possible. Isolation would enable them to be disciplined more closely while more rigorous conditions would heighten the punitive aspects of transportation.

All this contrasted with the policies of Macquarie whose views on other subjects, including the appointment of emancipists to the magistracy, were also rejected by the commissioner. The full extent of the differences between the two men did not become apparent until after Macquarie's return to England and the publication of Bigge's reports. Their relationship had, however, been troubled long before this. At first Macquarie had welcomed the appointment of a commission because he believed its findings would vindicate his actions. Yet within weeks of Bigge's arrival the governor was showing resentment at the presence of a man who, though younger and less experienced, had an authority equal to his own. Bigge's assertiveness and the relationship he established with leading citizens aroused further suspicions and although the two men concealed their differences in public the rift remained. An enquiry into the state of New South Wales was overdue, but of all the governors Macquarie least deserved the indignity of having much of his work and many of his cherished ideals openly questioned.

None of these problems arose in connection with Bigge's investigation of Van Diemen's Land where he spent four months beginning in February 1820. His enquiry covered similar ground to that on the mainland, except that he was required to report on Sorrell's liaison with Mrs Kent. Accusations of misconduct had been made by the troublesome and vindictive Anthony Fenn Kemp, a farmer and merchant who, while serving on the mainland as a captain in the New South Wales Corps, had played a prominent part in the overthrow of Bligh. The commissioner had little time for Kemp and wrote highly of Sorrell's work. On the other hand he refused to visit him socially and criticised his private life as betraying a 'culpable insensibility to the dignity of his public station'. Despite this Sorrell proved co-operative and Bigge was able to conduct his enquiries with a minimum of trouble. He believed that Van Diemen's Land should remain a penal settlement and gave qualified support to the idea of its becoming independent of Sydney.

> Without positively stating it as my opinion that the two governments ought immediately to be separated . . . [he wrote] I conceive that it is a measure which should be kept in view, and that the future adoption of it should be regulated by the increase which may take place in the amount and respectability of its population.

Bigge sailed for England on 14 February 1821 carrying a vast collection of material which engaged his attention on the voyage home. His reports, which took over three years to complete, appeared as three parliamentary papers, the first entitled *The State of the Colony of New South Wales,* in June 1822, the second and third, entitled *The Judicial Establishments in New South Wales and Van Diemen's Land* and *The State of Agriculture and Trade in the Colony of New South Wales*, in July 1823. They formed the most comprehensive body of information about the two colonies that had ever been published. They also contained detailed recommendations that had an important influence on the course of British policy, not least in connection with the penal system which had been the subject of a further parliamentary enquiry in 1819.

A More Rigorous Penal System

During the 1820s crime showed no signs of abating in the rapidly growing cities of Britain. There, particularly in the north where most of the new industries were located, men and women were forced to congregate under miserable conditions. They worked long hours for a mere pittance and lived in overcrowded, poorly built tenements where damp and the lack of sanitation presented a constant threat to health. Neglected by a government which shared the prevailing view that it was no part of the function of the state to protect the poor, they were also exploited by unscrupulous employers. The belief of economists that a fixed sum was available for wages and that this could not be exceeded without harming the economy reacted further to their disadvantage, as did the absence of a strong trade union movement. In these circumstances the surprising fact is not that crime increased, but that the number of offenders was not considerably larger. The mass of the proletariat proved law abiding, despite the degradations to which they were subjected and the absence of an effective police force. Nevertheless, more did turn to crime either from necessity or because they preferred the life of the criminal to that of any other.

The countryside also had problems. The end of the Napoleonic wars was followed by a drop in the price of foodstuffs. The introduction of the Corn Laws helped the wheat farmer but did not prevent the dispossession of substantial numbers of the smaller agriculturalists who had survived the late eighteenth-century enclosure movement only because the war created an artificially strong demand for grain. Contrary to popular belief enclosures at first increased the demand for labour since a variety of tasks had to be performed before the new system of farming could be introduced. This need was now declining and for the first time machinery was being introduced on a scale sufficient to reduce the opportunities for work in the villages. Rural England, therefore, was the scene of unrest and misery. Alternative employment was available in the towns and these provided a safety valve which helps explain why the incidence of crime was lower in country than in urban areas. Moreover, in small village communities, where everyone knew his neighbour, a stranger was immediately noticed and detection

was more likely than in the anonymity of a large urban centre.
Nevertheless men did commit offences by stealing and by poaching.
Others took part in demonstrations and machine breaking.

The highest incidence of rural crime was in Ireland which,
after the Act of Union of 1801, had been brought more closely
under British control. Secondary industry scarcely existed because
the country possessed little capital, no coal or iron and few natural
resources. Nothing occurred to parallel either the industrial revolution or the growth of urbanisation that together were helping to
transform the economy and society of England. Ireland remained
almost exclusively a land of villages whose inhabitants made their
living from the soil. Most of the land belonged to a small group of
wealthy individuals many of whom, particularly in the north,
were men of English extraction. The mass of the community
were either landless labourers or tenant farmers whose heavy
rentals ate deeply into their scanty resources. As was the case
everywhere in Europe the nineteenth century was marked by a
steady increase in population, but whereas in England this was
countered by an expansion in productive output, in Ireland little
scope existed for resources to grow. Nor did landlords, many of
whom were absentees, do much to improve methods of husbandry
or introduce the techniques of the agrarian revolution. The result
was a Malthusian situation in which population grew at a rate
which exceeded the capacity of the country to feed it. The existing
food supply, already only able to support the masses at subsistence
level, had constantly to be spread further. By 1831 one fifth of the
population was redundant. Small wonder that bitter resentment
should have been aroused amongst a people whose religion, history
and culture separated them from the English. Almost exclusively
Roman Catholic the Irish staunchly opposed the Anglican
ascendancy. Still vivid in their memories were the many examples
of British injustice and brutality that stretched back beyond the
days of Oliver Cromwell. Small wonder that they lacked respect
for laws imposed by men whom they regarded as enemies. Such
attitudes and conditions helped produce crime of every variety,
ranging from brutal assaults and murder to thefts and political
demonstrations.

Throughout the 1820s the British authorities faced the problem
of coping with the large numbers of men and women who were
sentenced by courts in all parts of the kingdom. One solution would
have been to construct more gaols but this was costly and since
the end of the war the government had been under pressure to

curtail spending. All government departments were closely watched by parliament whose members were aware that the property owning electorate would strongly resist any reimposition of the wartime income tax. Despite its drawbacks transportation had since 1788 provided a relatively cheap means of ridding Britain of substantial numbers of convicts. Not all sections of opinion approved the system but, until a better one could be found, banishment was kept on the statute books as a punishment in its own right and as a merciful alternative to hanging. Whether or not this particular sentence was imposed depended upon individual judges and juries. On average about 35 per cent of those convicted in England during the 1820s were ordered to serve periods of transportation ranging from seven years to life. Of these about one quarter went no further than the hulks in which they were housed while awaiting ships to carry them to the antipodes. The system was less haphazard than it had been and a higher proportion of convicts underwent the punishment imposed upon them.

Between 1821 and 1830 some 21 780 convicts were despatched to New South Wales. The conditions under which they served their sentences changed considerably after the publication of the Bigge reports. The commissioner's recommendations were accepted by the British authorities and despatched to Sydney with orders that they be implemented. For the first time an attempt was made to introduce uniformity and order into a system which had depended upon the personal inclination of individual governors. Scope still existed for administrators to exercise initiative, but the guidelines within which they were expected to operate had been laid down.

The main object of penal policy during the 1820s was to increase the deterrent effect of transportation by making life in the colonies more of a punishment. The harshest treatment was reserved for those who broke the law after their arrival. In New South Wales such people had either suffered capital punishment or been sent to Newcastle. By 1821 this region could no longer be used as a place of confinement. Graziers and small farmers were moving into the Hunter Valley and a land route to Windsor, along which convicts could escape, had been opened. Macquarie had earlier decided on a new site further north at Port Macquarie which had been discovered and explored by John Oxley in 1818. Preparations for the transfer of the penal establishment from Newcastle were begun in 1821, but it was not until the end of the following year that the first convicts were moved. As Bigge had recognised, the area was not sufficiently isolated. Although it was used for penal purposes until 1829 most of the worst characters were sent either to Moreton Bay, which Bigge had favoured, or to Norfolk Island whose re-opening as a penal settlement was ordered by Earl Bathurst in July 1824.

Nature had endowed Norfolk Island and Moreton Bay with scenic beauty and natural advantages which later made the one a tourist centre and the other the site for the capital of Queensland. The task for penal administrators was to ensure that the convicts sent there enjoyed none of the benefits of surf and sun. Moreton Bay, opened by Lieutenant Henry Miller in September 1824, was the most used during the 1820s. Under its second commandant, Captain Patrick Logan who took office in March 1826, a system based on rigorous punishment was introduced. Overcrowding and an impure water supply caused hardship and a high death rate. Norfolk Island began the second phase of its history on 6 June 1825 when a military detachment arrived from the mainland to begin clearing-up operations. The penal establishment, however, did not begin functioning effectively until the 1830s when the island gained an unenviable reputation for degradation and brutality.

The number of prisoners who actually underwent the rigours of confinement at one of these centres between 1821 and 1830 was only small. For most convicts they existed as a nightmare to be avoided rather than a reality which they experienced. On the mainland the strengthening of the police force and the appointment of additional magistrates with greater powers to punish summarily closed many loopholes. Improvements in day-to-day administration resulted in the keeping of better records and the maintenance of a closer watch over prisoners. Emancipists and convicts were no longer employed in the office of the superintendent of convicts and there was less likelihood of clerks falsifying documents. One of the first to suffer as a result of this change of policy was Principal Superintendent William Hutchinson, an emancipist who had been appointed by Governor Macquarie in April 1814. Charges of favouritism and misuse of public money were investigated by Bigge who found no evidence to sustain them. The commissioner, however, considered that Hutchinson's convict background debarred him from office and in 1823 he was replaced by Frederick Augustus Hely, an Irish-born free man who was recruited in England. An able and efficient official he acted as superintendent until his death in 1836. While Brisbane was governor he served under the colonial secretary, but Governor Darling gave him full responsibility for convict affairs.

Conditions were made less pleasant for convicts by the decision to place them in remote parts. Those kept in government employ were organised into small gangs each of which was closely supervised. Brisbane anticipated Bigge's recommendations in hiring some of these gangs out to settlers who were prepared to pay for having their land cleared and put into use. The plan was designed to use convict labour to increase the productive resources of the colony at no expense to the government. Another of its aims was to improve 'the moral condition of the convict(s)' by scattering them 'in small bodies removed at a distance from all temptation'. Brisbane laid great stress on the fact that he had devised it without 'the least communication with Bigge' and privately described it as his 'happiest' innovation. Most government convicts, however, were used for public purposes on the construction of roads, buildings and amenities. Their treatment was severe, as befitted men who were kept in the government's hands partly because they were of such vicious disposition that private persons would not employ them. While working they were chained together and at night they were

A government gaol gang, Sydney, typical of the gangs the government hired out to settlers prepared to pay for labour, although most were used for public works.

locked up in wheeled vehicles each of which housed twenty-five prisoners under cramped conditions. Talking was forbidden during the day and even a minor offence earned a severe flogging.

Although the authorities shouldered responsibility for the worst convicts they had no desire to bear more burdens than necessary. Bigge had recommended in favour of assignment and his proposals were given added force by the need to keep costs low. Throughout the 1820s governors were ordered to economise in every direction and allot as many convicts as possible to private settlers. Since there was a strong demand for labour, there was little difficulty in implementing this last instruction. Brisbane inherited the problem of assigning the large number of post-war convicts whom Macquarie had been obliged to keep in government hands. He followed the normal practice of allotting their services to any settler who could maintain them. He also introduced a new scheme under which settlers who sought land grants were obliged to employ one convict for each one hundred acres issued. Bathurst had doubts about this scheme which was designed also to curb the growing appetite for land and introduce regularity into a situation which Macquarie had allowed to grow out of hand. The settlers, however, accepted Brisbane's stipulation, so glad were they to obtain labourers.

Like their counterparts in public employ, assigned convicts found themselves dispersed further and further afield. Movement was restricted, tickets of leave and pardons were made more difficult to obtain. To make matters worse, convicts were no longer permitted to bring property with them to the colony. As a result they were unable to acquire not only comforts but also the capital that the more enterprising of their predecessors had used to set themselves up in business. Some of the emancipist dealers had gained a start by selling merchandise which they had purchased on the voyage to Botany Bay. This opportunity was no longer available. Moreover, after 1825 governors were no longer authorised to issue grants of land to those who had completed their sentences or been otherwise pardoned. This was a result of Bigge's investigations which had revealed an incidence of failure among grantees so high as to suggest that former convicts were unlikely to succeed as smallholders. The commissioner had recommended that in future holdings of thirty acres or more should be given only to emancipists who had saved some capital. This would ensure that they could support themselves and it was also a guarantee that they were above average. The rest might receive ten-acre plots located close to towns where they could supplement their farm earnings by working as labourers. The government, however, decided to abandon rather than modify the earlier scheme. There was now ample employment for ex-convicts and with plenty of land under crop there was no need for them to become settlers. Accordingly, all mention of land grants for emancipists was dropped from Darling's instructions which were the first to be drawn up after the publication of Bigge's reports.

Most of the changes introduced on the mainland were duplicated in Van Diemen's Land. Sorrell was recalled by Earl Bathurst who, while appreciative of his achievements, believed that his private conduct was having a bad effect on colonial society. On 14 May 1824 he left Hobart, two days after the arrival of his successor Colonel George Arthur. Before coming to the antipodes this distinguished soldier had fought in the Napoleonic wars and served as superintendent and commandant of British Honduras which he had administered effectively, if overbearingly, between 1814 and 1822. He remained in Van Diemen's Land for a record term of thirteen years and retained the support of his superiors. 'Of all the Governors which this department has employed in my time', wrote the knowledgeable James Stephen, under-secretary and former legal adviser to the Colonial Office, 'you have enjoyed the most uninterrupted reputation for all the qualities which a Governor ought to possess and the strongest hold upon the favourable opinion of your official superiors'. Their confidence was such that after his return to England in 1836 he was first appointed lieutenant-governor of Upper Canada and then, in March 1842 governor of the Presidency of Bombay. Few other rulers of an Australian colony were entrusted with so many high responsibilities.

Arthur's reputation in Van Diemen's Land rested chiefly on his success in administering the penal system and in ensuring that the requirements which had been laid down by Commissioner Bigge were adequately met. The lieutenant-governor had a deep interest in the management of convicts and devoted much of his time to perfecting a system that would serve a reformative as well as a deterrent purpose. Convicts were classified according to behaviour and treated accordingly. The worst were at first despatched to Macquarie Harbour which was located in bleak, isolated surroundings on the west coast. This region had been selected by Sorrell and occupied in 1822 after being approved by Bigge and Earl Bathurst. Arthur, however, considered it too inaccessible and in 1832 abandoned it for the better-known establishment which he had founded two years earlier at Port Arthur. Situated on Tasman

Peninsula this dreaded spot was easier to reach but almost impossible to escape from. Here convicts lived under physical conditions that were matched in severity by the treatment meted out by their gaolers. Kept under tight control they spent their days engaged in unremitting labour, mining coal, cutting timber and building boats. Few of those incarcerated at Port Arthur were prepared to run the risk of a second sentence.

Of the remaining convicts, some 93 per cent in all, the most intractable performed hard labour in government chain gangs. The majority, however, were allotted to settlers. Arthur was a firm believer in assignment which he regarded as beneficial to convicts and settlers alike. At the same time he recognised that employers should not be given too much control over the convicts. Regulations were introduced to ensure that masters treated their servants justly and that the latter were obedient. Convicts found guilty of misconduct were severely punished while those who improved were rewarded by tickets of leave, or remission of sentences. Arthur kept a close watch over their behaviour and constantly regraded convicts. A sincere Calvinist he tried to persuade churchmen of all denominations to come to the colony. By this means its moral tone would be raised and the convicts might further be reformed. Many of his hopes were not realised and doubt was later cast on the wisdom of depending so heavily on assignment. Nevertheless he remains an exemplary administrator who gave priority to the task of making Van Diemen's Land an effective gaol. To a greater extent than his mainland contemporaries he involved himself personally in the conduct of penal affairs and deserves full credit for the improvements that were introduced.

Growth of Private Enterprise

The fact that the British authorities sent convicts in increased numbers to eastern Australia during the 1820s did not mean that they saw its future as exclusively penal. New South Wales and Van Diemen's Land had already, by the opening of the decade, revealed a potential for other purposes and, with Bigge's findings at hand, there could be no turning the clock back. Not that there was any wish to do so. Having played a major part in the defeat of Napoleon, Britain with its rapidly developing industrial resources had emerged as the most powerful nation in Europe. Energies formerly devoted to war were directed to peaceful expansion. British goods were exported all over the world in increasing quantities. Markets were constantly sought and so too were new sources of raw material. In addition, British capital looked for fresh avenues of investment. Society was expansionist and outward looking and pressure was brought on governments to help provide new opportunities for industrialists and financiers.

British policy towards New South Wales and Van Diemen's Land, therefore, was formulated within a new framework after 1821. Penal considerations weighed heavily, particularly in the case of Van Diemen's Land, but it was clear that both colonies could also serve objectives more directly related to the needs of the British economy. Their temperate climates and reserves of land suited them to large-scale pastoralism. Locally grown wool promised to become an export staple which could reduce British dependence on foreign supplies and provide the colonies with a means of contributing to their upkeep. One way of accomplishing this was to encourage the migration to both regions of settlers with means and enterprise. Such people would also fulfil another role. The penal system, as recast during the 1820s, depended for its successful operation upon the availability of respectable free settlers who could support, control and, hopefully, reform assigned convicts. In view of the rate at which transportation was proceeding, migrants of a superior type were likely to be needed in numbers larger than before.

There were, however, limits to the kind of encouragement which governments were prepared to offer. There was no likelihood of the Colonial Office becoming involved in any scheme that involved expense. On one occasion after the end of the war assistance had been given to a settlement scheme at the Cape of Good Hope. This proved a failure and further strengthened the determination of the authorities to avoid commitments of this kind. Migrants to eastern Australia had to pay their own way and they also had to guarantee that they had enough capital to establish themselves after their arrival.

The principal inducement which the authorities were prepared to hold out was one that cost them nothing, namely land. In law all the territory in Australia which had been claimed by the British belonged to the Crown. It could be disposed of in any way that King George III and his ministers saw fit. Before 1821 land was given away free, subject only to the payment of an annual due known as a quit rent that was not levied until a stipulated period had elapsed. This generous practice was followed in most parts of the empire, but it also reflected the demands of local circumstances. Selling the land might, if introduced too early in so distant a land, inhibit prospective settlers and result in their migrating elsewhere. Moreover, if these people were obliged to use their capital in buying land they would have less money with which to purchase stock and other necessities. In this way development would be retarded. These arguments worked less powerfully during the 1820s and the government began slowly to alter its policy. Bigge and Macquarie had pronounced in favour of allowing settlers to purchase land when their needs and capital warranted acreages in excess of 2000. Governor Brisbane in October 1824 promulgated fresh regulations based on this principle. In 1825, however, these were superseded on orders from the secretary of state. Instead of using sales to supplement grants Lord Bathurst drew a clear distinction between the two methods of alienating land. Settlers with limited capital could still receive grants of up to 2560 acres, but richer graziers were obliged to purchase their land at auction in quantities of up to 9600 acres. It was also made clear that the latter system would eventually replace the former. In fact Bathurst had acted precipitately and in the face of strong opposition was forced to climb down. Sales were suspended after 1826 and the majority of settlers continued to receive their land on the old easy terms. In addition to obtaining grants which vested them with freehold rights they were able to lease tracts of waste land in return for a fee. Governor Brisbane, acting on the recommendations of Commissioner Bigge, issued tickets of occupation which enabled settlers to run stock on specified areas of Crown land. Darling substituted for this scheme one which allowed graziers to lease land within the settled areas on payment of an annual rental of 2s 6d per 100 acres. Many rather than incurring this expense simply allowed their stock to graze on the vast areas of easily accessible waste land.

These advantages were publicised in the United Kingdom by a variety of individuals, prominent amongst whom were colonists of free origin who sought to counter the convict influence by persuading respectable persons to migrate to the antipodes. The first important work written with this intent was W.C. Wentworth's *Statistical Historical and Political Description of the Colony of New South Wales* which contained a brilliant analysis as well as vivid descriptions of the colony. Originally published in 1819 it passed through three editions by 1823. Its success stimulated other writers. Several books dealing with life in the antipodes appeared during the 1820s. Four on Van Diemen's Land were printed between 1820 and 1824, the most significant being Edward Curr's *Account of the colony of Van Diemen's Land principally designed for the use of emigrants,* better known under its later title *Three Years Residence in Van Diemen's Land.* Amongst the works on New South Wales was James Atkinson's informative *Account of the State of Agriculture and Grazing in New South Wales* which remains one of the best and most widely consulted treatments of its subject. Such authors helped to dispel the unfavourable impression of life in the antipodes created by earlier writers. They did much to remove the ignorance that had been one obstacle to immigration and provided abundant information on every facet of life ranging from social habits to natural and economic conditions. Often written with verve and enthusiasm their books beckoned the adventurous and the enterprising to a land of promise.

Between 1821 and 1830 migrants came to eastern Australia in numbers larger than ever before. In 1821, 320 arrived, but from then the annual figure only once fell below 500 and in two years exceeded 1 000. The total intake of men was 7 554. At first Van Diemen's Land received the largest proportion but the greater resources of New South Wales and the appearance of writings which dispelled rumours of the superiority of its southern neighbour resulted in its share increasing. Migrants chose the antipodes for many reasons. Some had friends or relatives already established there and came to join them. Others sought to improve their social standing by making their home in a colony where they would be numbered among the leading families. Whatever their pretensions practically all possessed capital ranging from a few hundred pounds to several thousand. They were attracted by the certainty of acquiring large acreages on which they could raise stock. Some brought pure-bred sheep not only of the merino but also of the Saxon variety which became increasingly popular during the 1820s after first being imported by Edward Riley.

The decade also saw the first attempts by companies to exploit the natural resources of New South Wales and Van Diemen's Land. In June 1824 the Australian Agricultural Company was granted a charter by parliament enabling it to occupy one million acres of pastoral land in New South Wales in return for an investment of one pound for each acre and the employment of 1 200 convicts. Founded by a group of wealthy London bankers it had the support of the Macarthurs and other prominent graziers who had an interest in the wool industry. Operations began late in 1825 on a site selected near Port Stephens by the company's agent, Robert Dawson, a school friend of John Macarthur junior and former manager of the Berkshire estate of Viscount Barrington. Setbacks, however, were experienced despite the company's success in capitalising on Bigge's recommendation that the Newcastle coal-mines, formerly worked by the government, should be handed over to private enterprise. The company gained a monopoly over coalmining but its pastoral activities made slow progress as a result of the low quality of its livestock and the unsuitability of much of its land. Dawson fell foul of the committee of management which suspended him in April 1828 after James Macarthur had unjustly accused him of incompetence. In 1829 the board of directors in London gave full charge to Sir William Parry, a former naval officer and Arctic explorer. Fresh land was selected on the rich Liverpool Plains and by 1833 the company's activities had become centred on two properties, Warah near Quirindi and Goono Goono on the Peel River near Tamworth. Drought and stock losses hit its activities hard, but by the time Parry handed over to Colonel Henry Dumaresq in March 1834 recovery was under way.

Meanwhile, a second company had been floated by a London syndicate whose object was to develop the agricultural and pastoral resources of Van Diemen's Land. The chief instigator and first agent of the Van Diemen's Land Company was the author Edward Curr, who was a friend of Lieutenant-Governor Sorrell. Curr arrived at Hobart in May 1826 with permission to select 250 000 acres in the north-west of the island. By September a base had been established on a 20 000-acre block at Circular Head, but the rugged nature of the terrain and opposition from Lieutenant-Governor Arthur, who feared the company would take all the best land, delayed further expansion. By 1830 six locations were occupied, but stock losses had been heavy and it was long before activities got under way. Curr worked hard incurring much hostility from other colonists. In 1841 he moved to the Port Phillip district where he became a leading grazier and a prominent political figure.

The presence of additional entrepreneurs, the infusion of substantial quantities of private capital and the arrival of more convicts than ever before, combined to make the 1820s a decade of heightened economic activity. New South Wales at first experienced a boom as men and money flowed in. Manufacturing remained of small importance, but the increased demand for clothing, leather goods and furniture resulted in some expansion of secondary industry. Government permission was also given for the establishment of a distillery which produced spirits from locally grown grain. This was an innovation that had long been sought by landed interests who saw it as a means of enlarging the wheat market. The British authorities, conscious of the dangers of allowing liquor to be manufactured in a penal colony, had resisted the settlers' demands. Under pressure from Macquarie, however, Earl Bathurst finally gave way, although not until he had received assurances from Bigge that convict discipline was unlikely to be threatened. After 1823 the illicit stills that no earlier governor had been able to eradicate found themselves in competition from one that was officially recognised.

Agriculturalists benefited from the increased demand which was further stimulated by the growth of population. The increase in the number of mouths to be fed also enlarged the outlet for meat. This, together with the fact that the Australian Agricultural Company was busily stocking its runs, created a 'mania' for sheep and cattle that was vividly described by the Reverend John Dunmore Lang:

> Barristers and attorneys, military officers of every rank and civilians of every department, clergymen and medical men, merchants, settlers and dealers in general, were seen promiscuously mingled together every Thursday, and outbidding each other in the most determined manner, either in their person or by proxies of certified agricultural character, for the purchase of every scabbed sheep or scarecrow horse, or buffalo cow that was offered for sale in the colony.

Additional credit was sought to finance purchases and in 1826 the Bank of Australia was created by the exclusives in opposition to the 'emancipist' Bank of New South Wales which was experiencing financial difficulties.

The boom burst in 1827 as a result of an English financial crisis which reduced wool prices and interrupted the flow of British capital to the colony. To make matters worse, a severe drought struck New South Wales. For three years, observed Lang, 'the heavens became as brass and the earth as iron'. In 1830 a group of landed proprietors described how 'Three seasons of unprecedented drought have conspired with other causes to produce much distress and to occasion great depression throughout the colony'. Property depreciated, land and stock had to be sacrificed and many settlers were bankrupted.

These events which marked the culmination of what has been described as 'Australia's first trade cycle' did not inhibit further expansion. By 1830 there was more than twice as much land in productive use as in 1821. During this same period sheep had multiplied roughly five times, cattle four times, while agricultural output had also increased greatly. Most of these new resources were located outside the Cumberland Plain which before 1821 had been the centre of economic life. This region had almost reached saturation point by Macquarie's departure and in the next ten years it lost its supremacy to other parts. With land scarce in the older localities settlement spread creating serious difficulties for the overworked surveyor-general's department. The staff found it impossible to measure land in time for settlers to occupy it, so strong was their demand for fresh pasture. To keep them waiting was unwise because it would have forced them to spend their capital. Accordingly, settlement was allowed to precede survey and the land situation, already chaotic when Governor Brisbane arrived, became more so while he and, later, Darling held office. Quit rents which had been in arrears for decades could not be collected because both the staff and the means of enforcing payment were lacking. Nor was the government able to ensure that the terms of grants were heeded. In 1829, in a vain attempt to give the surveyor-general a chance to restore order, Governor Darling forbade settlement beyond the nineteen counties, an area which stretched along the coast from the Manning River to Moruya and inland for some 240 kilometres.

Despite this, the official bounds of the colony were many times larger than they had been in 1821. The economy too had been established on a more secure footing due partly to an increase in the volume of exports. The quantity of wool sent overseas expanded despite lower prices and greater competition from European sources. In 1826 the one million lb mark was reached and although there was a drop in the following year the next three saw a steady upward movement to just short of 2 million lbs at the end of the decade. More significant in terms of value were exports derived from the fisheries which in 1830 returned £59 471 to the colonists, as compared to the £34 907 received from wool. Sealing had declined during the 1820s as overkilling by avaricious hunters depleted resources. Whaling, in contrast, attracted the attention of local interests. For the first time colonial entrepreneurs, like the prosperous free merchant and landowner Richard Jones, found the capital to invest in deep-sea whaling. In addition, a new phase of bay whaling opened due to the activities of newly arrived graziers whose land was located close to appropriate parts of the shore. These men engaged in whaling while waiting for their herds and flocks to begin returning a profit.

The importance of the fisheries has been overlooked by historians who once regarded wool as the first and only staple. Not until after 1834 did this commodity become the leading export earner. Before that date it was overshadowed by seal skins and whale oil. These and other less important articles such as timber, coal, bullock horns and bark, however, came nowhere near paying for imports. In 1830, as in 1821, New South Wales was vitally dependent for its survival upon the money spent by the home government on the penal establishment. Increased British expenditure on the convicts was in fact an important element underlying the heightened economic development of the 1820s.

TABLE 3
Exports of Wool and Fisheries Products from New South Wales 1830–50

| | Fishery products | | Wool | |
	Value(£)	% of total exports	Value(£)	% of total exports
1830	59 471	42	34 907	25
1835	180 349	26	299 587	44
1840	224 144	16	566 122	40
1845	96 804	6	1 009 242	65
1850	29 368	1	1 614 241	67

Source: B. Little, 'The Sealing and Whaling Industry in Australia Before 1850', *Australian Economic History Review,* Vol. 9, No. 3, September 1969.

This was no less true of Van Diemen's Land where large numbers of convicts were directly maintained by the Crown and where government played an important part in economic life. As was the case on the mainland, however, private persons contributed greatly to expansion. Outstanding among them was Joseph Archer who arrived in March 1821 with a capital of £3 250 and a flock of pure merino sheep. He received a 2 000-acre grant on the Lake River adjoining that of his brother Thomas, a commissariat official and by 1831 was one of the most prosperous settlers. Important too was Charles Swanston, founder of the Derwent Bank, merchant, land speculator and company director. Another was Edward Lord who by 1821 already owned 35 000 acres of land, 6 000 head of cattle, 7 000 sheep and three trading vessels. Small wonder that he should then have been described as 'the richest man in all the island'. These men together with migrants, wealthy emancipists and the

Van Diemen's Land Company were behind the varied developments that occurred during the 1820s. Nearly 1 million acres of land passed into private hands in this period and settlement spread along the route from Hobart to Launceston, keeping close to water. By 1830 all the best locations were occupied and the only good land still available was along the north coast and in the north-west. Whereas New South Wales was on the verge of its greatest era of pastoral expansion, Van Diemen's Land settlers soon found good grazing land hard to obtain.

The administration of land regulations in Van Diemen's Land left much to be desired. Lieutenant-Governor Arthur was accused of favouritism; quit rents were rarely collected; and large areas were bought up by speculators and others who failed to develop it. Nevertheless output expanded despite an agricultural depression that arose from a shortage of currency and the abolition of a fixed price for grain. Subsequently the colony was hit by the English financial crisis that affected New South Wales. Even so, the number of sheep trebled and the export of wool exceeded that from the mainland in each of the years from 1829 to 1831. The fisheries yielded only about half as much as in New South Wales but the gap between the two regions in terms of productive resources and output of primary industries was much less than might be supposed, given the disparities in area and population. The economy of Van Diemen's Land with its small manufactures, its flourishing primary industries and developing trade was as well balanced as that of its northern neighbour. Only in the 1830s did size seriously affect its relative position.

Political Issues in the 1820s

The increasing size and complexity of the Australian colonies necessitated successive modifications in their government. Three times in less than ten years institutions that had remained untouched for over a generation in New South Wales were changed. The first occasion was in 1823 when an Act was passed authorising the king to issue a new Charter of Justice, separating the judiciaries of New South Wales and Van Diemen's Land and placing each under a chief justice, thereby laying the foundations for present-day legal systems. The Act also established in New South Wales a nominated Legislative Council of up to eight members. At first all were government officials, but in 1825 Earl Bathurst appointed three representatives of the merchants and gentry. During the same year an Executive Council composed of the lieutenant-governor, the chief justice, the archdeacon and the colonial secretary was established while in 1828 the Legislative Council was enlarged to fifteen members and its powers were increased.

Governors were increasingly expected to consult with both councils and heed their advice. In exceptional circumstances the opinions of members might be disregarded, but if the British government considered such a course unwarranted governors could find themselves in difficulties. There were, therefore, effective restraints on local rulers and these were at first heightened by the need to secure from the chief justice an assurance that their enactments did not contravene the laws of England. A stipulation to this effect was incorporated in the 1823 Act but so many problems were created that it was dropped in 1828.

These reforms were designed not to liberalise government but to make it more effective. The previous system had worked well while the colony was small and amenable to discipline. New pressures had grown since the first settlement and the actions of governors were increasingly questioned by disgruntled elements in the colony and by their allies in the House of Commons. To allow this situation to continue at a time when the number of free and freed in the colony was rapidly increasing might weaken the local government. Bigge had drawn attention to these dangers. The actual framing of the 1823 Act, however, was undertaken by Francis Forbes, first chief justice of New South Wales, who acted in close collaboration with James Stephen and the Colonial Office. The Act embodied some of Bigge's proposals, but not his suggestion that governors should consult with the magistrates when drawing up regulations relating to discipline. The idea behind this proposal, namely that the governor would be more likely to act wisely, did however find partial expression in the decision to create a Legislative Council. Bigge had not proposed such a step and it was James Stephen, legal adviser to the Colonial Office, who suggested it. In common with the later moves of 1825 and 1828 it was an attempt to ensure that no governor acted without first seeking and heeding expert advice. By this means the mistakes of the past could be avoided and the ministry at home might escape the embarrassment of having governors' actions challenged in the House of Commons. To strengthen the whole structure parliament was involved in the changes of 1823 and 1828. Previously the system of government had derived its authority from the king acting through his ministers. Now the constitution of New South Wales was based on an Act of Parliament rather than Royal decree.

The inaugural meeting of the Legislative Council of New South Wales took place in the council chamber, Government House, Sydney, on 25 August 1824. The Executive Council did not assemble until 19 December 1825. From these two dates both bodies met regularly and, although there were occasions when their views were disregarded or overridden, for the most part they effectively discharged their duties. The right to initiate legislation, however, was still vested in the governor. He, acting within the framework of instructions received from London, continued to dominate the legislative and the executive processes and vitally to influence the course of development.

The first administrator to face a Legislative Council was Major-General Sir Thomas Brisbane. He had been appointed as successor to Macquarie in 1821 on the recommendation of the Duke of Wellington under whom he had served with distinction during the Napoleonic wars. A mild-tempered, handsome officer, of ancient Scottish lineage, he was also a Fellow of the Royal Society and a man of high intellectual capacity. One of his reasons for coming to New South Wales was to pursue his interest in the study of astronomy. His enemies accused him of spending less time governing than star-gazing from the observatory which he built at Parramatta and placed under his German assistant, C.C.L. Rumker who became the first government astronomer. This criticism was unfair to a man whose high sense of responsibility did not allow him to neglect his duties. Brisbane encouraged exploration, applied most of the reforms advocated by Bigge, tightened the administration of the convict system, introduced tickets of occupation to assist graziers, established an Agricultural Training Centre, reduced expenditure and introduced currency reforms—all in the space of four years. In addition, he began to reorganise the colonial public service. Forgetful and imprecise, he was not a purposeful or efficient ruler and was unable to impose himself on his subordinates. He had the misfortune to clash with John Macarthur, the Reverend Samuel Marsden and Archdeacon Scott, all of whom had the ear of the Colonial Office. Worse, he came into conflict with Frederick Goulburn, first holder of a position newly created within New South Wales, namely that of colonial secretary. Goulburn was an overbearing, interfering, inexperienced, political appointee, whose brother had been under-secretary to Lord Bathurst. By the time the clash became acute the government was already concerned at Brisbane's handling of affairs. Goulburn, besides demonstrating his incapacity, had incurred the enmity of John Macarthur who also disapproved of Brisbane. The Macarthur influence helped bring about the recall of both men, Goulburn to be replaced by the distinguished entomologist and public servant, Alexander McLeay, and Brisbane by a stern disciplinarian, Lieutenant-General Ralph Darling.

Apart from a brief interlude as acting governor of Mauritius during 1818 and early 1819, Darling had given his life exclusively to the army. He saw active service against the French in the West Indies, was awarded a gold medal for commanding Sir John Moore's old regiment, the 51st Foot, at Corunna in 1808 and took part in the disastrous Walcheren expedition in 1809. He spent most of the Napoleonic wars at the Horse Guards in London, however, where he rose to be deputy adjutant general, and from 1811 to 1818 was in charge of the all-important recruiting department. His capabilities as a staff officer won the approval of his superiors, including the Duke of York, while the creditable manner in which he ruled Mauritius earned him the support of Earl Bathurst and the admiration of Wilmot Horton. He came from a poor family, his father Christopher having risen from the ranks to become adjutant of the 45th Foot in which he himself was once a private and later an ensign. He had none of those powerful connections that were then so important to advancement and owed his rise to talent rather than family.

Darling's high administrative ability was soon put to good use after his arrival at Sydney in December 1825. Brisbane, while allowing departmental heads to exercise initiative, had not provided that overall control which was necessary to give the public service direction. Darling immersed himself fully in the task of establishing order. He was handicapped by the reluctance of his superiors to provide additional money so that salaries could be raised and by the inefficiency and corruption of some of his subordinates. It was partly because there was a shortage of reliable officials that he appointed his private secretary, Lieutenant-Colonel Henry Dumaresq, to the position of clerk of the Executive and Legislative Councils, and William Dumaresq to the post of acting civil engineer. The fact that the two were related to Darling through his marriage in October 1817 to their sister Elizabeth gave rise to the charge of nepotism. Certainly the governor did work closely with these two men and with Alexander McLeay who was also connected with the Dumaresqs. He appointed his nephew, Charles Henry, as his private secretary in succession to Henry Dumaresq. But these were all competent men whose talents justified their appointments. The

Dumaresqs came from one of the two leading families in Jersey. They had a distinguished record of military service and they made a mark in the colony as settlers. Charles Henry Darling was later to govern three British territories including Victoria. By turning to such a quarter Darling was able to surmount some of his problems and find respite from his quarrelsome subordinates. Although some departments such as the surveyor-general's did not function as effectively as he would have liked, the public service did improve. The colonial secretary's office gained from losing responsibility for convicts and the creation of a land board smoothed the administration of land policy. The whole system ran more efficiently thanks to Darling's strictures and inexhaustible attention to detail, although the governor's health suffered from never-ceasing toil. He introduced important reforms in the convict system, and laid down town planning regulations for Sydney. He encouraged Captain Stirling to examine the Swan River and, much to the chagrin of Surveyor-General Thomas Mitchell who became one of his bitterest critics, appointed Captain Charles Sturt, his relative and military secretary, to lead expeditions in 1828 and 1829 which resulted in the discovery of the Darling and Murray Rivers. Under his aegis Allan Cunningham, who had already done much to advance botanical knowledge, made his famous journey north between January and August 1827 and discovered the Darling Downs. This widening of the colony's horizons was a tribute to Darling's foresight and opened the way to further expansion.

Like the French king whose every gift to a subject made one disappointed man and nine enemies, the New South Wales governors of the 1820s found that even their most enlightened measures sometimes went unappreciated. The situation indeed bore a faint resemblance to eighteenth-century France where powerful figures jostled the monarch when their interests were threatened. The Macarthur clan was a constant source of worry. Their patriarch John, no longer the fiery rebel of Bligh's day, was still capable of causing trouble. In London his lawyer son John, who numbered amongst his influential friends Under-Secretary Wilmot Horton, was well placed to catch the ear of the Colonial Office. At home Macarthur was at the centre of a group known as the exclusives which in the early 1820s numbered among its central figures Archdeacon Scott, James Bowman, the principal surgeon, Attorney-General Saxe Bannister and Surveyor-General John Oxley. Macarthur's intimates were in British politics, the professions, the wool industry and the church as well as in the Legislative and

Samuel Terry, the wealthy convict, one of the leading ex-convict entrepreneurs and a public figure.

Executive Councils. Few colonists could rival his power, but there were others of similar views like the Reverend Samuel Marsden whose influence was considerable. When directed against a governor their rancour could have serious effects as Brisbane discovered to his cost.

On some matters, personal as well as public, these men were divided. On others that touched their economic interests they were often at one with the leading ex-convict entrepreneurs such as Samuel Terry, Daniel Cooper and his partner Solomon Levey. There was, however, a division between the exclusives and the emancipists. This last word had a double meaning. It was used in a narrow sense to label men and women who had completed their sentences. Politically, however, it had a wider connotation and was used during the 1820s and 1830s to refer to a group composed partly of former convicts, partly of respectable migrants. Among its leaders was the native-born W.C. Wentworth, whose great energies, wide vision and political skill made him a dominant figure for over a generation. The son of a wealthy New South Wales landholder and surgeon, D'Arcy Wentworth, who had family connections with such powerful aristocrats as Lord Fitzwilliam and the Earl of Rockingham, he was trained at the English bar and at first seemed destined for a patrician life. His mother, Catherine Crowley, however, was a convict and while in England he suffered the double ignominy of being rejected as the suitor of Elizabeth Macarthur and discovering that his father had narrowly escaped transportation for highway robbery. Shattered by these blows he espoused the cause of the Australian-born and the emancipists. His patriotic poem *Australasia* and his book urging representative government and trial by jury won him widespread support and on his return to New South Wales in 1824 he quickly established himself as a popular leader.

No less prominent in the same cause was Sir John Jamison of Regentville near Penrith on the Nepean River. He had been knighted by the Swedish government for his services as a surgeon before coming to the colony in 1814 to take over the property of his father, Thomas Jamison, former surgeon's mate on the *Sirius*. An enemy of Macarthur, whom he considered to have cheated his father in a mercantile transaction, Sir John incurred the displeasure of the Colonial Office by making false charges against Governor Brisbane. Debarred from holding any official position under the existing system of government he espoused the popular cause. Governor Bourke described him as one of the 'many free emigrants of great wealth and intelligence who advocate liberal principles'. Others included John and Gregory Blaxland, William Lawson, William Cox, Archibald Bell and James Atkinson. The presence of such people in the emancipist camp meant that the split between this group and the exclusives reflected differences of political outlook as well as of social origin.

The exclusives, all of whom had arrived free, had affinities with the English Tories. They favoured a strong executive and opposed representative government. They had reservations about the use of the jury system in the criminal and civil courts and about the idea of emancipists serving as jurors. They considered such reforms unsuited to a colony that was still primarily penal in character. No colonist who had been transported to the colony could be relied upon to act impartially. Indeed, if given power they might well use their numerical preponderance to swamp settlers of free origin. Self-interest as well as questions of principle underlay the conservatism of the exclusives.

If the exclusives were sometimes described as Botany Bay Tories, the emancipists equally well deserved the label Whig. They were mainly moderate reformers who sought to make the government more responsive to property owning groups by establishing a legislature whose members were chosen by such people. They were not democrats and like the exclusives abhorred violence and revolution—a fact made clear by their outspoken criticisms of the 1830 uprising in Paris. They did, however, wish to gain a voice in government for propertied colonists, free as well as former convict, and secure for both the right to participate in trial by jury. As loyal British subjects they resented the fact that in New South Wales they were debarred from the political and judicial rights to which they would have been entitled in England. The belief that they were being denied their birthright gave added force to their arguments.

The issues of trial by jury and constitutional reform were debated during the 1820s more vigorously than ever before. A change had occurred in the climate of opinion due partly to the presence of large numbers of educated migrants, partly to the development of the press. Before 1821 there was only one newspaper, the *Sydney Gazette* that had appeared since 5 March 1803 under the editorship of George Howe, an emancipist who had once worked for *The Times* in London and who had been appointed government printer in 1801. The *Sydney Gazette* was at first run along semi-official lines as a vehicle for the publication of official notices and regulations. Its columns also included private advertisements, local news items, extracts from English papers and comment of a non-political nature on subjects of importance to farmers, graziers and the like. The 1820s saw the establishment of the *Australian* by W.C. Wentworth and his friend Robert Wardell, a Cambridge Doctor of Laws, then of the *Monitor* under Edward Smith Hall, a migrant and lay missionary, grazier and cashier and secretary of the Bank of New South Wales. Both papers had a political objective. The first altered its emphasis during the 1820s as a result of changes in editor and owner, but remained broadly liberal. The second under the outspoken Hall who in 1829 became the first colonist to be convicted for criminally libelling a public official, namely Archdeacon Scott, took a more radical line. The presence of two such papers forced the *Sydney Gazette* to enter the political arena and, although its links with the government were severed, it mostly sympathised with official policy.

Of the two questions that figured most prominently in the press trial by jury made the greatest headway. Commissioner Bigge had recommended reform once enough suitably qualified people were present. During the 1820s the cause was taken up not only by popular elements but also by liberal-minded officials including

Governor Brisbane who sympathised with the emancipist cause. The British government, aware of the peculiarities of the colony and of the deep divisions of opinion, moved only slowly, but by 1828 it had sanctioned the use of juries in civil cases at the option of either litigant and in criminal cases where seditious libel was involved. It was also made clear that no obstacle would be placed in the way of any further changes that were supported by the governor-in-council. The initiative had been given to the men on the spot who were considered best placed to judge the moment for reform. By 1831, when Governor Darling returned home, steps had been taken to allow suitably qualified pardoned convicts to serve on civil juries, but most cases in the criminal court were heard by a board of seven naval or military officers.

If emancipists and their supporters had cause to be dissatisfied with this situation, they were even more displeased by the 1823 and 1828 Acts which ignored their demand for representative government. The struggle that centred around this issue became bitter and tarnished Darling's reputation, exposing weaknesses that had earlier become evident in his administration of Mauritius. Shortly after agitation for reform of the 1823 Act started in 1826 the governor had the misfortune to punish two soldiers, Joseph Sudds and Patrick Thompson who had committed theft in the hope of being discharged from the 57th regiment. Determined to stamp out this practice before it spread, Darling commuted their court sentences to seven years hard labour and ordered them to be drummed out of the regiment clad in irons at a parade on 22 November 1826. Unknown to Darling, Sudds was ill, and subsequently he died. Although at first reasonable in their response the anti-government press and the emancipists, led by Wentworth, seized the issue as a means of belabouring institutions that they hoped would be reformed when a new constitution was introduced. Feelings were aroused and emotions ran high. The governor, who like his predecessor had at first taken a lenient attitude towards the press, now introduced repressive legislation—a move that Lord Bathurst had recommended on the grounds that a free press was out of place in a penal colony, particularly as restraints were imposed in England. This step aroused a greater public outcry than had the Sudds-Thompson affair and sealed the growing breach between the governor and Chief Justice Forbes who acted in what Darling considered an underhand manner by declaring two of his four newspaper Bills unconstitutional. The penalties imposed under the remaining measures and a more severe Act of 1830 partly curbed the press, but at the cost of alienating liberal opinion. Darling, a Tory in politics, considered that representative government was ill-suited to a penal colony and saw his main task as that of maintaining order and discipline. His administration, which had opened promisingly on a note of conciliation, ended in discord, with Wentworth threatening impeachment and other enemies such as Captain Robison, who resented being dismissed from the Royal Veterans, making loud accusations. Darling was later cleared of all charges and knighted, but the fact remains that under pressure he had overreacted and stirred up feeling. Accustomed by long service in the army to be obeyed, he lacked the finesse to handle astute political adversaries like Wentworth.

No challenge of such magnitude had by 1830 emerged to trouble the even more autocratic rule of George Arthur in Van Diemen's Land. At first this region was unaffected by the constitutional changes introduced on the mainland. The framers of the 1823 Act adopted Bigge's cautious stance and merely empowered the Crown to establish a separate administration when the time was considered opportune. In the meantime, although some of the more irksome restraints were removed at Arthur's insistence, the government remained linked to that of New South Wales in a subordinate position. The expansion in population, difficulties in communication between Sydney and Hobart and the growing need for prompt decisions on important issues underlined the disadvantages of such an arrangement. Throughout his early months in office Arthur chafed at the restrictions imposed upon him and supported by leading colonists pressed hard for independence. This was effected by an Order in Council dated 14 June 1825 which separated the government of the two regions. Arthur, while retaining the title of lieutenant-governor, was vested with powers that in practice were as great as those of the mainland rulers.

The two governments were now similar in form. An Executive Council and a Legislative Council modelled on those of New South Wales were established. Arthur, however, was not one to heed others. He held decisive views, particularly on matters connected with the convicts, and was determined to run the colony as he chose. The British authorities, recognising the need for firm control in a community that contained so many criminals, placed less emphasis on the need to consult colonial opinion than was the case on the mainland. Indeed, Earl Bathurst stated categorically that 'the free inhabitants, whether immigrants or prisoners free by emancipation or servitude should be looked upon as visitors and liable to submit to the rules established for general peace and order of the colony'.

This attitude necessarily created problems but, without a substantial politically conscious free population, they assumed only minor proportions. Most settlers were too busy and too dependent upon government for convict labour to risk offending Arthur. Nonetheless, his authoritarianism, strictness, high moral tone and determination to stamp out corruption antagonised important figures such as Andrew Bell, emancipist proprietor and founder in 1816 of the *Hobart Town Gazette,* and Robert Lathrop Murray, a former military officer who had been transported for bigamy. Their attacks in the press resulted in his encouraging George Terry Howe, brother of the proprietor of the *Sydney Gazette*, to establish a rival paper. This bore the same name as Bell's publication, undercut its circulation and eventually forced its owner to restyle it the *Colonial Times.* Meantime, Bell was imprisoned for libel and the lieutenant-governor, with the all-important concurrence of Chief Justice Pedder who unlike Forbes was no liberal, had taken steps to curb the freedom of the press. The fact that the civil and judicial authorities were agreed upon the need for such a move ensured that it succeeded with far less trouble than was the case on the mainland. Opposition still existed but by the time his New South Wales counterpart returned home in January 1831 Arthur was still fully in control of the situation.

four: New Policies and Settlements

Wakefield and Imperial Policy

By the early 1830s New South Wales and Van Diemen's Land, although still primarily penal colonies, had acquired more of the characteristics associated with free settlements. The former, with its greater natural resources and larger numbers of free and freed persons, had progressed furthest in this direction, setting a pattern that was to persist until the middle of the century. Both colonies at first continued along their well-trodden path, but penal elements retained an influence in Van Diemen's Land that they progressively lost on the mainland. These divergences were partly a result of differences in the potential of the two regions, partly of alterations in Colonial Office policy that were in turn influenced by changing conditions and attitudes in Britain. After 1830, as at every stage of their early history, the course of events in the Australian colonies was vitally influenced by the situation in the mother country.

The social and economic conditions that prevailed in Britain throughout the 1830s and the 'hungry forties' continued to spawn poverty as well as crime. Misery and suffering were widespread, nowhere more so than in Ireland where the failure of the staple potato crop after 1845 resulted in widespread deaths and starvation. There was nothing new in the existence of distress among the lower orders, but a change of great importance to the Australian colonies occurred in the government's handling of this problem. The continuing high birth and falling death rate of the early nineteenth century brought fears that Britain was in danger of becoming overpopulated. The conclusion earlier drawn by the Reverend Thomas Malthus that population growth would exceed the increase in productive resources by a widening margin seemed to many to be confirmed by the evidence of their own eyes. The mercantilists of the eighteenth century had seen strength in numbers, but to nineteenth-century economists and social reformers, population expansion if left unchecked would breed disaster. During the 1820s voices were raised in favour of employing Britain's overseas possessions as a safety valve for the release of the pressures that were building up at home. Amongst those to urge this course was R.J. Wilmot Horton, under-secretary for the colonies, who recommended that paupers be encouraged to migrate to North America as one way of relieving Britain's problems and at the same time providing her dependencies with labour. In the event, his proposals foundered on the rock of expense which sank all such projects during this decade.

The principle was nonetheless appealing, particularly to the parish authorities who were responsible for the paupers. Before governments could be prevailed upon to sanction migration schemes, however, some means had to be found of financing them. Local authorities had little cash to spare and the limited revenue raised in the Australian colonies from quit rents, duties and fines was already committed to other ends. Where then was money to be found? The answer came from an unexpected direction.

In 1831 Viscount Goderich (later first Earl of Ripon), secretary of state for the colonies since September 1827, announced that henceforth Crown land was to be sold by auction in lots of 640 acres at a minimum price of 5s an acre. The free land grant system was now regarded by the Colonial Office as wasteful and inefficient. It brought the government little financial return and was difficult to administer. Moreover colonists obtained unduly large acreages so that too much land lay idle and settlement was impeded. By substituting sale for grants Goderich planned to remove these disadvantages. The Ripon regulations, as they became known, were designed to promote more intensive cultivation of the soil, prevent undue dispersal of settlement, reduce transport costs and, by making land more difficult to obtain, ensure that a larger proportion of colonists were available as labourers.

Once the principle of land sales was established the question arose as to what use might be made of this new source of revenue. The government had not earmarked it for any specific objective, but eventually it agreed to use some to promote emigration to Australia. In 1831 an emigration commission was set up to collect and spread information and assist those who wished to depart. Although this body operated for only a year, it laid down important regulations and helped establish the basis for a new system of government-sponsored emigration that was financed in part from the land fund.

It was once believed that the inspiration for these developments came from a writer who had no official connection with either the Colonial Office or the colonies. This was Edward Gibbon Wakefield whose career as a minor diplomat had been terminated in 1826 when he was sentenced to three years in Newgate for abducting a sixteen-year-old heiress. While in prison he read widely and made a detailed study of the emigration movement. As a result of his research and of his discussions with fellow inmates he developed an interest in Australia. Gradually he evolved a theory of colonisation which so closely resembled subsequent policies that historians postulated a causal connection between the two.

Wakefield was a convinced upholder of the British Empire which he saw as essential to the continued economic development of Britain. Without new outlets for capital, profits would fall and without additional sources of employment the workers, whose plight Wakefield discussed in terms that foreshadowed Marx, would be condemned to perpetual want. His theory was intended to benefit not only the mother country but also the dependencies. He advocated planned colonisation and strongly criticised Wilmot Horton for seeking merely to shovel out paupers. Migrants were to be carefully selected to ensure a satisfactory balance between sexes, classes and occupation groups. Once in the colony they must be placed in communities whose compactness provided a necessary guarantee that they would develop along civilised lines. Nor must migrants be allowed to obtain land too readily. New South Wales was at that time experiencing a labour shortage and according to Wakefield's analysis this was a result of the ease with which grants had been obtained. To solve this problem and guarantee a continuing supply of workers, land had to be sold at a price 'sufficient' to occasion,

> Neither superabundance of people nor superabundance of land, but so limiting the quantity of land as to give the cheapest land a market value that would have the effect of compelling labourers to work some considerable time for wages before they could become landowners.

Such were the broad features of the Wakefield theory. His supporters saw him as a major innovator whose advocacy of the sale

Emigrants at dinner aboard ship. Migration to New South Wales increased
as people seized the opportunity to escape hardship at home.

of land, recommendation that the proceeds be used to finance large-
scale migration and plea for the careful selection of migrants altered
the course of imperial policy. His detractors, who include some
recent historians, view him as 'an ignorant, self opinionated, self
seeking busybody' who sensed the direction in which policy would
move and capitalised on this in an attempt to carve out a new career
now that his old one had ended in ignominy. Certainly his views
lacked originality; his concept of the 'sufficient price' was not properly worked out; and the analysis on which he based his case for
the sale of land was demonstrably erroneous. It is unlikely that he
caused the government to change its policies and it is questionable
as to how much influence he exerted upon Colonial Office officials.
Much has been made of a statement by Under-Secretary Viscount
Howick (later the third Earl Grey) who expressed admiration for
Wakefield's ideas. Recently, however, it has been shown that Howick
was speaking incautiously and over-generously long after the event
and that he was unaffected by Wakefield when he urged Goderich
to introduce land sales in 1831. The effects of Wakefield's persuasive writings on public opinion during the 1830s should not be
underestimated but governments were more difficult to move. He

and his followers had an influence on some of the details of policy but its course was determined by other factors.

One consequence of the changes which occurred in British policy was that migration to New South Wales increased as more people seized the opportunity to escape from hardships at home. Between 1832 and 1837 some 6 546 men and women were brought out under the government system. This was supervised by a member of the Colonial Office staff, T.F. Elliott, who was assisted by a voluntary organisation, the London Emigration Committee. The colonists, however, complained that many arrivals had been poorly selected and were unsuited to local needs. Accordingly, in 1836 Governor Bourke inaugurated the bounty system under which settlers arranged passages for migrants of their choice and received a bounty from colonial funds to cover the cost. This proved more popular and less expensive than the government system which it supplemented; but it too became liable to abuse after a change was introduced allowing the bounty to be paid to shipowners. These men commercialised the operation by conveying whole boatloads of labourers to Port Jackson and persuading the colonists to accept them. By 1842 a further 48 081 assisted migrants had arrived but their quality was sometimes poor and a halt had to be called due to the depression and dwindling funds. Meanwhile, the British authorities had taken firmer control over emigration. In January 1840 Lord John Russell, influenced by Wakefield's views concerning the interconnection of land and labour, established the Colonial Land and Emigration Commission. This co-ordinated developments in both fields on an imperial basis and improved the machinery of selection. A shortage of funds at first prevented New South Wales from benefiting from the continued exodus of migrants from Britain and only 4 648 arrived between 1843 and 1847. Thereafter money again became available and between 1848 and 1850, 26 225 men and women were brought out. In addition, substantial numbers paid their own passages as had been the case throughout the period.

Reform of the Penal System

By 1850 many more migrants were living in New South Wales than ever before. The number of convicts, in contrast, had become negligible. In 1847 they amounted to only 6 664 and formed a mere 3·2 per cent of a total population of 205 009. Twenty years earlier they comprised 40·1 per cent of the population and in 1840 the proportion stood at 29·6 per cent. Transportation had in fact continued on a substantial scale for most of the 1830s and during the years 1830–40 some 34 623 convicts landed at Sydney. The replacement of Darling by Bourke made little difference to the way in which they were treated. Admittedly, Bourke tried to reform those sent to Norfolk Island by providing clergymen and offering plots of land to the better prisoners. But the island, under its stern commandants, Lieutenant-Colonel James Morisset who had earlier been in charge of Newcastle and Major Joseph Anderson, was still notorious for its depraved inhabitants and rigorous punishment. On the mainland, Bourke sought rather to make the penal system uniform than to soften it. Supervision of the road gangs was tightened to make escape difficult and the work was made more arduous.

These improvements did nothing to make transportation acceptable to the growing number of Englishmen who urged its abolition. From the earliest days there had been opposition to the use of banishment as a weapon in the struggle against crime. The barbarity of the custom was increasingly felt to be out of place in a society that was becoming more tolerant and humane. Criminals should be kept in England and reformed, not shipped overseas and forgotten. The Benthamites had long urged a change in the system and during the 1830s they were joined by humanitarians, evangelicals, penal reformers and systematic colonisers, all of whom had their own reasons for wanting an end to transportation.

None had made a detailed analysis of the system which they condemned. All based their criticism on theoretical rather than empirical grounds. Their writings while containing a stratum of the truth also embodied wild assertions and erroneous facts. At first they focused on the inadequacies of transportation from the economic and penal standpoint. Figures of questionable validity were produced to show that it was cheaper to keep convicts in Britain than send them to the antipodes. Rises in the crime rate were cited as proof that the threat of transportation did not deter would-be law breakers. Criticism was levelled against assignment which, it was argued, impeded uniformity of discipline or control. While some convicts were treated like slaves, others were given substantial personal freedom. Assignment was described as a lottery which encouraged men to commit crimes in the hope of being sent to the Australian colonies. During the 1830s these themes were expanded, but attention was also given to the harmful effects exerted by criminals on the community at large. New South Wales and Van Diemen's Land were depicted as societies whose every facet of life was tainted by convicts. Transportation, wrote one critic, 'has produced the most degraded community in the universe; the most demoralised society on record in the history of nations'. Now that free people were arriving in increasing numbers it was essential that the convict blight be removed.

Ill-founded and exaggerated though many of these opinions appear when viewed from the present day, they were accepted by Whig opinion as justifying a radical change in the penal system. In April 1837 Lord Melbourne's Whig ministry appointed a House of Commons Select Committee to enquire into transportation, especially 'its efficacy as a punishment, its influence on the moral state of society in the penal colonies, and how far it is susceptible of improvement'. The committee was composed mainly of men who opposed transportation. Its chairman, Sir William Molesworth, and a substantial number of members were Wakefieldians who saw convictism as an obstacle to free migration and a threat to the economic progress of the colony which they had recently helped to found in South Australia. Not surprisingly the Molesworth Committee's Report, which appeared in August 1838, recommended that convicts no longer be sent to the mainland or to the settled parts of Van Diemen's Land. Most were to serve their time in Britain under carefully supervised conditions. Long-term sentences might, however, be spent under close control in penitentiaries that were to be built at Norfolk Island and on Tasman Peninsula away from contact with private settlers.

The government was not prepared to go to the extreme of abolishing transportation to both of its antipodean possessions. Even before receiving the committee's proposals, however, it had decided that New South Wales was no longer suitable for convicts. Once the Molesworth Report had cleared the ground, the government acted and on 22 May 1840 an Order in Council removed New South Wales from the territories to which such people could be sent. This did not at once end the responsibility of governors for supervising the convict system. Quite apart from the presence of criminals who still had sentences to complete, fresh arrivals continued to be sent to Norfolk Island which came under New South Wales jurisdiction. Between February 1840 and 1844 control was in the hands of Captain Alexander Maconochie a former naval officer and foundation professor of geography at University College, London. While private secretary to Lieutenant-Governor Sir John Franklin, Maconochie had, at the request of the English Society for the Improvement of Prison Discipline, carried out an investigation into the convict system. His report was so condemnatory of official policy that Franklin dismissed him in 1838. In contrast to many

English reformers he regarded assignment as a severe punishment which uniformly degraded and demoralised convicts by making them slaves. He accepted the need for transportation but recommended that those sent to the colonies should be subject to treatment that would 'return them to society, honest, useful and trustworthy members of it'. After initial confinement accompanied by religious and moral instruction they were to receive vocational training and be allowed progressively greater freedom as their conduct improved. Restraints in the form of supervisors and corporal punishment were to be abolished and the responsibility for discipline was to rest on the prisoners themselves. The length of a man's sentence would be determined not by the courts but by his own behaviour and he would be released once he had been reformed. This scheme and the evidence which its author gave before the Molesworth Committee aroused the interest of Lord John Russell who appointed Maconochie administrator of Norfolk Island.

Between 1840 and 1844 this island, hitherto the scene of the worst horrors of the convict system, became the centre of an enlightened experiment which embodied many of the principles of modern penology. The Colonial Office had previously agreed that the conduct of convicts should determine how long they stayed there, but Governor Gipps of New South Wales was to decide what latitude Maconochie was to receive. While not prepared to permit experiments with the 1 200 twice-convicted felons from New South Wales who were already on the island, Gipps, although sceptical of the commandant's ideas, gave him a free hand to treat the 679 prisoners recently sent from England. Maconochie ignored the instruction to segregate old from new. He brought all under a system that eschewed brutality and allocated daily marks which earned partial and eventually total remission of sentences when the requisite total was reached. Convicts were allowed to occupy responsible positions and, but for the opposition of Gipps, would have been permitted to exchange marks for money. Maconochie claimed with justice to have converted the island from 'a turbulent, brutal hell' into 'a peaceful, well ordered community'. He was criticised, however, for awarding marks too lavishly and arousing expectations that could not at once be fulfilled. Disappointment bred scepticism among the convicts and partially undermined discipline, giving rise to claims that the island had lost its punitive value. Concerned at these premature reports and alarmed at increasing costs the government decided to abandon the experiment before it had been given a fair trial. In February 1844 Captain Joseph Childs replaced

Maconochie and Norfolk Island became merely a dumping ground for convicts. It functioned as a penal settlement until 1853, first under Childs, whose ineffective administration culminated in a convict uprising that brought about his removal in July 1846, then under John Price, a police magistrate from Van Diemen's Land. Both men resorted to brutality and the deterioration in convict morality and behaviour highlighted the value of Maconochie's approach.

During its last nine years as a penal settlement Norfolk Island came under the government of Van Diemen's Land which, since 1840, had become the chief repository for transported felons. Throughout the 1830s convicts continued to arrive at Hobart where they were mostly distributed among free settlers. The autocratic Lieutenant-Governor Arthur had been replaced in February 1837 by Sir John Franklin, a naval officer and Arctic explorer whose sensitive disposition and liberal views contrasted sharply with those of his predecessor. An advocate of assignment and a supporter of representative institutions, Franklin presided over Van Diemen's Land at a time when official thinking was moving in a different direction to his own. Having ended transportation to New South Wales the authorities were unwilling to accept the Molesworth Committee's recommendations concerning Van Diemen's Land. Unwilling to retain all convicts in the United Kingdom and lacking any alternative outlet, the government decided to continue sending them to this region. Instead of following the course taken by the mother colony, the island was tied more closely to the English penal system, thus ruling out any possibility of its constitution being liberalised.

During the early 1840s some 5000 convicts poured in annually. The task of catering for them presented increasing difficulties. Even before the Molesworth Committee started taking evidence, the home and colonial secretaries, Lord John Russell and Lord Glenelg, had decided to abolish assignment. From 1837 convicts arriving in Van Diemen's Land worked in government gangs before being distributed among settlers. In 1839 the practice of allowing convicts into private employ was ended and Franklin was ordered to increase the number of gangs. This meant that the financial burden of maintaining prisoners fell exclusively on the British Treasury. Concerned at this situation the secretary of state for the colonies, Lord Stanley, in November 1842 introduced the probation system under which prisoners who behaved for two years while in public service were given a 'probation pass' enabling them to work for wages. Continued good conduct earned a ticket of leave and a remission of sentence, provided the convict did not leave the island. Those who failed to respond to treatment were sent to Norfolk Island. The man responsible for administering this system was Sir John Eardley-Wilmot, a sixty-year-old county magistrate and former member of parliament who had some knowledge of juvenile delinquency. He replaced Franklin in August 1843 and was recalled in 1846 after the probation system had broken down due partly to his incompetence, partly to the government's failure to send enough supervisors to maintain discipline and partly to the economic depression of 1842 which reduced the demand for labour. So many convicts were unemployed that transportation was suspended for two years after 1846 while alternatives were being considered and while first the temporary commandant, C.J. La Trobe, and then Lieutenant-Governor Denison found means of absorbing prisoners already there. Van Diemen's Land with its limited resources was clearly incapable of meeting the needs of the English penal system as they had existed since 1840. The whole issue of transportation, however, was by now bound up with local politics and the developments of the next few years are best considered later in a different context.

New Settlements

Meanwhile, new mainland settlements which owed nothing to convicts had been established. Least successful were the attempts to found on the northern coast a centre for trade with the East Indian archipelago. In 1815 the Dutch, recently united with the reluctant Belgians under the House of Orange to form the Kingdom of the Netherlands, had regained their East Indian possessions. They faced formidable competition from the British who, under the energetic and far-sighted Sir Stamford Raffles had acquired the swampy, malaria-ridden Singapore. So successful was this entrepôt that merchants began searching for other means of increasing their share of eastern trade. They were particularly anxious to obtain trepang which would enable them to penetrate the highly prized Chinese market. In 1823 William Barnes, a seaman adventurer, urged the opening of a second Singapore at Melville Island. Such a step had earlier been recommended by Lieutenant Phillip Parker King, whose explorations of 1818 and 1824 had completed the survey of Australia's northern coast begun by Matthew Flinders in 1802. Barnes's proposals were supported by the East India Company and ultimately by the British government which was attracted by strategic as well as commercial considerations. The Dutch were old rivals and a second base near their possessions would prove useful in the event of hostilities. Moreover, the proposed settlement would forestall any Dutch claim to northern Australia which might be difficult to resist in view of their prior discovery of this region. In January 1824 an expedition under Captain James Bremer was despatched aboard the *Tamar* to Melville Island with orders to call *en route* at Port Jackson to collect troops, convicts and supplies. The party arrived off the north coast on 20 September 1824 and a year later the boundary of New South Wales was extended from the 135th meridian to the 129th to bring the new settlement within the British sphere of influence.

Fort Dundas, named and selected by Bremer at Melville Island, was badly chosen. Situated on a part of the coast rarely visited by the Malays, it was off the route of European vessels and proved unsuitable for white people who found the climate oppressive and unhealthy, the soil unproductive and the natives troublesome. In April 1826 Earl Bathurst, anxious to maintain a British presence in the north, ordered the opening of Raffles Bay on the mainland. After an uncertain start in June 1827 the settlement, whose centre was at Fort Wellington, gradually established itself. Due largely to its second commandant, Captain Collet Barker, a man cast in the mould of Arthur Phillip, the early difficulties were overcome and by 1829 trade had developed with the Malays. By then, however, the British government, influenced by unfavourable reports despatched months earlier from Raffles Bay, had decided to abandon the region. Captain Barker reluctantly withdrew in 1829 leaving Fort Wellington to the elements.

Midway through the following decade interest in the north coast of Australia was revived by rumours of an impending occupancy by the French who were fitting out an expedition at Toulon. Concern was also aroused by the Dutch who had won a commanding position over Torres Strait. Prominent among those anxious to break their hold was George Windsor Earl, a writer and trader with extensive first-hand knowledge of the region. Backed by the newly formed and influential Royal Geographical Society, he revived the idea of a second Singapore and between 1835 and 1837 vigorously campaigned for its establishment in the eastern archipelago. The Colonial Office was difficult to convince, but it did favour a settlement on Australia's north coast and now believed that the earlier one could have succeeded. In February 1838 Captain Bremer was again given command of an expedition, this time to Port Essington which had

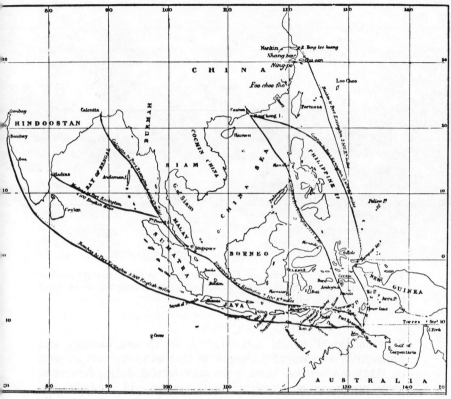

A contemporary map showing the advantages of Northern Australian settlement, 1840s.

been recommended by Lieutenant King in 1818 but rejected in the mistaken belief that it lacked fresh water. After establishing a township named Victoria, Bremer departed, leaving Captain John Macarthur, a marine and nephew of the founder of the Australian wool industry, in command.

The new settlement led a tenuous existence for eleven years. Few trading vessels arrived, the government invested little money and land was granted on such unfavourable terms that few settlers came. The population remained small and the market so restricted that merchants would not bring goods for sale. It was difficult to graze sheep or cattle and the colonists found the climate uncongenial.

Victoria Square, Port Essington. This settlement was set up mainly to allay fears of French or Dutch occupation and as a second Singapore, an entrepôt to encourage trade with China.

'Day and night', wrote T.H. Huxley, the famous biologist and philosopher who visited the region in 1848 as an assistant surgeon on HMS *Rattlesnake*, 'there is the same fearful, damp, depressing heat, producing an unconquerable languor and rendering the unhappy resident a prey to ennui and cold brandy and water'. By the late 1840s fears of French or Dutch occupation had evaporated. The British claim to Australia was clearly established and there was no threat to its sovereignty. Accordingly, in December 1849 Port Essington suffered the fate of Raffles Bay. Years were to elapse before the problems of colonising the tropical north were surmounted.

More successful was the attempt to found a settlement in Western Australia which had lain vacant for four decades since the British arrived at Port Jackson. The reports of Dutch discoverers and English explorers were sufficiently discouraging to deflect the interest of European powers who were preoccupied by war until 1815. The British found ample land and resources in the east and had no desire to extend their commitments unnecessarily. Although no formal claim had been laid to Western Australia, however, the area was seen as coming within the British sphere of influence and any attempt to challenge this was bound to provoke a reaction. The eastern colonies were already isolated from other parts of the empire. Were a foreign power to establish itself along the southern coast the security of New South Wales and Van Diemen's Land might be jeopardised. Such a possibility seemed to have arisen when two French vessels, the *Thetis* and the *Esperance* sailed along the coast in 1825. They were followed a year later by the corvette *L'Astrolabe*, commanded by Dumont D'Urville, who was on a voyage of discovery around the world. These were scientific expeditions but the British government was in no mood to take chances. Napoleon had been replaced by the Bourbons but France had rapidly recovered from defeat and its agents were actively furthering their monarch's interests in Europe and the Pacific. Despite protestations to the contrary, the presence of French vessels might foreshadow settlements that could affect British trade in the Pacific as well as her possessions in eastern Australia. Such a prospect aroused deep concern in London and Sydney prompting Governor Darling to recommend in October 1826 that all the mainland be brought under his jurisdiction.

Most of the southern coast was 'barren and devoid of all circumstances which could invite settlement', but two localities were considered liable to French occupation. The first was Western Port which had been surveyed by Baudin in 1802 and which occupied a commanding position on the northern shore of Bass Strait. Acting on orders from London, Darling on 9 October 1826, after a preliminary survey, despatched an expedition there under Captain Wright. At the other extremity of the continent a settlement had been contemplated for convicts who committed offences which warranted isolation under conditions less rigorous than those applied at Norfolk Island. Shark Bay was the site first contemplated but before this could be examined attention shifted to King George's Sound which was considered more suitable. In October 1826 Major Lockyer and a small contingent of troops and convicts left Sydney and on 21 January 1827 raised the Union Jack in Western Australia. Their object was not to found a new colony but to reinforce British claims to this part of the continent and keep the French out. Yet, as was so often the case, the government found that expansion, once started, was difficult to halt. Within eighteen months of Lockyer's arrival what had begun as a venture in strategy had become an essay in colonisation.

The first step was taken by Captain James Stirling who in April

1826 was brought out of half pay and given command of HMS *Success* with orders to convey currency to New South Wales and transfer the Melville Island garrison to a new site. Arrived at Sydney in December 1826 he persuaded Governor Darling to permit him, while waiting for the monsoons in the north to pass, to explore the west coast where the French were still active. Accompanied by the government botanist, Charles Frazer, he sailed on 17 January 1827 and returned to Port Jackson on 15 March 1828 having discovered and surveyed the Swan River area. Both men made glowing reports and won Governor Darling's support for their belief that a settlement should be established under Stirling. Its strategic importance was stressed and so too was its commercial potential as a base for trade with the East Indies.

In London the admiralty and the Colonial Office were impressed by these reports but neither could see any justification for settlement. King George's Sound was sufficient for immediate purposes and since it came under the government at Sydney was cheaper than the colony proposed by Stirling which would require a separate administrative machinery. 'I am decidedly of opinion', minuted the under-secretary for the colonies in December 1827, 'that it would be inexpedient on the score of expense and that it is unnecessary with a view to any urgent interest to attempt any further settlement'.

Stirling was bitterly disappointed by this decision which frustrated the ambitions he entertained for his own future and that of his brother William, an English manufacturer who had been bankrupted by the cotton crisis of January 1826. After completing his mission to Melville Island he served briefly with the East India naval squadron and was then invalided home. Married to the daughter of a wealthy merchant he was too energetic and ambitious to accept a life of leisure and was determined to found a colony at Swan River. His presence in London provided him with greater opportunities to expound his views; moreover a change in government brought to power as under-secretary and as secretary of state for the colonies two family friends, Horace Twiss and Sir George Murray. After protracted discussions, which involved the Admiralty, the government agreed to despatch Captain C.H. Fremantle on the *Challenger* to take possession of Western Australia—a mission which he accomplished on 2 May 1829. Meanwhile the decision had been taken to establish a colony and in February 1829 an expedition under Stirling sailed for Swan River to carry out preliminary work while more detailed plans were drawn up.

One motive was concern lest France capitalise upon Stirling's discovery. More important was the interest shown by private business men. Stirling himself, in an effort to counter the government's refusal to become involved in expense, had tried unsuccessfully to form an association of investors. The main initiative came from Thomas Peel, son of a wealthy cotton manufacturer and cousin of Robert Peel, then home secretary and future prime minister. He sought a 4 million acre grant in return for settling 10 000 migrants, but the government rejected so large a request and his four financial backers withdrew their support. He found a new silent partner in Solomon Levey, a wealthy New South Wales Jewish emancipist then visiting London. After further negotiations the government agreed to a scheme which, although less ambitious than his first proposal, was based on the same principle. Other groups put forward their own suggestions and prospective settlers also materialised. This was a period when the flow of migrants to the antipodes was increasing. Some of those who had contemplated going to the eastern colonies, including Peel himself, switched their attention to the west which was closer to home, free of convicts, had a congenial climate and an abundance of good land.

By 1829, therefore, the government favoured the settlement of Western Australia. It would have to bear the cost of administration but private interests would shoulder the burden of opening up the land and transporting migrants. Once this had been accepted plans were quickly finalised. In November 1831 the legal system was established and a constitution was proclaimed confirming Stirling in office as governor.

The new colony was the first in Australia to be designed solely for free people. From the outset one theme common to the varied proposals had been that convicts should be debarred. There were already convicts at King George's Sound, but in 1831 the garrison was withdrawn and for the next two decades only migrants were allowed into Western Australia. The same was true of neighbouring South Australia where a settlement also existed.

Although the coastal region of South Australia had been known since 1627 it aroused no interest until 1831 when reports reached London of a journey made in the preceding year by Captain Charles Sturt. He had left Sydney on 3 November 1829 with orders from Governor Darling to investigate the Lachlan-Murrumbidgee river systems and had discovered and named the Murray River, following it to its outlet on the coast at Encounter Bay where the paths of Matthew Flinders and Nicholas Baudin had crossed in April 1802. News of his discoveries reached England where plans for the settlement of Spencer's Gulf had been put forward in February 1831 by Captain Anthony Bacon. While serving a sentence in debtors' prison this army officer had learned of the southern coast from Captain Henry Dixon. After his release he asked the government to found a new colony there under his command. This and a later proposal were rejected but Bacon continued to work in conjunction with other groups.

Prominent among these were the Wakefieldians. Shortly before Bacon's proposals had reached the Colonial Office a plan for the settlement of Gulf St Vincent had been submitted by a former cell-mate and associate of Wakefield, Robert Gouger, who had been imprisoned for failing to pay a debt arising from the printing of *A Letter from Sydney*. This plan which had been drawn up in consultation with Wakefield was turned down by the British authorities. In May 1831, however, a further scheme was presented by Gouger and Bacon. This had the backing of the National Colonisation Society, an organisation founded in 1830 by Wakefieldians in conjunction with Wilmot Horton and his supporters, who later withdrew after a quarrel over how to promote colonisation. The Wakefieldians were interested in establishing a settlement embodying the principles of 'Selection, Concentration and the Sale of Waste Lands for the purposes of Emigration'. The pattern of life in the eastern colonies, however, was too well established for an experiment to be conducted there. Even less suitable was Western Australia whose colonisation was proceeding along lines diametrically opposed to those recommended by Wakefield. Indeed, his analysis of what had gone wrong there played a part in shaping his general theory. The region recently explored by Sturt possessed none of the disadvantages of other parts. Its virgin soil was capable of sustaining white inhabitants and, while accessible by sea and land, it was far enough from existing colonies for new ideas to be tried without outside interference.

Such was the theory. In practice, four years were to elapse before the British government overcame its reluctance to sanction another Australian settlement. Supporters of the new colony faced a more difficult task than those who had worked for the opening of Western Australia. The period was one in which the extension of imperial commitments was opposed inside and outside parliament. Many believed that colonies would inevitably leave the mother country thereby providing only limited return for the money spent on them. The new settlement at Western Australia was already in some difficulties. What justification could there be for a further venture which did not even possess strategic value? Understandably, the government was difficult to convince and its final approval was given only after a plan was formulated that promised to minimise its financial involvement while giving the Colonial Office some control over developments.

The National Colonisation Society planned to raise £500 000 and form a company which, in return for a Royal Charter, first choice of land and control over a governor nominated by the·Crown, would bear the cost of a settlement to be run in accordance with Wakefield's principles. Although supported by prominent figures such as Jeremy Bentham, the proposal foundered because it proved impossible to meet the government's stipulation that the necessary money must be raised before permission for settlement could be given. Some of the promoters, including Major Bacon, whose underhand tactics had heightened the suspicion of officials, withdrew but others prepared for a new approach. Steps were taken to form a South Australian Land Company that was to finance a colony modelled on the earlier plan. This suggestion was rejected chiefly on the advice of James Stephen who in a lengthy and damning indictment adjudged it dangerous, ill-founded, 'wild and impracticable'. A later attempt in June 1833 to take advantage of the replacement as colonial secretary of Viscount Goderich by Lord Stanley met with similar opposition and resulted in the collapse of the South Australian Land Company.

The flagging energies of the colonisers were given fresh impetus when Charles Sturt visited England and published in 1833 *Two Expeditions into the Interior of South Australia*. This book, which described his explorations and those made in 1831 by the late Captain Collet Barker, who after the withdrawal from Raffles Bay had taken charge of the penal settlement at King George's Sound, provided detailed information about the southern coast. Moreover, Sturt placed his own weight behind those who were urging settlement. In October 1833 Wakefield anonymously published a two-volume work, *England and America*, which examined the reasons for the failure of the company's proposals, further discussed his principles of colonisation and aroused renewed interest in the project. In December 1833 the committee of the recently formed South Australian Association drew up a proposal for a colony which it was prepared to administer, but which would belong to the Crown. The idea of a joint stock company was dropped and it was announced that the settlement would be open to all. By January 1834 some thirty individuals with a combined capital of £200 000 had announced their support and a variety of lesser persons had volunteered their services. Protracted nego-

tiations and several changes of plan were necessary before the
government, after first securing financial guarantees, was prepared
to move. In August 1834, however, the South Australian Act was
passed. It provided for a cumbersome governmental machinery in
which power was divided between a governor appointed by the
Colonial Office and a resident commissioner responsible to a group
of commissioners nominated by the South Australian Association.
These men had power to sell land at a minimum price of 12s an
acre and the proceeds were to finance administration as well as
pay for the passages of migrants. Opposition was voiced by the
colonial under-secretary of state, R.W. Hay, who feared that the
government would be involved in expense, and by James Stephen
who considered it no more feasible to settle a new country by an
immediate sale of land than it was 'to undertake the building of a
bridge across the Swan River by the sale of the waters'.

Although the Wakefieldians had obtained their colony the result
was not entirely to their satisfaction. They believed in self-government which they advocated on the grounds that only the men on the
spot could fully appreciate the needs of the community. Their early
plans had been based on the assumption that interference from
London would necessarily inhibit development. The Colonial Office,
however, insisted upon the government maintaining some control.
As Wakefield wrote,

> It was clear to us that the part of our South Australian plan to
> which the Colonial Office most objected, was a provision for
> bestowing on the colonists a considerable amount of local self
> government. As we could not move an inch without the sanction
> of that office, we ... resolved to abandon the political part of
> our scheme, in the hope of being able to realise the economical
> part.

In the event Wakefield discovered that this compromise did not
work to his satisfaction and after the Act was passed he dissociated
himself from the venture. He believed that the minimum price
charged for land was too low. He resented the government's decision, taken while he was caring for his dying daughter in Lisbon,
to appoint as chairman of the commission Colonel Robert Torrens,
the radical parliamentarian and political economist who had hopes
of becoming governor of South Australia. The two men advocated
systematic colonisation, but while Wakefield was concerned with
the social and cultural aspects of transplanting communities over-

seas, Torrens thought chiefly of colonies as sources of raw material and outlets for British capital, goods and settlers. A second source of contention arose from Torrens's belief that the land fund should be used to meet all the costs of the South Australian settlement. His 'self supporting principle' was opposed by Wakefield who wanted the proceeds of land sales to go exclusively to financing migration. With Torrens in a position of power there was little likelihood of Wakefield's view prevailing.

Historians have been unable to agree in their assessments of Wakefield's contribution towards the founding of South Australia. While R.C. Mills saw his as 'the controlling mind', Douglas Pike argued that others were more important and pointed to the absence of Wakefield from England while important negotiations were being undertaken. This last view is unduly harsh. Wakefield was involved in most of the plans; he helped to arouse public interest by means of his writings; and he was active at crucial moments such as those on which the final bill was being debated by parliament: Certainly he deserves a place among the founders of South Australia.

Wakefield turned his attention to other facets of imperial affairs but his followers were included among the commissioners in London and the officials appointed to the colony. Robert Gouger who became the first colonial secretary of South Australia had been closely associated with Wakefield since January 1829, when the two men met in Newgate prison and discussed Gouger's plans for migrating to the Swan River. It has been said that Wakefield's theory of colonisation was the product of these discussions and that Gouger played an equal part in formulating it. This, however, was more than was claimed by Gouger or any other contemporary. Gouger was a highly intelligent man of philanthropic bent who was deeply interested in alleviating the lot of the poor by encouraging them to migrate. He was capable of originality but his role in relation to the settlement of South Australia was practical rather than ideological. He assisted in propagating Wakefield's theories, helped establish each of the organisations which were formed to promote the new colony, acted as secretary to these societies and worked hard behind the scenes to rally support for them. His appointment was a tribute to his dedication and to the financial burdens which he had borne over the years.

Not all of the men involved in the settlement of South Australia were inspired by such high ideals. The speculative impulse had also been at work since the impecunious Major Bacon had put forward his abortive proposal. Amongst the supporters of each of the plans

were men who looked for financial return. Many of those wishing
to migrate to South Australia did so because they hoped to benefit
materially. Yet to most of its pioneers the colony had a wider appeal.
From the outset the plans of its founders included provision for
elective government, freedom of the press and religious freedom.
The chance of fashioning a new society where there would be no
state church, no aristocracy and none of the inequalities inherent
in nineteenth-century England attracted much support for South
Australia. Dissenters whose religious beliefs disadvantaged them at
home, political radicals who considered the English government
too oligarchic and society too hierarchical figured prominently
among the first South Australians. They came in the hope of fashioning a society that would be progressive, egalitarian and free
from vested interests. It was this which gave South Australia its
peculiar flavour. Nowhere else in an Australian colony was the
utopian element so strong among the first settlers. Wakefieldian
idealism, political radicalism and the quest for social and religious
equality all left their mark on early South Australia.

If the colonisation of Western and Southern Australia resulted
from the initiative of British interests, that of the future colony of
Victoria stemmed from the expansionist activities of graziers in Van
Diemen's Land and New South Wales. Port Phillip, which became
the nucleus of the new settlement, had been visited by Baudin in
1802, explored in April of the same year by Matthew Flinders and
rejected by David Collins in October 1803. The area was not again
visited until December 1824 when the English explorer and settler,
W.H. Hovell, and the Parramatta-born Hamilton Hume came
overland from Sydney on a trip marred by Hume's competitive
behaviour. Their discovery of good land between Lake George and
Corio Bay did nothing to interest settlers. The only whites attracted
to Port Phillip were a handful of Van Diemen's Land whalers and
sealers who had long used it as a base. Ten years were to elapse before
their pursuits and those of the Aboriginal tribes were disturbed by
the arrival of permanent residents.

The first settlement, made in 1834, was a result of the land shortage in Van Diemen's Land. For some time graziers had looked
enviously across Bass Strait to Port Phillip Bay, but it was difficult,
costly and risky to transport possessions and stock there. In 1832,
however, there arrived in Van Diemen's Land a wealthy Sussex
farmer and banker, Thomas Henty, accompanied by five of his six
grown-up sons. They had sold their English farm in 1828 and acquired a 84 413-acre property at the Swan River with the intention

of raising merino sheep. James, the eldest son, arrived in 1829 but two years later, despairing of success, he transferred the family's possessions to Van Diemen's Land where he was joined by his father and brothers. By then land sales had replaced free grants and prices were rising. Accordingly, the Hentys sought permission to acquire holdings on the southern mainland. Their first request was rejected by the Colonial Office which opposed a settlement so far from Sydney. While their second proposal was under consideration, Edward sailed with supplies and stock for Portland Bay which he and his father had chosen as a site for their farm.

This move spurred other Van Diemen's Land settlers into action. Amongst them was the local-born John Batman, who had been promised a 2 000-acre grant for his services in the 'black war' between the whites and Aboriginals of Van Diemen's Land. His interest in southern New South Wales had been aroused by his friend and compatriot, Hamilton Hume, and he had already tried unsuccessfully to obtain land at Western Port. Others similarly inclined included Charles Swanston, former captain in the East India Company's forces who had arrived at Hobart in mid-1831 and established himself as controller of the Derwent Bank, property owner, and agent for British firms in India and China. In addition there was J.H. Wedge, the government surveyor, the Robertson brothers who were mercers, and J.T. Gellibrand, a barrister, property owner, newspaper editor and disappointed applicant for a grant at Western Port. These men formed the Port Phillip Association and in May 1835 despatched Batman to Port Phillip. Their object was to purchase land from the Aboriginals, thereby securing a title that they hoped would be accepted by the British authorities. By June 1835 negotiations with the tribal elders were complete and the association had acquired some 600 000 acres of land, including the site of Melbourne.

It was not Batman, but a later arrival, John Pascoe Fawkner, who can claim to be the founder of Melbourne. The son of a convict who had sailed with the expedition commanded by David Collins, Fawkner had visited Port Phillip as a boy and was among the pioneers of Hobart. His father became a small farmer and he himself ran a bakery until his deportation to the mainland in 1814 for helping seven convicts to escape. His career after returning to Hobart in 1816 was noted for its colour, variety and enterprise. He worked as baker, timber carrier, builder and sawyer, experienced financial difficulties and had two further brushes with the law. By 1835 he had become a successful innkeeper, advocate and defender

of the emancipists. For a time he also owned a newspaper. A man
of great energy and forcefulness, Fawkner's interest in expanding
his activities to the southern mainland was aroused by the reports
of whalers and sealers. He purchased the *Enterprise* and set sail
for Western Port in late August 1835 after being delayed for more
than two months by court cases involving assault and debt. Western
Port was not to his liking and he diverted his attention to Port
Phillip where John Batman was already established. Undeterred he
took over land on the Yarra River on 30 August 1835, erecting the
hut which became Melbourne's first edifice.

The actions of the Hentys, Batman and Fawkner presented the
government of New South Wales with an unwelcome problem.
Each of these men and their associates were making use of land
which belonged to the Crown. Admittedly, the Port Phillip Association had purchased its holdings but the right of the Aboriginals
to own land was not recognised in law. On 26 August 1835 Governor
Bourke issued a proclamation declaring the sale void. He warned
the other settlers that they would be punished as trespassers unless
they withdrew. This sharp response, designed to assert the rights
of the Crown, has been seen as an attempt by Bourke to establish
jurisdiction over an area which Lieutenant-Governor Arthur of
Van Diemen's Land hoped to control. Bourke, however, knew
from experience that once news of the availability of good land at
Port Phillip spread there would be no stopping an inrush of pastoralists. The best policy was to anticipate this by first extending
the government's authority over the region. 'Dispersion will go on',
he observed realistically, 'notwithstanding the discouragement, but
accompanied by much evil, that might be prevented by the guidance
and control of authority opportunely introduced'. His superiors
were anxious to prevent a dispersal of settlement, but after considerable hesitation accepted his advice. In 1836 Bourke was
authorised to place Captain William Lonsdale, an army officer with
experience as a civil magistrate, in command of Port Phillip.
Shortly after, the first surveys were carried out preparatory to land
being offered for sale at auction. Of the men who had already
settled, the Hentys had a long struggle before their titles were
recognised, while the members of the Port Phillip Association were
eventually allowed a reduction of £7 000 on any land for which they
might bid.

Once doubts had been removed the region was quickly opened.
In March 1837 Bourke paid an official visit and approved the site
of a township which he named after the prime minister, Viscount

Melbourne. By that stage other settlers had crossed Bass Strait and the first overlanders had moved down from New South Wales. Their interest had been aroused by the reports of Major Thomas Mitchell, the surveyor-general, who in June 1836 had explored the area stretching south from the Murray towards the coast and discovered land so rich that he named it Australia Felix, a title it retained until the area of which it formed part was separated from the rest of New South Wales and renamed Victoria. This took a decade to accomplish. Before the middle of the century the Port Phillip region was an appendage of the mother colony and the economic and political developments which occurred there were vitally influenced by decisions taken at Sydney.

Between 1830 and 1850, therefore, important changes occurred in British policy towards the eastern colonies, the rest of the continent was brought within the empire and new settlements were established. These developments reflected a growing British interest in the potential of Australia for purposes of investment and migration as well as for markets and raw materials. They also served to illustrate how the scope of activities in the antipodes was widening and how the pace of life was quickening. In other ways too, important changes took place and these were to make the pre-gold rush era of vital significance to the economic, social and political history of Australia.

five : Economic Development

Squatting

The land hunger which brought about the occupation of Port Phillip persisted throughout the 1830s and 1840s driving settlers outwards in their search for fresh pastures. By 1850 migrants from the United Kingdom, pastoralists from Van Diemen's Land and overlanders from New South Wales had established themselves on much of the best land around Port Phillip. In the north of New South Wales equally important advances had been made. The initial impetus came from the Australian Agricultural Company, whose holdings in the Port Stephens district proved unsuited to sheep. Unable to find land close to their existing grant the company's agents were obliged to look further afield. Their search, which was spearheaded by the surveyor and Hunter River settler, Henry Dangar, lasted from 1830 until 1832 and resulted in the occupation of vast grants on the Liverpool Plains. This opened the way to northward expansion, first by squatters who were driven off the plains by the company and secondly by new arrivals who appreciated the fresh opportunities. Between 1830 and 1840 the New England Tableland was breached and Armidale, Guyra and Tenterfield were successively settled.

Even greater steps were taken during the next decade following the 'rediscovery' of the Darling Downs by Patrick Leslie, an Aberdonian migrant and former Highland officer. He had sold his commission while in India and came to New South Wales where he managed the Collaroi estate of his uncle Walter Davidson, a friend and former associate of John Macarthur. He married into the Macarthur family and established himself in colonial society, but his activities as a pastoralist fared badly and he quarrelled with his uncle. Meantime, his brothers, Walter and George, had also arrived. In January 1840 he headed north and by following the route charted by Allan Cunningham in 1827 reached the Darling Downs where he located a property 'large enough to form a principality' extending from Toolburra to the headwaters of the Condamine. In June 1840 he and Walter, together with their twenty-two ticket-of-leave convicts, 'four hundred breeding ewes, one hundred ewe hoggets, one hundred rams and five hundred wedders, three and four year old' established themselves on their station and named it Canning Downs.

The Leslies were not the first to settle beyond the later border between New South Wales and Queensland. In January 1840 a pastoralist, John 'Tinker' Campbell, had moved his cattle from the Gwydir Valley to Bebo on the north bank of the Dumaresq River. Others followed, particularly after 1842 when Governor Gipps decided to close the penal establishment at Moreton Bay because graziers were entering the region. Hitherto free persons had not been permitted to travel via Moreton Bay, which meant that the only access to the Darling Downs was overland. Now they were able to bring stock and possessions by sea. By 1850 much of the area from Moreton Bay to the mountains was settled and the Darling Downs were almost fully occupied. Brisbane developed as an administrative and service centre as well as a port, providing amenities for the growing numbers of colonists.

The opening of these areas was accompanied by the spread of pastoralists into western New South Wales. Between 1836 and 1840 a wide belt, stretching north from near the junction of the Lachlan and the Murrumbidgee Rivers to the intersection of the Gwydir and Namoi Rivers, was occupied. The next ten years saw pastoralists move along the Darling and settle on parts which lay between that river and the Lachlan. Although suitable for sheep and cattle these localities, with their hot, dry conditions, had less to recommend them than either Port Phillip or the Darling Downs. As a consequence, the growth of settlement in the west of New South Wales was more gradual. By 1850, however, most of the best land was occupied.

In the forefront of this expansion were the squatters who became a dominant element in New South Wales during the 1830s. Although the term squatting had only recently come into use, the phenomenon which it described already had a lengthy history. Colonists had long been accustomed to occupying vacant Crown land for their own purposes. Wealthy graziers who already owned large acreages might seize an empty plot adjacent to their grants, or send stock under the care of herdsmen to more distant localities where good runs were available. Smaller settlers sometimes did the same, especially in time of drought. Poorer colonists who were unable to obtain grants or purchase holdings were known to occupy small areas of Crown land, principally in the settled districts. They included lesser migrants, emancipists and a handful of ticket-of-leave holders.

The early squatters were a mixed group who had in common only the fact that they were illegally occupying Crown land. At first governors turned a blind eye to a practice which they had neither the desire nor the means to prevent. Before 1821, while settlement was mainly confined to the Cumberland Plain, the incidence of squatting was only slight and occasioned no problems. The subject was never mentioned in official despatches and the authorities in London remained ignorant of it. During the 1820s, however, as land usage increased attempts were made to regularise the situation. Governors Brisbane and Darling introduced schemes under which pastoralists could lease prescribed areas on payment of an annual fee. Governor Bourke who approved of this idea was concerned lest the rights of the Crown were not adequately protected. While in command at the Cape of Good Hope he had seen how lessees converted occupancy into ownership, thereby depriving the Crown of its property. He was determined that this should not happen in New South Wales and drew up a bill which the Legislative Council passed in 1833. It provided for the creation of commissioners of Crown land whose duties were to supervise the waste lands and safeguard the government's interests.

These measures applied only to the nineteen counties. Within this area the occupancy of unalienated Crown land had been legalised and, although many settlers continued illicitly to use vacant spots, the more respectable took out licences. Outside the nineteen counties Crown land could be neither sold nor leased. The local authorities were unable to supervise outlying regions and the British authorities opposed the spread of settlement. They considered that the nineteen counties were adequate and feared that unnecessary dispersal of population would increase the government's burdens and expose the colonists to danger and hardship. These opinions were reinforced by the Wakefieldian theorists who advocated con-

The squatting districts of New South Wales, 1846.

centrating settlement within prescribed bounds. Yet already colonists were using Crown land well beyond the settled regions. Each year saw more graziers move further afield in the search for fresh pastures. Their actions created problems which came to a head under Governor Bourke.

For Bourke's superiors and for colonial theorists in far-off London the solution was simple. Movement beyond the limits of occupation must be banned. Wakefield believed that it would be no more difficult to keep squatters off the Crown lands of Australia than it was to prevent trespassers encroaching on the king's estates in England. In fact, the colony was so vast that it would have taken an army to enforce such a policy. Bourke was aware of this but he also showed more understanding of the graziers' needs than did officials at home. His experiences at the Cape had familiarised him with the problems of running stock on land whose carrying capacity was only limited. He sought to encourage the pastoralists and had no objection to their using waste land provided the Crown's rights were safeguarded.

In 1836 the Crown Lands Occupation Act, framed on Bourke's orders, was passed by the Legislative Council. This measure strengthened the control of the government over its lands, not only within the settled districts, but also outside. Complaints voiced by wealthier graziers and the evidence collected by a Select Committee of the Legislative Council, appointed in June 1835 to enquire into the incidence of crime in outlying areas, had shown that ne'er-do-wells were occupying vacant land and engaging in illicit pursuits. The problem was in fact greatly exaggerated by landowners who hoped to eradicate the smaller men by branding them as wrong-doers. Bourke appreciated this and his Act, while aimed at checking abuses, also included provisions intended to protect the less wealthy elements who wanted to run stock on unalienated land. Anyone who wished to do so could use such land, provided they were of good character, took out a licence and paid an annual fee. Policing was entrusted to the commissioners of Crown land whose task was to maintain order and ensure that the smaller occupiers were treated justly. Although the Act ran counter to official policy it was accepted in London, just as the unwelcome opening of the Port Phillip region had been earlier. Within the Colonial Office, James Stephen had come to recognise the impossibility of preventing squatting. His superiors did not agree and their approval of Bourke's Act resulted from a failure to appreciate its wider implications.

The 1836 Act extended government recognition of squatting to the regions outside the nineteen counties and inaugurated a new phase in its history. Henceforth, anyone of sound repute who could afford a licence was allowed to graze stock on unoccupied land of their choice anywhere in the colony. The immediate consequences of this should not be overstressed. There was no sudden rush to the more distant parts of New South Wales. At first most of the occupation licences were for land within the nineteen counties close to labour, markets and the amenities of townships. The more venturesome did, however, spread themselves, and as runs became scarcer in the settled districts so the interior was penetrated more deeply. Not all who moved into these parts heeded the obligations imposed by the 1836 Act and in March 1839 Sir George Gipps, Bourke's successor, took action to strengthen it. The interior was divided into districts, each under a commissioner who was assisted by the newly created border police. Governmental control which had been nominal under Bourke was now actual. Lawlessness declined and more pastoralists paid their licence fees.

These developments gave the word 'squatting' a new meaning in contemporary usage. In the mid-1830s it had been used principally to abuse small squatters whom the large landowners described as 'the instigators and promoters of crime—receivers of stolen property —illegal vendors of spirits, and harbourers of runaways, bushrangers and vagrants'. During the 1840s it lost its derogatory

The squatter's first home usually consisted of a rough timber hut where he lived with his workers, but more substantial houses were also built.

meaning as crime was curbed and as increasing numbers of respectable graziers took out occupation licences. Henceforth the term described pastoralists who, with government permission, ran stock on Crown land to which they had no permanent title. A number also owned properties within the settled districts, but an increasing proportion lived exclusively on their leaseholds.

Such people came from all walks of life and included emancipists as well as migrants. The practice was for them to select suitable land, delineate its bounds by rough marks and then, having obtained a licence, begin stocking their run. Some built substantial houses and solid dairies, barns and other outhouses. A visitor to John Henty's station near Port Phillip as early as 1839 was ushered into 'one of the prettiest rooms I ever recall seeing—it was carpeted, curtained, and looked the very picture of neatness and comfort'. In this particular district the existence of Melbourne brought the squatters into contact with civilised life. The same was true on a lesser scale of other regions where townships developed. In general, however, life was lonely and the nearest neighbour perhaps kilometres away. The Aboriginals could be troublesome and injuries and fatalities were not uncommon. If the squatter's existence was occasionally dangerous, it was also invariably harsh. He often lived with his workers in a rough one or two-roomed timber hut which contained no comforts. Cut off from books and intellectual diversions even men of good family sometimes degenerated into rowdies. Few women braved the bush which at first was almost exclusively a male preserve.

Isolation and the fact that the squatting districts had only recently been occupied were among the reasons for their primitive state. Important too was the insecurity of the squatters' tenure which discouraged improvements. The land titles conferred by the Crown Lands Occupation Act were proof against intrusion by other squatters, but not by the Crown. The government could resume the squatters' leases after six months notice and there was no obligation to pay compensation for any improvements they had effected. Increasingly the squatters resented these uncertainties. But for them, vast areas would have remained unproductive. In the face of great hardship and at considerable cost they had opened up and stocked the land, thereby performing a service of benefit to the whole community. Their efforts deserved rewarding by leases of sufficient duration to ensure a satisfactory return on capital and labour. If their land was put up for sale, they considered that they should be given first option of purchasing it. If it was sold, they should be compensated for the buildings, yards and fences which they had constructed and for the areas they had cleared.

These demands for long leases, pre-emptive rights and compensation for improvements crystallised during the conflict between squatters and government under Governor Gipps. In an effort to obtain more revenue at a time when land sales were dropping and money was urgently needed to finance migration, Gipps on 2 April 1844 published regulations that were to regulate the leasing of Crown land from July 1845. As matters stood, the payment of an annual licence fee of £10 entitled the squatter to as much land as he chose. The new 'occupation' regulations, as they have become known, stated that no run should exceed twenty square miles or be capable of carrying more than 4000 sheep or 500 head of cattle. Except where the region was acknowledged by the commissioner to be unusually poor, a squatter seeking a larger area would be obliged to take out a separate licence for each twenty square miles that he leased. By this means the government would earn more rent and the small graziers would no longer pay the same fee as the large squatter.

Gipps opposed long leases which would tie up land in a few hands and impede would-be purchasers. On the other hand he saw that there was justice in the squatters' claims and recognised that they needed security if they were to build decent houses and make permanent improvements. He drew up a second set of regulations that were not to be applied unless approved by the British authorities. After despatching his proposals to London Gipps decided to notify the colonists of his intentions and on 13 May 1844 his recommendations were published in the *Sydney Morning Herald*. Known as the 'purchase' regulations they offered licensed squatters of five years standing the opportunity to buy at least 320 acres of their leaseholds. Each purchase was to be by public auction at a minimum price of £1 per acre and would guarantee possession of the rest of the run for a further eight years. At the end of this and successive eight-year periods the process could be repeated until the whole of a property was bought. There was no guarantee that the present occupier would be able to buy his land at public auction, but an opportunity to do so had been offered and under conditions that would prevent existing interests monopolising the interior. Compensation was to be paid to squatters who lost possession of their stations.

The justice of these proposals was recognised by the press but not by the large squatters. Some occupied so many runs that the cost of buying 320 acres on each would have been prohibitive. Others feared they would be outbid at auctions and lose the whole of their properties. The opposition to the 'purchase' regulations, however, was mild compared to the furore aroused by the 'occupation' regulations. Rarely had any government measure united so many sections of the community. Squatters large and small, landowners, merchants, shopkeepers and even some artisans strongly voiced their objections to Gipps's decision. At first glance this appears surprising. Small squatters might reasonably be expected to have appreciated the decision to charge them lower licence fees than the large graziers. Under normal conditions landowners would scarcely have opposed regulations directed against men whom they considered were treated over-generously by the government. Yet times were not normal. The colony was suffering from a severe depression and the belief that the governor had acted unfairly in increasing the licence fee made the squatters close ranks to protect themselves. Gipps had earlier antagonised landowners by trying to keep land prices up and collect quit rents more systematically. These men used the publication of the 'occupation' regulations as a means of raising protest against Gipps's land policy in general and they were joined by merchants and others whose welfare depended on the continued prosperity of the squatters.

It was, therefore, the timing as well as the content of the 'occupation' regulations that created problems. Had the governor made his intentions clearer by publishing both sets simultaneously, he might have taken the edge off the opposition. But the situation was difficult and it was made worse by the fact that agitation for self-government was growing. Those who urged that the colonists be given greater powers made political capital out of Gipps's actions, adding a further dimension to the opposition movement. Constitutional as well as economic considerations also influenced the squatter-dominated Legislative Council in its condemnation of the 'occupation' regulations following the publication of a biased report prepared by its own Committee on Crown Land Grievances.

The final decision, however, had to be taken by the British government which controlled the unalienated lands. Recognising this, the large squatters carried the fight to London, where Francis Scott, MP for Roxburgh and a man with important connections, was appointed by the Legislative Council to further members' ends. They also persuaded merchants, manufacturers and bankers that Gipps's measures would adversely affect the industry. Their combined influence, exercised through the press, parliament and in direct negotiation with the Colonial Office, eventually won over a government conscious of the importance of Australian wool. At first sympathetic to Gipps, the government in August 1846 introduced the Australian Waste Lands Bill which amounted to a capitulation to the squatters. In March 1847 an Order in Council divided the colony, for purposes of pastoral occupation, into three zones— settled, intermediate and unsettled. Squatting leases of one, eight and fourteen years respectively were permitted in these three areas subject to the payment of a fee based on the stock carrying capacity of the land.

In the colony this measure aroused strong opposition from middle-class politicians and townsfolk who saw it as giving the squatters a monopoly over the interior. Much bitterness was aroused, but it was nearly a decade before urban interests secured enough political power to challenge the government's verdict. In the meantime the squatters enjoyed untroubled possession of their lands and began making permanent improvements. After 1847 they erected attractive stone houses some of which still stand as picturesque additions to the landscape. They built better barns and out-houses, fenced larger acreages and sowed a variety of grasses to create lush pastures. The squatting districts themselves took on more the appearance of settled regions as roads were constructed and small townships, schools and churches were established.

Within the space of less than two decades between 1833 and 1847, therefore, the squatters who originally were no more than trespassers had triumphed first over the British government which sought to restrict settlement, then over Governor Gipps. Although they gained much from these victories they also benefited the colony by pushing its boundaries further afield and developing its potential. There were less than 2 000 squatters out of a total population of over a quarter of a million. By 1850, however, they occupied over 73 million acres of land and owned approximately 5 500 000 sheep in addition to 888 000 head of cattle. They stimulated economic development in mainland eastern Australia and added colour and vitality to its history.

These achievements were not duplicated in any other part of the continent. Elsewhere squatters did exist, some having come from New South Wales. One such person was Joseph Hawdon who had migrated in 1834 and settled at Burgalia near Bateman's Bay in partnership with his brother John. In 1836 Joseph, in company with two other settlers, John Gardiner, an Irish-born pastoralist from Van Diemen's Land, and John Hepburn, became the first to over-land cattle to Port Phillip where Hawdon acquired land and a contract to carry mail to Yass. Two years later he mapped out an overland cattle route from Port Phillip to Adelaide. In 1839 he discovered a quicker route from Melbourne to Adelaide opening up a path for squatters. By 1850, 293 squatters and more than 1 million sheep were spread over 30 000 square kilometres of the interior of South Australia.

Neither here nor elsewhere did these squatters occupy a position comparable to that of those in New South Wales. In Van Diemen's Land separate districts were not set aside for their use and only limited areas of vacant land were available for leasing in the settled regions. Western Australia was slower to develop and although settlers did allow their stock to wander over Crown land few problems were created. In each of these colonies legislation reflected the weak position of the squatters. Although varied in points of detail the acts, while conferring some rights on occupants of Crown land, left them vulnerable to purchasers and gave them little prospect of security or compensation. In general, they remained less prosperous, less influential and more mobile than their counterparts in New South Wales.

The Pastoral Age in New South Wales

The opening of the rich interior of New South Wales provided the pastoral industry with the means of attaining a position of unprecedented importance in the economic life of the colony. The foundations for that supremacy had been laid during the 1820s but its achievement was a result of later developments. The introduction of assisted passage schemes brought New South Wales within reach of working-class migrants. Graziers complained that these people were often poorly selected and preferred to remain in the towns rather than face the hardships of the bush. Moreover, the number of arrivals varied and in some years demand exceeded supply. Nevertheless in a period when convicts were being transported in larger numbers, more free labourers were also available than before. Their presence made pastoral expansion easier.

More important was the fact that capital was available in greater quantities. Some was brought by migrants who occupied land in which they also invested their own labour and expertise. These migrants sometimes formed partnerships with friends, relatives or associates who remained in England and contributed part of the capital in exchange for a share of the profits. Most funds, however, were provided by British financiers who were attracted by the good returns. In England interest rates were restricted by law, but in New

South Wales, where capital was urgently needed, this limitation was removed by the Forbes Act of 1834. Named after the chief justice, the measure was enacted in response to pressure from British investors and colonial borrowers who henceforth were able to set their own rates of interest. Funds for investment flowed into the colony and five new banks were created. They included the Sydney Bank established in 1834 by Charles William Roemer, a Leipzigborn merchant and pastoralist, the Commercial Bank of Sydney and the Union Bank of Australia, both of which were founded by London financiers. In addition the existing Bank of New South Wales and the Bank of Australasia expanded their activities.

TABLE 4
Total Immigration into New South Wales 1830–50

	Men	*Women*	*Children*
Assisted immigrants	32 063	35 369	24 783
Unassisted immigrants	14 776	7 291	5 708

Source: R.B. Madgwick, *Immigration into Eastern Australia, 1788-1851*, p. 223.

Capital and enterprise alike were largely attracted to the production of wool for the English market. Many graziers concentrated on crossbred sheep which produced mutton as well as wool. Others reared the merino, but an increasing number turned to Saxon sheep whose fleeces were of good quality and earned high prices. In England the demand for New South Wales wool became steadily stronger. During the 1830s the textile mills of Yorkshire expanded and increasingly adopted machine methods to manufacture more cloth and to take advantage of widening markets. The German states of Saxony and Silesia remained their principal suppliers, but the cost of carrying wool through the numerous European customs barriers reduced its competitiveness. Ocean freight rates had fallen and Australian wool could be brought more cheaply to England than could that of Germany. Transport and handling expenses of Australian wool, including brokerage and insurance, amounted to $3\frac{3}{4}$d per lb compared to $4\frac{3}{4}$d per lb for German wool. Moreover, Australian packaging and sorting had improved. Australian exports rose from 2 500 000 lbs in 1831 to 9 750 000 lbs in 1840. The largest quantity came from New South Wales whose fleeces outstripped in value those of Van Diemen's Land and increased from roughly £40 000 in 1830 to over £400 000 ten years later. British expenditure on the colonies was still a major source of New South Wales revenue, but after 1834 wool supplanted the fisheries as the principal earner of overseas income. In that year fishery products amounted to only 26 per cent of total exports, while wool amounted to 44 per cent and realised more than a third as much in monetary terms.

TABLE 5
Expansion of Population, Agriculture, Sheep and Cattle
Raising in New South Wales (including Port Phillip) 1830–50

	Population	Acreage cultivated	Cattle	Sheep	Wool exported (lbs)
1830	46 402	70 695	248 440	504 775	899 750
1835	71 592	79 256	n.a.	n.a.	3 893 927
1840	129 463	122 906	n.a.	n.a.	8 610 775
1845	173 377	138 237	1 159 432	5 604 644	10 522 921
1850	265 503	144 647	1 374 968	7 092 209	14 270 622

Sources: New South Wales Colonial Secretary, Returns of the Colony, 1830 to 1850.
NOTE: The figures for 1830 come from the 1828 census—no census was taken in 1829 or 1830.

The importance of the pastoral industry was not determined solely by wool. Not all graziers possessed either the expertise or the capital needed to enter the costly and hazardous business of exporting wool to a distant market. Raising sheep for mutton, or cattle for beef and dairying were safer occupations that attracted even those who devoted part of their attention to wool. The demand for meat and dairy products grew continually and prices remained remunerative. There was also a small but significant export trade in hides as well as a local market for leather goods. A history of the cattle industry is still to be written but it is clear that, although overshadowed by wool, this industry was important and attracted capital. The expansion of settlement was a response to the demands of the cattle man as well as to those of the sheep farmer.

In 1841 the boom ended and pastoralists were hit by a depression which lasted until 1843. Historian S.H. Roberts attributed this to a combination of excessive speculation and falling wool prices. Brian Fitzpatrick, in contrast, believed that the main cause was the 1839 crisis in the English money market which resulted in a sharp drop in overseas investment. The first of these interpretations was based too heavily on the despatches of Governor Gipps who sought to account for his government's inability to meet the cost of migration rather than offer a reasoned exposition of the causes of the depression. The second was unduly influenced by Fitzpatrick's antipathy towards British capitalists. S.J. Butlin has discounted both views by showing that, while wool prices did not decline unduly in the early 1840s, new British investment increased during 1840 and 1841. In his view the major cause of the depression was that pastoralists had expanded beyond the point at which they could realise profits. Their plans were founded on an expectation of continued high returns. This was a miscalculation and the ensuing disappointment produced a psychological reaction which ended the boom. Investors either withdrew their money or refused to lend more and those graziers who were heavily extended suddenly found themselves in a vulnerable position. Banks foreclosed and credit was impossible to obtain.

To make matters worse, the depression followed a three-year drought. Property values fell, sheep sold for as little as 1s a dozen, cattle for 7s 6d each, and prize Arab stallions for 18s. Many pastoralists were ruined and, like the fictitious Billy Barlow, the subject of a contemporary ballad, watched the bailiffs sell their stock 'at sixpence per head and the station given in'. An atmosphere of despair hung over some districts as conditions deteriorated. Lamented Patrick Leslie in December 1843,

> As to the state the country is in, I really do not know what to say for it is getting worse every day and yet I sometimes say to myself how can it be worse? and then the next steamer fetches the accounts of some fresh disaster. Nothing can be sold and if by chance anything can be sold there is no money to be had, nothing but bills, bills.

Because the pastoral industry occupied a central position, its misfortunes were felt throughout the economy. Land sales dropped, immigration funds dried up and the government was unable to pay the passages of migrants whom it had contracted to bring out. In 1843 three of the colony's seven banks, the old-established Bank of Australia and the more recent Sydney and Port Phillip Banks, collapsed, threatening the economy with ruin by the beginning of 1844. Unemployment had risen, wages had fallen and ruin faced those shopkeepers, publicans and businessmen who had overstretched their resources. Merchants at Sydney and Port Phillip were hit by a fall in prices which forced them to sell their wares at a loss.

Amongst others who suffered were the assisted migrants who

unexpectedly found that their services were not wanted. Large numbers were forced to congregate under miserable conditions in Sydney because they lacked the means of travelling further. Particularly serious was the plight of single women who were unable to find positions. The government had no plans for assisting these migrants and the task fell to one of the more remarkable women in Australia's history, Caroline Chisholm. In September 1838 she had arrived from Madras with her husband who was employed by the East India Company and settled at Windsor. A Roman Catholic convert of great character and compassion, she established a Female Immigrants House at Sydney which became a refuge for the needy. Not content with temporarily alleviating their plight she wrote letters to pastoralists and travelled widely to find permanent employment for migrants. Despite indifference and sectarian opposition she accomplished much and by 1845 when she left for England had become one of the most respected figures in the colony.

By then New South Wales was beginning to recover from the depression. Pastoralists had benefited from the unemployment which had led to a fall in wages. Expedients, such as boiling down sheep and cattle into tallow which sold in London at £2 to £3 per hundredweight provided graziers with some income. They also used their influence in the Legislative Council to enact relief measures. Three bills were proposed in January 1843 by W.C. Wentworth who was himself a leading pastoralist. One, the Usury Act, aimed at reducing interest rates, was rejected by the council, but its intention was partly realised when two banks voluntarily cut their rate by 2 per cent. The other two measures were reluctantly accepted by Governor Gipps who did not believe that legislative action could alleviate economic distress. The Solvent Debtors' Act made it more difficult for creditors to seize the property of debtors whose assets exceeded their liabilities. The Lien on Wool Act was intended to facilitate borrowing. Many squatters were unable to obtain credit because they did not own their land and had few other acceptable assets. The new Act allowed squatters to mortgage the coming wool clip, thereby securing an advance sufficient to tide them over their difficulties. This was an imaginative move which worked because the demand in London for wool remained strong and prices continued to be profitable.

The depression, then, had serious but only temporary consequences for pastoralists. As confidence returned recovery began, losses were recouped and fresh ground was broken. Expanding population provided a growing labour force as well as an increasing market for meat. In England manufacturers eagerly purchased wool and by 1850 the value of the clip amounted to £1 614 241 compared to £566 122 in 1840. Sixty-seven per cent of the colony's export income was now coming from wool and part of the rest derived from pastoral products such as tallow and hides. The return on capital was high enough for the pastoral industry to absorb a growing proportion of investment funds. This meant there was less capital available for the fisheries which by 1850 were contributing only 1 per cent to export earnings.

A further casualty to the popularity of grazing was agriculture and particularly wheat farming whose returns on investment were insufficient to attract large-scale capital. Nevertheless agriculture had diversified and expanded. So too had other branches of the economy which had an urban base. The spread of settlement after 1830 was accompanied by a proliferation of country towns whose number rose from some half dozen in 1830 to nearly fifty by the middle of the century. Some were mere hamlets containing only a

Collins Street, Melbourne, 1840, when Melbourne was described as being 'a kind of big settlement' of clustered houses, tents and sheds, with poorly paved streets.

handful of residents and a general store. Others which occupied strategic positions had become more extensive. Goulburn, for example, which commanded the south-western districts, and Bathurst, which lay on the principal route to the west, each boasted several hundred permanent inhabitants and a variety of shops and businesses. More important was Maitland, the principal Hunter Valley town and the second largest in New South Wales proper. Its position on a river navigable to the sea and in a wealthy, populous region helped it to grow more rapidly than any other centre outside Melbourne and Sydney.

Melbourne, provincial capital of the Port Phillip district, changed substantially in the space of little more than a decade. A contemporary wrote in 1840 that it was then,

> Certainly not a city, and could hardly be called a town: nor did it even partake of the characteristics of a village or hamlet. It was a kind of big 'settlement', in groups pitched here and there, with houses, sheds and tents in clusters, or scattered in ones or twos.

By 1851 it had become a sprawling township catering for 23 000 townsfolk. Municipal institutions were granted in 1842, but finance remained scarce because the New South Wales government did not provide adequate revenue. As a result streets were poorly paved and conditions often poor. Nevertheless, improvements did occur and in 1849 gas lighting was introduced in the streets.

'The application of gas as an agent of light' had been made some eight years earlier in Sydney which overshadowed Melbourne in other ways too. Its supremacy derived from its greater age and from the fact that it was the seat of government, the chief port as well as the home of the manufacturing industry. Its population grew from 11 500 in 1830 to 52 000 in 1850. To house this increase new suburbs were built at Woolloomooloo, Surry Hills, Paddington and Redfern. The city proper, depicted so minutely by the artist Joseph Fowles in his *Sydney in 1848*, has been described as 'a lovely colonial town of clean, chaste Georgian architecture'. It had its more down-trodden and disreputable parts, particularly around the Rocks, but even before the establishment of the Sydney Municipal Council in 1842 something had been done to improve health standards, ensure an adequate water supply and pave the streets. After 1842 further progress was made in all of these directions, although by 1850 much remained to be done.

The increase in population, especially in the urban areas of New South Wales, stimulated building and associated industries and the retail trade. Secondary industry also underwent further changes. Most manufactured articles were imported from England whose factories flooded the world with articles of a quality and price that made them highly competitive. A number of products were, however, made locally, principally in Sydney where by 1838 all but twelve of the colony's manufactories were located. In that year this city contained 'seventy seven grain mills, two distilleries, seven breweries, five soap works, twelve tanneries, five brass and iron foundries, seven woollen factories, one salt, one hat and one tobacco works'. Demand was too small for large-scale methods of production to be introduced but steam power was used more and more, particularly in milling where the number of engines increased from four in 1830 to seventy-five in 1850. Most units of production were only small, but some larger businesses were founded, amongst them the Australian Gas Light Company in 1841 and the Australasian Sugar Company, better known by the later name of the Colonial Sugar Refining Company.

Economic Development in Van Diemen's Land

The expansion which occurred between 1830 and 1850 increased the New South Wales lead over its southern neighbour across Bass Strait. By the middle of the nineteenth century the population and livestock industry of Van Diemen's Land was only a third that of the mainland colony. In 1829 more wool had been sent to England from Hobart than from Sydney, but by 1837 only half as much was being despatched and by 1850 the proportion had dropped even further.

These trends were a result more of a quickening in the pace of New South Wales development than of any slackening in that of Van Diemen's Land. During the 1830s the island colony received some 10 000 migrants principally under assisted passage schemes financed from land sales. In the following decade the number of arrivals declined due to a surplus of labour, but convicts continued to be sent. Nearly 20 000 were shipped between 1830 and 1840 and a further 33 505 had been landed by the time transportation stopped in 1852. At first they were assigned on a full-time basis to settlers who could maintain them. Subsequently, after the probation system was introduced, they were available for hire once they had satisfactorily completed a term in government employ. For a time the change from one system to the other created difficulties but for most of the period cheap labour was abundant. Competition from convicts forced wages down and in the 1840s free persons actually migrated from Van Diemen's Land to other colonies in search of work.

TABLE 6
Expansion of Population, Agriculture, Cattle and Sheep
Raising in Van Diemen's Land 1830–50

	Population	*Acreage cultivated*	*Cattle*	*Sheep*	*Wool exported (lbs)*
1830	24 504	55 976	85 942	680 740	993 979
1835	40 283	87 283	82 217	824 256	2 428 500
1840	46 057	124 103	n.a.	1 089 987	3 636 900
1845	n.a.	140 953	76 417	1 253 481	3 662 100
1850	69 187	168 820	82 761	1 822 320	5 274 300

Sources: Statistical Returns of Van Diemen's Land, 1824–1835, Hobart, 1836; Statistics of Van Diemen's Land, 1844–1853.
NOTE: No population census was taken between 1842 and 1847. The total number of residents in 1847 was 67 918.

Capital and labour although available in smaller quantities than on the mainland was enough for additional expansion. Private as well as banking capital flowed in and government expenditure remained high. While pastoralists pushed into the west, farmers occupied the remaining vacant land along the Derwent and Tamar valleys in the eastern third of the island. There was not, however, the same division between grazier and farmer that existed in New South Wales. Pastoralists also produced crops and grazing did not enjoy so marked a dominance. Van Diemen's Land developed a mixed farming, rather than a pastoral economy. Its income came from the export of wool to England and also of wheat to other colonies, principally New South Wales. Wheat acreage increased from 31 156 in 1830 to 64 700 in 1848, by which stage production exceeded that of New South Wales and Port Phillip combined.

These developments were accompanied by variations in the level of prosperity. Events on the mainland precipitated a slump late in 1841. Overseas investors temporarily lost confidence and withdrew funds. The result was a fall in revenue, a rise in unemployment, the collapse of some financial institutions and large numbers of bankruptcies. Recovery did not begin until 1845 and thereafter prosperity slowly returned, a process helped by a rise in wool prices and renewed British investment.

By 1850 the Van Diemen's Land economy was able to sustain a community that was shortly to lose the financial and other advantages of being a penal settlement. Most of its 69 187 inhabitants were free and 'the use of natural resources (apart from minerals) was more advanced . . . than in any other Australian colony'. Over 4 million acres had been granted, 167 820 acres were farmed and on the remaining land 1 822 320 sheep and 82 761 cattle grazed. Hobart had grown into a major commercial centre second only to Sydney in terms of its size and the volume of its trade. There were two locally owned banks, the Bank of Van Diemen's Land and the Commercial Bank, both Hobart centred, and two that were London-based, the Bank of Australia and the Bank of Australasia, all of which were to enjoy a lengthy history. In addition, five local and two English insurance companies operated in the colony.

As in New South Wales secondary industry was of peripheral importance but the number and variety of firms had increased. Since 1830 makers of agricultural implements had grown from four to forty-six, breweries from eleven to forty-six, foundries from one to six, steam mills from none to nineteen, wind and water mills from thirty-six to fifty-six and tanners from thirteen to thirty-eight. Ship building, which had begun during the 1820s with the construction of small coastal vessels, had expanded, particularly during the 1830s when the foundation of new colonies on the mainland opened up fresh avenues of trade. Ships of up to 560 tons were now built in yards located both at Launceston and Hobart. According to one contemporary 'a fleet of not less than 390 vessels, carrying 23 200 tons, besides small craft, yachts and boats innumerable' were constructed between 1839 and 1859. This in turn stimulated the expansion of rope and sail-making, cooperage, saw-milling and allied trades, adding to the range of local industries.

The Economic Problems of Western and South Australia

Meanwhile the colonists of Western and South Australia had been establishing their economies. Since neither received convicts they were cut off from the supply of cheap labour and public finance that facilitated the growth of New South Wales and Van Diemen's Land. From the outset, their progress depended upon their ability to attract free migrants and private investment. Although South Australia succeeded in obtaining enough manpower and capital for developmental purposes, Western Australia was less fortunate and by 1850 was obliged to turn to the British government for assistance.

During the 1830s while the eastern mainland was enjoying a boom Western Australia was struggling. The original planning was inadequate and migrants arrived too rapidly. Land had not been properly surveyed or explored and, after the best spots close to Perth were occupied, settlers had to turn to areas less suited to primary production. One of the casualties was Thomas Peel who arrived too late to obtain a 250 000-acre grant on the Swan River and had to take his land further south in a region of sand and scrub. Many of the 450 migrants who accompanied him were unable to find suitable land and were forced to turn to other forms of employment. Their misfortunes were publicised by the press in eastern Australia and in England. Edward Gibbon Wakefield described the colony as the 'best example of the worst method of colonisation' and gave it unwelcome notoriety at a time when favourable publicity was needed. These adverse reports undermined the confidence of prospective migrants, and investors turned elsewhere, creating problems that took long to surmount.

TABLE 7
Expansion of Population, Agriculture, Cattle and Sheep
Raising in Western Australia, 1835–50

	Population	Acreage cultivated	Cattle	Sheep	Wool exported (lbs)	Wool exported (£)
1835	1 231	n.a.	n.a.	n.a.	n.a.	n.a.
1840	2 311	3 000	2 318	30 961	50 000	2 500
1845	3 853	n.a.	6 508	95 681	144 390	7 219
1850	5 886	n.a.	15 315	128 111	309 640	15 482

Source: Blue Books for Western Australia; *Statistical Register of Western Australia, 1900.*

Developments during the rest of the decade did nothing to compensate for the setbacks of the early years. The British government's decision in 1831 to sell Crown land dealt a serious blow to the colony. Capital which colonists would have spent on stocking and clearing holdings was needed for the purchase of land. To make matters worse the government sought to persuade grantees who had acquired excessive acreages before 1831 to hand some back. This action resulted from fears that these people might dispose of their surplus land at less than 5s an acre thereby preventing the sale of Crown land. Although the government offered to compensate those

The Flourishing State of the Swan River Thing. Suitable land was hard to find and adverse publicity, such as this cartoon and Wakefield's report of the Swan River Settlement as being 'the best example of the worst method of colonisation', did little to help overcome the problems.

who surrendered property, it met vigorous resistance from settlers and clashes developed which lasted throughout the 1830s adding to the general malaise.

Between 1832 and 1838 only £1 336 worth of land was sold which meant that practically no funds were available for migrants. Capitalists were deterred from coming not only by the new regulations but also by evidence that Captain Stirling had given a misleading impression of the quantity of good land. Patches of rich soil were so interspersed with barren areas that it was often difficult for a settler to use all his holding. There was also little natural fodder and much of what was available proved poisonous. These natural drawbacks had been overlooked by Wakefield. Their existence does something to explain the reluctance of settlers to give up part of their holdings.

Under these conditions, the number of migrants fell sharply after the first two years. Between 1832 and 1840 only 885 arrived, compared with the 2 419 who had come earlier. Some, like the Hentys, soon left for other parts of Australia. Most, however, remained either because they were more persevering or, more generally, because they lacked the means of going elsewhere. Such people had made little progress by 1840. In that year out of 1 500 000 acres alienated 3 000 were under crop. On the rest grazed 506 horses, 2 318 head of cattle and 30 961 sheep. With a population of only 2 311 demand was limited and trade slow to grow. Perth after ten years was little more than a village and Fremantle had failed to develop as a port because it was located away from the main shipping routes. Albany, on the southern coast, became the principal point of call but it had few visitors and had made little progress.

Nevertheless, the colony had survived the first decade. Pastoralists exported their first wool to England aboard the *Shepherd* in January 1840. Additional stimulus was provided in the following May when the West Australian Society was founded in London by business-men who numbered Wakefield among their directors. They sought to establish a new Wakefieldian settlement on Colonel Lautour's abandoned grant on the shores of Leschenault Inlet on Koombana Bay, 1 500 kilometres south of Perth. Plans were laid for an attrac-tive city, to be named Australind; land was offered for sale in one-hundred-acre blocks at £1 per acre and half of the proceeds were to be used to bring labourers from Britain. Although considerable acreages were sold, many purchasers reneged when they heard that the land was likely to be resumed by the government. This rumour proved groundless but those who did migrate aboard the *Parkfield* and the *Parmelia* in 1841 and 1842 found Australind ill-suited to agriculture. Mismanagement and over-optimism spelled doom for the venture but not before it had attracted much-needed colonists most of whom proved permanent acquisitions.

The failure of the Society confirmed the unfavourable view of Western Australia already current in England. Fortunately, this did not completely deter additional immigrants. Indeed, the number rose to 1 416 during the 1840s partly because more funds were available, partly because economic conditions deteriorated in England. Moreover, good agricultural and pastoral land had been found east of the Darling Range and north of Perth in the Champion Bay district. Land sales increased threefold despite the British government's decision to raise the price to 12s and then £1 per acre. The acreage cultivated rose to over 5 000 by 1850, the number of sheep to 128 111, wool exports to 309 640 lbs and the value of the clip to £15 482. The colony was gradually taking shape. Small townships were established and Perth took on more the appearance of a capital as new buildings were constructed and amenities improved.

Progress, however, had been slow and the position was still precarious. The increase in land prices, although uniform throughout Australia, made it even more difficult for the west to attract migrants with capital. Such people preferred better established colonies where the chances of success seemed greater. Disappointed colonists were still leaving Western Australia and in 1845 their number exceeded arrivals by 129. The basic problem was a shortage of labour. In desperation property owners petitioned the British government in 1846 to proclaim the settlement a penal colony, assume financial responsibility for running it and despatch convicts and migrants in equal numbers. Anxious to find an outlet for convicts now that New South Wales was closed and Van Diemen's Land overcrowded, the government agreed and in May 1849 Western Australia ceased to be exclusively free. By thus surrendering its birthright it guaranteed its existence. British capital and convict labour enabled private enterprise to place the colony on a secure footing.

TABLE 8
Expansion of Population, Agriculture, Cattle and Sheep
Raising in South Australia, 1840–50

	Population	Acreage cultivated	Cattle	Sheep	Wool exported (£)
1840	14 630	2 503	16 052	166 770	n.a.
1845	22 460	26 218	31 150	681 374	72 000
1850	63 700	64 728	100 000	1 000 000	131 000

Source: F. Proeschel, *Atlas of Australasia*, London, 1863.
NOTE: No figures are available showing the actual quantity of wool that was exported.

Developments in South Australia followed a different course. Its founders were anxious to avoid the mistakes committed in the west. Moreover, the government insisted on financial guarantees, and a substantial amount of capital had been raised before settlement commenced. This was a result partly of the interest shown by individual migrants, partly of the activities of the South Australia Company which channelled further capital and enterprise into the venture. The existence of the company gave the colony an advantage over Western Australia, so too did the fact that it had the support of a powerful and vocal group of theorists, business interests and politicians who lost no opportunity to counter English sceptics and opponents in the other Australian colonies.
Despite all this, South Australia experienced difficulties during

its first two years. The division of authority between Governor John Hindmarsh and Commissioner James Hurtle Fisher created friction that did not end until both men were replaced by Governor George Gawler who arrived on 12 October 1838. By then chaos reigned. William Light, the first surveyor-general, and most of his staff had resigned. A man of great ability, Light had previously served with distinction in the British army and the Egyptian navy. The demands imposed upon him in South Australia, however, were too great and he met opposition from Hindmarsh as well as from the commissioners in London. Before leaving office in June 1838 he had selected a site for Adelaide, drawn up plans for the city and surveyed and apportioned town lots for settlers. As yet he had been unable to mark out country sections and as a result most of the colonists were forced to live idly in or around the capital. As the supply of goods dwindled, shortages developed and prices rose. All this pointed to a flaw in the original plan. 'South Australia ... began at the wrong end', observed one of the colony's early writers, J.F. Bennett, 'they commenced by building a town ere there was any country population or country produce to support it'.

Under Gawler this process was reversed and the colony experienced a boom. The governor overcame the lag in surveying by reorganising the surveyor-general's department and appointing additional staff. He began a vastly expanded programme of public works to provide additional employment and capital. Adelaide took shape as a graceful, attractive city with well laid out streets, spacious parks and handsome public buildings. Country districts were also progressively opened. Agriculture and pastoralism expanded rapidly helped by an influx of labourers and other migrants whose presence increased the population from 6000 in 1838 to over 14000 by 1841. The export of wool which had begun in 1838 steadily grew. A contemporary journalist, riding through the countryside in July 1840, passed,

> Substantial farmhouses on all sides ...—hundreds of acres under thriving and healthy crops—scores of ploughs preparing for future cultivation—fencing proceeding with vigour and activity ... flocks and herds grazing in all directions ...

Small wonder that Gawler's administration should at first have proved highly popular among colonists who attributed their prosperity to his policies.

The steps which Gawler had taken resulted in a sharp increase in public expenditure to which his own extravagance and inability to curb his subordinates contributed. On his arrival authorised expenditure for 1838 had already been exceeded and over the next two years the gap widened. The commissioners in London who bore financial responsibility for the settlement at first accepted this as necessary for economic expansion and met the deficit by raising loans on the security of future land sales. Expenses, however, continued to mount and in 1840 bills poured in so rapidly that they grew alarmed. The government authorised a loan of £120 000 in July 1840, but rumours that the commissioners were in difficulties and fears that war was about to break out with France stopped subscribers coming forward. Other means of raising money could have been explored but the commissioners were panic-stricken and after failing to honour bills they were declared bankrupt. They were as much responsible as Gawler for the débâcle but they failed to give him their support and it was he who suffered the disgrace of being recalled.

The collapse of the commission brought the self-supporting system in South Australia to an end. There was no inherent reason for the scheme to have failed. With better management and better fortune it could have succeeded. Responsibility for the settlement

The Kapunda copper mine. The discovery and mining of rich silver lead and copper deposits during the 1840s resulted by 1850 in the predomination of ore over wool and wheat exports.

was now shouldered by the Colonial Office determined to minimise costs. An era of retrenchment was inaugurated by the new governor, George Grey, a former army officer and explorer of north-west Australia, who took office on 14 May 1841. The boom was over and like their counterparts in the east the colonists were plunged into a depression. Wages fell, unemployment rose, capital and currency were scarce and a system of barter had to be introduced. Distress and misery prevailed in all ranks of society. Property values dropped in town and country and whole sections of Adelaide were deserted. As fewer foreign vessels arrived so the port declined, adding further to the problems that confronted the city.

These setbacks were the result not of any deep-rooted problems such as continued to plague Western Australia but of temporary difficulties. After Grey placed finances on a sound footing and improved administration, confidence gradually returned and the number of migrants rose after 1842. Of major importance was the discovery of rich deposits of silver-lead at Glen Osmond near Adelaide in 1841 and of copper at Kapunda in 1842 and Burra Burra in 1845. By 1850 some thirty mining companies were operating and the value of ore exports was more than twice that of wheat and wool combined. Overseas earnings from the export of metals did much to promote development and encourage further migration. By 1850 the total population had reached 63 700.

Important too was the continued expansion of the landed industries which absorbed the energies and capital of the majority of the colonists. Natural conditions favoured agriculture more than pastoralism and the land system was geared to moderate-sized rather than large holdings. Sheep raising was important and wool formed one of the earliest exports, bringing the colony an annual income of £148 000 by 1851. Costs, however, were high, profits only moderate and there was not that abundance of cheap land that made the industry so attractive on the eastern mainland. In contrast, the mediterranean climate of the coastal region proved ideally suited to vines, figs, olives and above all wheat. Agriculture made steady progress during the 1840s but wages were high. Admittedly for the wheat farmer there existed an important labour-saving device, the stripper, claimed to have been invented by J.W. Bull, a Mount Barker farmer, but named after John Ridley who first manufactured the machine. It was not widely used, however, because it was better suited to some varieties of wheat than others and to large rather than small farms. Heavy wage bills impeded wheat growing and so too did high freight and insurance rates as well as inter-colonial duties which restricted exports. Even so, by 1850, 41 000 acres were under wheat and exports yielded £59 000. The colony was in fact fast becoming economically self-sufficient.

TABLE 9
Australian Wool Imports into England
1830–50

	Australia	Germany	Spain	Total	Australia (%)	Germany (%)
1831	2 493 337	22 436 105	3 474 823	31 651 999	7·9	70·7
1835	4 209 301	23 798 186	1 602 752	42 168 142	9·9	56·4
1840	9 721 243	21 812 099	1 226 905	49 393 967	19·6	44·2
1845	24 151 287	18 465 131	1 074 540	75 551 950	31·9	24·4
1850	38 590 413	9 153 583	440 751	72 674 483	53·0	12·6

Source: P. Burroughs, *Britain and Australia 1831–1855, A Study in Imperial Relations and Crown Lands Administration,* Oxford, 1967.

Between 1830 and 1850, therefore, settlement in Australia expanded at an unprecedented rate as men and money came in quantities greater than ever before. By 1850 Van Diemen's Land was almost fully occupied, as was a broad belt stretching northward from Port Phillip to Moreton Bay on the eastern mainland. Along the west coast colonisation had spread from north of Perth to Albany and in South Australia scarcely a block of land was to be had within a 1 500 kilometre radius of Adelaide. Outside Western Australia substantial development had occurred as grazing, agriculture, trade, commerce and manufacturing expanded. Besides offering a valuable outlet for British capital and migrants the colonies had also provided the mother country with raw materials. Since 1845 Australia had emerged as Britain's largest supplier of wool and by 1850 exports amounted to over 38 million lbs, which represented 53 per cent of the British market. In the German states production had declined as pressure of population and secondary industry made inroads on pasture land. In 1850 they supplied only 12·6 per cent of Britain's needs. The Australian continent, which in 1830 had been valued chiefly as an outlet for convicts, was now of great importance commercially and economically. This change which was important in itself had significant effects on the course of political development in the colonies.

six : Government and Politics

Political Conflict in New South Wales and Van Diemen's Land

The non-elective system of government that had been established in New South Wales and Van Diemen's Land during the 1820s persisted throughout the ensuing decade. In England the current of thought and action was flowing in a liberal direction. Eighteen thirty-two saw the passage of the first Reform Act which widened the franchise and redistributed seats to make the House of Commons more representative of property-owning interests. Two years later local government institutions were reformed along similar lines. Neither of these developments had any immediate effect in the eastern Australian colonies. Circumstances there were different and this made irrelevant innovations that were introduced in the mother country. So long as these colonies were receiving convicts further changes in the basis of their governments were unthinkable. The fact that the proportion of free and freed was increasing did not alter the need for firm control. Nor was much weight attached to the argument that free citizens were entitled to the same rights as their counterparts in England. Their presence in a penal colony meant they accepted its constitution and forfeited the advantages enjoyed by those who lived in Britain.

In New South Wales opinion was still divided as to the desirability and form of constitutional change—a fact which gave the government additional reason for acting cautiously. Until late in the decade the division followed existing lines. Liberal elements, including ex-convicts as well as migrants, formed the group commonly labelled emancipist which pressed for representative government and further extension of trial by jury. Under the leadership of W.C. Wentworth and other figures who had risen to prominence during the 1820s they held public meetings and submitted petitions to the British government. The first of these documents arose from a meeting at Sydney on 9 February 1830 in protest against the Act of 1828. A copy was despatched to London at the close of the year and laid before the House of Commons on 28 June 1832 by Henry Lytton Bulwer MP who was interested in colonial affairs. Neither this petition nor a second one in 1833 gained anything for the emancipists who decided that their organisation should be improved. The outcome was the formation on 5 August 1835 of the Australian Patriotic Association. Originally intended to unite all sections of opinion, it became a vehicle for the expression of the emancipists' aims. A corresponding committee was established under the chairmanship of Sir John Jamison to coordinate activities and despatch instructions to Bulwer who had volunteered his services as their London representative. Draft proposals for a new constitution were drawn up in 1835 and submitted to parliament a year later.

The arrangement did not work well. Bulwer made little headway against the opposition and indifference which he encountered. He knew too little about his constituents and was more 'a theorist . . . an aspirant for place', as the emancipist Edward Eagar complained, than 'a man of business, of detail, of application'. In December 1837 he resigned in favour of the Wakefieldian, Charles Buller, who proved little better. A friend of the exclusive James Macarthur, he was scarcely an appropriate choice for the position.

The exclusives continued to have doubts about allowing ex-convicts to serve on juries and they also opposed a wholly elective Legislative Council. Their ideas were given cogent expression by James Macarthur, whose *New South Wales, Its Present State and Future Prospects,* ghost-written by Edward Edwards and published in 1835, became the counterpart to William Charles Wentworth's *Historical, Statistical and Political Description of New South Wales.* Macarthur did not completely oppose constitutional change. He accepted that the Legislative Council should be enlarged and he was prepared for some of its members to be elected; but under conditions designed to ensure that only persons of substantial property and high character were returned.

The exclusives had support in the Colonial Office and parliament. In the colony, however, they were confronted by a governor whose political colouring was different to their own. In December 1831 Darling had been replaced by Richard Bourke who, after serving

with distinction in the British army from 1798 until 1815, had
been acting governor of the Cape of Good Hope between 1826 and
1828. The intervening period was spent on his property at Thornfield
in Limerick to which he had a deep attachment. Educated at West-
minster School and Oxford University, Bourke had wider intellectual horizons than his predecessor who lacked his advantages
of birth and social position. Darling's stiff demeanour was replaced
by an open, gracious manner that broke down some of the barriers
between governor and governed. Moreover, whereas Darling
had been a Tory, Bourke inclined more towards the liberals despite
the fact that his cousin was Edmund Burke the leading conservative thinker of the late eighteenth century. This did not mean
that he planned to take sides in the conflict that divided New
South Wales. His sense of duty was too strong and he recognised
that as governor he had to stand above party divisions. He did,
however, appreciate the need for moderate change and sympathised
with those who were trying to bring it about.

Between 1831 and 1836 Bourke supported liberal reform.
Unlike Darling, he favoured representative government and in 1835
sent to London a constitution bill, which had been drafted by Sir
Francis Forbes, containing provision for a predominantly elective
Legislative Council in which emancipists could play a part. This
measure was not accepted but, although he could not change the
composition of the council, Bourke summoned it more often than
had Darling and liberalised its procedures. He also opened the way
to wider public discussion of issues by refusing to invoke an act
of September 1831 which had imposed heavy penalties for seditious
libel. Relations between the press and the governor improved
considerably and Bourke found support in the *Australian,* the
Sydney Monitor and the *Sydney Gazette,* although this last journal
became more critical after a change of editor in 1836. The main
opposition came from the *Sydney Herald* (later the *Sydney Morning
Herald*) which began its long history on 18 April 1831. By 1836
under the direction of two of its founders, Ward Stephens and
F.M. Stokes, it was fast becoming the colony's leading paper.
Its mottoes were two couplets from the poet Pope:

> In Moderation placing all my Glory,
> While Tories call me Whig—and Whigs a Tory.

and

> Sworn to no Master, of no Sect am I.

These proclaimed the virtues of moderation and freedom from the dictates of party, but its stand was anti-Whig and it found little to commend in Bourke's views.

Despite the presence of such a governor, the exclusives still wielded considerable power. Six of the seven non-official members of the Legislative Council belonged to this group, which also had the support of Tory-appointed government officials such as the colonial secretary, Alexander McLeay and C.D. Riddell, the colonial treasurer. Both of these men sat on the Executive Council as did the Anglican archdeacon, W.G. Broughton, who was another Tory sympathiser. McLeay and Broughton also belonged to the Legislative Council which thus had a permanent exclusive majority. Since the governor was obliged to consult this body, the exclusives were strongly placed to influence policy. This was particularly important in relation to Bourke's attempts to extend the use of juries in the law courts. The governor believed that all accused persons were entitled to a civil jury and that emancipists should have the same rights as free persons to sit on such juries. Owing to opposition in the Legislative Council, however, he was unable to move as far in this direction as he would have liked. Nevertheless, some reforms were introduced. In July 1835 a measure was passed with the governor's casting vote allowing suitably qualified emancipists to become jurors. The use of juries in criminal cases was also extended, but the option of a military jury was preserved to meet the exclusives' reservations. By 1836 a dual system operated in both civil and criminal courts. Juries could be used if requested but alternative methods still existed. In this, as in other respects, the legal system differed from that of Great Britain.

Bourke's administration was the last in which the division between the exclusive and emancipist political factions had any real significance. Even while he was governor the split lost some of its meaning and sharpness. This was partly a result of his own conciliatory behaviour which did much to heal differences and bridge gaps. Although strongly attacked by embittered settlers like 'Major' James Mudie of Castle Forbes who resented being censured for undue harshness to his convict servants and, although attacked by other Hunter River graziers for restricting their power to punish convicts, Bourke was respected and liked by most sections of the community. His decision to leave the colony in December 1837 after his superiors had failed to give him the backing he considered he deserved in a conflict with C.D. Riddell was widely regretted. While he was in command political debate was conducted more rationally and in a calmer atmosphere than had been the case under Darling.

Moreover, his reforms of the legal system went far towards removing one of the sources of contention between exclusives and emancipists. The two factions were still divided on the question of representative government but the gap was narrowing. James Macarthur was prepared to accept some elected members and was less hostile towards wealthy emancipists being included in the council. Wentworth who had always favoured a franchise restricted to property owners was beginning to appreciate that he might have more in common with Macarthur than with some of his own followers. At the early meetings of the Australian Patriotic Association he was opposed by Richard Hipkiss, a chartist and former member of the Birmingham Political Union. Hipkiss had arrived in May 1832 and was one of a growing class of migrants who settled in Sydney and found employment as skilled tradesmen, shopkeepers or small-business men. Their interests separated them from landowners like Wentworth and they sought a franchise based not on wealth but on intelligence. The fact that they posed a threat to the large emancipist property owners as well as to the exclusives was an additional reason for the groups to coalesce.

By the time Governor Sir George Gipps arrived in February 1838, therefore, signs of a new political alignment were evident. This process gained further impetus from developments that occurred after his accession. The abolition of military juries by an Act brought before the Legislative Council by Gipps in 1839 meant that the procedure of the law courts was no longer contentious. More important, the decision of the British government to abolish transportation forced exclusive and emancipist leaders to see that the economic interests which they shared were more important than any political differences that might still separate them. As large employers of labour they were anxious for a continued supply of convicts and they protested strongly when they heard that this was to be cut off. In Sydney, however, the government's action was welcomed by urban elements, particularly recently arrived migrants whose principal assets were their skills. They saw transportation as a threat to their economic and political wellbeing. So long as convicts were being sent, reform of the Legislative Council was out of the question, fewer jobs were available and wages were likely to be depreciated. The transportation issue, then, besides bringing the wealthy emancipists and exclusives closer together, opened a fresh division between urban elements on the one hand and, on the other, pastoralists together with their allies amongst those merchants, bankers and financiers who were connected with the wool industry. The conflict involved political and economic issues, but it also raised the question of what kind of society was to be developed in New South Wales—one fashioned in the image of urban groups, or one dominated by the squatters.

No such change of alignment occurred in Van Diemen's Land where the exclusive-emancipist split had never assumed significant proportions or cut so sharply across other lines of division. 'There is not at present any emancipist party', wrote Sir William Molesworth in 1838, 'that class being as yet few in number and without wealth or influence'. The whole political scene was different to New South Wales and it was made more so by the continuation in office of the existing lieutenant-governor. Until 30 October 1836 Van Diemen's Land was administered by George Arthur, whose superiors thought highly enough of him to ignore the new rule under which governors were recalled after six years service. Arthur was on good terms with the liberal Bourke, but he saw no reason to modify his policies in the light of practices on the mainland. Admittedly, on 15 November 1834 he allowed the use of juries in civil and criminal courts but membership was restricted to free persons of respectable character and the alternative system of a jury composed of military officers was preserved. The Act made fewer concessions than the one passed by Bourke, whose views on representative government and freedom of the press were also rejected by Arthur.

The reaction of the colonists provides some support for the view that many were more interested in their wellbeing than in political advancement. Economic conditions after 1830 were flourishing and transportation resulted in a high level of government expenditure as well as a steady influx of convict labourers. The restriction of political rights was an acceptable price to pay for the economic advantages of living in a penal colony. As was the case on the mainland, however, not everyone accepted the view that free institutions were incompatible with the continued arrival of convicts. Van Diemen's Land contained enough men of respectability to provide both an electorate and members to sit in the Legislative Council. What was needed was continued agitation to persuade the British government to change its mind.

Between 1831 and 1836 meetings were organised in Hobart by a group which included former New South Wales Corps officers, Anthony Fenn Kemp and Edward Abbott; the banker William

Gellibrand and his son who was a barrister; Thomas Horne, later puisne judge and a relative of Horne Tooke, the late-eighteenth-century English radical; and Thomas Gregson, a free settler and publisher from 1832 of the *Colonist* newspaper 'the journal of the people'. The first of their meetings held in 1831 on the 'Glorious twenty third of May' was convened by the sheriff to present an address to King William IV congratulating him on his accession to the throne. It culminated in the formation of a Grand Political Association and the despatch to London of a petition demanding an elected house of assembly. This document was rejected and the association itself foundered amidst ridicule after its members were seen wearing the tricolour and proclaiming themselves as liberators. Further meetings were held in Hobart in July 1832 and in July as well as August 1834, but the new petitions made no headway against the refusal of the British government to contemplate political reform while convicts were being sent.

The replacement of Arthur by Sir John Franklin who took office in January 1837 was seen by the colonists as promising change. The new governor was more pliant and less prone to allow the presence of convicts to determine his policies. Arthur had never taken seriously the agitation for representative government, which he believed was sought only by a handful of agitators and trouble-makers. He saw public meetings not as a reflection of genuine grievance but as an imitation of what was going on elsewhere. Franklin treated the demands of the free colonists with respect and claimed that 'the spirit of freedom and the love of free institutions exists here quite as strongly as it does in New South Wales'. His sentiments were liberal and he came to the colony anticipating that it would be granted representative government. Soon after arriving he permitted the public to attend debates in the Legislative Council. This he believed was a major step that would pave 'the way for some modification in the legislature of the colony'. Bourke had opposed such a move in New South Wales because he believed that there was a better chance of members reaching agreement if they deliberated in private. Franklin argued that, in opening the doors of the council, he had already subjected its members to popular control. Having conceded the substance of representative government, all that remained was for the Colonial Office to give it form.

Constitutional Change

By 1840, therefore, hopes were high in New South Wales and

Van Diemen's Land that the colonists might soon be allowed to elect representatives to the Legislative Council. The decision to make Van Diemen's Land the chief repository for transported felons, however, as Franklin was informed in August 1840, 'has rendered it inexpedient ... to propose at present any material change in (its) ... institutions'. The British authorities had always subordinated the interests of free settlers to penal purposes in Van Diemen's Land and now there was even less likelihood that the colonists would get their way. The reverse was true of New South Wales whose connection with the penal system was about to be severed. Political institutions devised to suit an earlier stage of the colony's history could now be reframed in accordance with its new status.

The future constitution of New South Wales had been under consideration for some time. The need to await the findings of the Molesworth Committee prevented a decision being taken in 1838 and thereafter government hesitancy in the face of a complex problem resulted in further delays. Not until late in 1841 did Lord John Russell's administration grasp the nettle. Russell, a statesman whose intellectual capacity and parliamentary skill more than compensated for his delicate, diminutive physique, was at the forefront of early and mid-Victorian politics. He led the progressive Whigs and had played a major part in bringing about the 1832 Reform Act. Between 1839 and 1841 he served as colonial secretary in Lord Melbourne's administration and in that capacity was responsible for the Order in Council which ended transportation to New South Wales. Two months later he prepared a new constitution based on proposals sent by Governor Gipps for a partly elected Legislative Council and for the division of New South Wales into three administrative regions. He dropped this measure in the face of his own misgivings and colonial opposition but resolved to settle the question after coming to power as prime minister. The actual details were worked out by Lord Stanley, an able parliamentarian but not a constructive thinker, who had reluctantly agreed to become secretary of state for the colonies. His Constitution Act, passed by parliament in 1842, was modelled on the one drafted earlier by Russell and established representative government in New South Wales.

This was not the only Australian colony to receive a new constitution in 1842. South Australia also experienced change—for the third time in six years. The original system of government had proved unworkable because it had created two sovereignties.

Clashes were bound to occur between the governor who was responsible to the Colonial Office and the resident commissioner whose duty was to the board of commissioners and shareholders in London. Each had his own sphere of jurisdiction but there were areas in which both sides could claim the right to intervene. What made matters worse were the personalities of the men on the spot. The first governor, Captain John Hindmarsh, was a man of singular courage who had earned the public thanks of Lord Nelson by saving (at the cost of one eye) HMS *Bellerophon* from destruction by fire at the battle of the Nile in Aboukir Bay in 1798. His application for the governorship of South Australia was supported by Lords Palmerston and Grey but his reputation rested more on his bravery than on his ability to command. Honest and warm-hearted, he had an abrupt manner and lacked experience in handling civilians. Resident Commissioner James Hurtle Fisher, a lawyer by training, had a legalistic mind which made him prone to hairsplitting and jealous of his rights. He proved unwilling to co-operate with Hindmarsh whose bluff manner provided a further irritant. Conflict began on the voyage aboard HMS *Buffalo* when Hindmarsh found it impossible to accommodate all of Fisher's large party at his table. Weeks of confinement together in the 589-ton vessel widened the gap.

Once ashore the two men found themselves in the small town atmosphere that coloured South Australian politics throughout the foundation years. Adelaide was the centre of political life and the population remained sufficiently small and confined for minor irritants to become magnified out of all proportion. The colony may have been established by settlers of high political ideals but in its early years this did little to raise the tone of public debate. Personality rather than principle divided men and petty squabbling took the place of reasoned discussion. Amongst the leading protagonists were staunch individualists whose strong views and easily aroused tempers gave an often virulent edge to their debates.

Between April 1836 and July 1838 the rivalry of Hindmarsh and Fisher provided the chief source of discord. The governor was determined to impose his will on the commissioner and the council. On arrival he found that Surveyor-General Light, one of the commissioner's staff, had already selected a site for the capital. At once he disputed the choice less because there was a better alternative than because he had not been consulted. When outvoted by the colonists after a lengthy dispute he surrendered ungraciously and named the poorer regions around Port Adelaide after the commissioners. Fisher engaged in similar pinpricking obstructing the council and making life difficult for the governor. Such a conflict necessarily involved public officials. Most at first ranged themselves on opposing sides according to whether they were appointed by government or commissioners. An important exception was Colonel Light who on grounds of former friendship supported the governor despite their disagreement over the location of Adelaide. Light, however, turned against Hindmarsh after the latter's private secretary, George Stevenson, began publishing the *South Australian Gazette* on 3 June 1837. Its bitter personal attacks on the governor's opponents also antagonised fair-minded officials including the colonial secretary, Robert Gouger, and the judge-advocate, Charles Mann, besides alarming the commissioners in London. Confidence in the governor was further undermined by a series of public meetings organised by Fisher's friends for the purpose of discrediting Hindmarsh.

By 1838 it was clear to commissioners and Colonial Office that the existing system of government was imperilling the future of South Australia. Accordingly, Hindmarsh was replaced by Lieutenant-Colonel George Gawler who also assumed the duties of resident commissioner. This change brought the government of South Australia closer to that of the eastern Australian colonies but it was still not identical with either. The governor's council contained only nominated members and there was also a board of commissioners in London with jurisdiction in the colony. Unlike his colleagues in other parts of Australia the new governor had two masters to please at home as well as a colony to keep in order.

This was a task for which Gawler was not ideally suited. A soldier who had distinguished himself in the Peninsular War, he became a religious convert in 1818 and was determined to attend to the spiritual as well as the material needs of the colony. A strict evangelical he insisted on sabbatarian observances at Government House and frowned on dancing and cards. Autocratic by temperament and a believer in order rather than liberty, he was hard working and conscientious. Yet these gifts were counterbalanced by a susceptibility to flattery and a lack of firmness. Nevertheless, under Gawler the situation improved. Admittedly dissension did not stop and the tone of political discussion remained sharp. The *Register* which had supported Hindmarsh attacked Gawler and was joined by its one-time opponent, the *South Australian*, which appeared on 2 June 1838 under the editorship of the former advocate-general, Charles Mann. A democrat and early supporter of South Australian colonisation, he believed that too much power was concentrated in the governor's hands. Yet political conflict no longer stultified government action. Fisher remained in the colony but his power was broken. Obstructive officials were replaced by others more cooperative, including Charles Sturt, the explorer, and Robert Richard Torrens, son of one of the colony's founders and the man responsible for the Torrens system of registering land titles that was later adopted in other colonies. Under their direction government offices functioned more effectively and so too did the council which became more pliant. A further innovation was the establishment in October 1840 of the Adelaide Municipal Council— the first of its kind in Australia. Founded by the commissioners to give colonists training in handling local affairs, it suspended operations in 1843 after its lack of effective power had bred disillusion.

Meanwhile Gawler himself had been recalled. Shortly after, the commission in London was abolished, and the Colonial Office took over the colony. In June 1842 Lord Stanley's Act for the Better Government of South Australia vested power in a governor and nominated Legislative Council of at least seven persons. This was less than had been conceded to New South Wales and it placed South Australia on a similar footing to Van Diemen's Land. It was not intended, however, that the province should permanently remain a Crown colony. On several occasions since 1836 the demand for representative institutions had been put forward by liberals such as Fisher and Mann. As yet, however, development was so limited and the financial problems were so great that control was left in the hands of the authorities in London.

Much the same was true of Western Australia whose small population depended on British assistance and accepted the need for Colonial Office tutelage. Only one constitutional change had been made when four colonists were added to the Legislative Council in 1839. Like the official members these newcomers, who included W.L. Brockman, a pastoralist and stockbreeder, George Leake, a merchant, William Tanner, a leading settler, and Thomas Peel, one of the founders of the colony, were all nominated. The system of government was typical of a Crown colony with Legislative and Executive Councils presided over by a governor who was responsible to the Colonial Office. Stirling, the first person to fill this office had been replaced in January 1839 by John Hutt, a former employee of the East India Company, follower of Wakefield and advocate of the colonisation of South Australia. A hard-working, austere man, he had the thankless task of presiding over the affairs of a region that at the time of his departure in February 1846 was still struggling.

Representative Government in New South Wales

By 1842 each of the Australian colonies had a form of government that suited its particular political and economic maturity. New South Wales, as the largest and most highly developed settlement, had been endowed with a reasonably liberal constitution. The Legislative Council was enlarged to thirty-six members of whom two thirds were chosen by a property owning electorate that included emancipists. The elected representatives had to qualify by having greater capital assets than the voters. They had a permanent majority on the council which could initiate legislation dealing with local issues. No such legislation could become law until it was approved by the council. On the other hand it had also to be accepted by the governor and the Imperial parliament whose powers were considerable. The governor could not be dismissed by the Legislature and each year £81 600 was set aside from the colonial revenues to support public worship as well as civil and judicial purposes. The Legislative Council had no control over this money. Nor could it dispose of Crown land or decide how to spend the money arising from its sale. Such matters were reserved to the Colonial Office which selected the governor, appointed the leading officials and had the final say on all matters. Herein were sown the seeds of a conflict that took over a decade to resolve.

The presence of a predominantly elective legislature had important effects on political life. It provided a new forum for debate and a fresh focus around which opinion could revolve. Proceedings and debates were reported at length and the colonists were given an opportunity to observe the legislative process at close quarters. The newly constituted council helped develop the political con- sciousness of the colonists and reinforced their faith in parliamentary institutions. Much of its time was taken up with matters of regional significance, which could cause heated debate and produce deep- seated rifts among members. The big issues, however, were connected with the powers and policies of the British government. In the 1830s the main demand had been for representative government. During the 1840s those who had benefited from this concession worked hard for the means of giving it greater substance.

The form which this struggle took was strongly influenced by the interests of those who dominated the Legislative Council. Under the Act of 1842 six seats (including one for Melbourne) were allotted

to Port Phillip, sixteen to the country regions of New South Wales
and two to the capital. Election day in Sydney, 15 June 1843, was
marked by disorder as a band of rowdies known as the Cabbage
Tree Mob ran rampage through the city, attacking and destroying
polling booths. Despite this the electorate returned two men of
substance, W.C. Wentworth and Dr William Bland, a leading
medical practitioner and emancipist who had fought hard for
liberal reform during the 1830s. From country electorates came
extremely able men including Dr J.D. Lang, the public-spirited
Presbyterian clergyman whose outspoken radical views kept him at
the forefront of colonial life for nearly half a century. Others of
high calibre were T.A. Murray, Irish-born landowner and later
speaker of the assembly and president of the council; Dr Charles
Nicholson, landowner, businessman, surgeon, scholar and a key
figure in the early history of the University of Sydney; Roger Therry,
a distinguished barrister and Catholic layman; Richard Windeyer,
a leading lawyer; and Charles Cowper who was to become premier
of New South Wales on five occasions. In addition to the elected
representatives were the twelve nominated members chosen by
the governor from among officials and 'gentlemen of independence'.
Amongst the former was Edward Deas Thomson, who had come to
New South Wales in 1828 as clerk of the Executive and Legislative
Councils. He served as colonial secretary from 1837 until 1856 and
won high praise as an outstanding administrator. In the Legislative
Council he acted as the chief spokesman for the governor's policies,
a task which called for tact and parliamentary skill. A less fortunate
choice from Gipps's standpoint was his selection of Robert Lowe,
later Viscount Sherbrooke and chancellor of the exchequer under
Gladstone. Originally a staunch supporter and friend of the
governor, Lowe turned his formidable debating skill to a different
end after Gipps attempted, by means of his squatting regulations,
to raise additional revenue. This move alienated Lowe who saw
it as increasing the power of the executive and undermining the
role of the legislature in whose rights he passionately believed.
After further dissension he resigned in August 1844, established
the *Atlas* newspaper and campaigned for an increased measure of
self-government.

The Legislative Council represented not the mass of the colonists
but the leading elements of society. Pastoralists predominated and
the man who spoke out most clearly on their behalf was W.C.
Wentworth. One of the wealthiest landowners in the colony he
quickly established his ascendancy in the Legislative Council. He

fought for the group to which he belonged economically but his interests were never purely sectional. His outlook was coloured by that patriotism which had been formed in his youth and he believed that, in order to realise its potential, the colony must be given more control over its own affairs. His support for self-government linked his views to those of progressives and rallied to his support, both within and outside the council, men who opposed other aspects of his thought. To a greater extent than any other figure he imposed himself on the 1840s.

Wentworth and his associates were particularly anxious to obtain for the Legislative Council control over the Crown lands of the colony. Land was a principal source of wealth and the pastoralists considered it unfair that the British government should determine how it was to be alienated. The colonists, who were directly involved in making the land productive, should have the right to decide what should happen to it. Indeed, they were better equipped to do so than officials and armchair theorists in far-off London. By raising the minimum price to 12s an acre in 1838 and £1 in 1842 and using land revenue for purposes other than encouraging migration, the home government obstructed progress. On several occasions the Legislative Council appointed committees to enquire into this matter and their findings, invariably condemnatory, were sent to London. The British authorities, however, viewed the lands of the empire as a trust best administered from outside the colonies. Care had to be taken to ensure that future as well as present generations were catered for and impartial officials in London were alone equipped to do this. They recognised that the Legislative Council in Sydney was dominated by the pastoralists and feared legitimately that their campaign was directed by self-interest. To allow them control of Crown land might be to deny others a share in its use.

No more successful were attempts to persuade the Colonial Office to give the legislature control over the land revenue and other sources of finance. The elected members believed that they should have a voice in the spending of money raised in the colony. The existence of a civil list reduced their ability to influence the actions of the executive and gave it too much independence. The Colonial Office, first under Lord Stanley and then after 1846 under the third Earl Grey, refused to accept these demands. A leading member of Lord John Russell's Whig cabinet, Grey had a high sense of responsibility. Although prepared to grant self-government to the Canadian provinces, he considered that New South Wales was not ready for this concession. The colonists needed to gain more experience of political affairs before they could be entrusted with greater power.

The reluctance of the British government to make concessions involved governors in severe difficulties. Their situation was bound to be delicate because in the Legislative Council they faced a large and often hostile majority which drew strength from its claim to represent the most important elements in the community. Of the two men who held office during the 1840s Sir George Gipps had the worst time. His relations with the nominated council between 1838 and 1842 had been favourable, but the partly elected one proved a constant thorn. This was inevitable given that Gipps had to carry out the orders of the Colonial Office but personal factors, the governor's own policies and a deterioration in the economic situation complicated matters. In 1840 he incurred the lasting enmity of Wentworth by frustrating his attempts to acquire for a pittance 20 million acres of the south island of New Zealand. Half a dozen other council members, including Robert Lowe, were slighted when by oversight they did not receive an invitation to dine at Government House. More seriously, the governor's stand against the squatters angered the council, eighteen of whose elected members belonged to the Pastoral Association. From the time of the council's first meeting until Gipps's departure in July 1846 there was constant turmoil which undermined his health and obscured his very real contributions to the colony.

The settlement of the squatting problem in 1847 improved matters for his successor, Sir Charles FitzRoy, an army officer and former member of parliament who had gained experience of civil command as lieutenant-governor of Prince Edward Island and the Leeward Islands. His conciliatory policies resulted in the Legislative Council moderating its stand, particularly after the Colonial Office gave it the right to appropriate the casual revenues of the Crown. Yet other sources of conflict remained and these were exacerbated by Earl Grey's failure to appreciate the depth of feeling that existed on constitutional issues. As New South Wales grew in importance and as increasing numbers of migrants arrived, so the demand for self-government became stronger among all sections of the community. The cessation of transportation brought an end to government spending on the convict system. The British authorities were anxious to cut expenditure and the colonists were expected to provide for services that had once been financed by the Exchequer. The police and gaol establishments, for example, had to be supported from revenue raised locally and contributions had to be made towards defence. All this was widely appreciated by the colonists who argued that if they were to provide money for these purposes they should have more say in how it was to be spent. Economic dependence on Great Britain had been reduced and, with exports rapidly rising, New South Wales was able to stand on its own feet. This in turn was believed to justify further changes in its political status.

The existence of agreement on these matters, however, should not be allowed to obscure splits over other questions. The antipathy of urban groups towards the squatters was heightened by the Order in Council of 1847 which was seen as a triumph for self-interest and backstairs intrigue. Even worse was the use which the squatters made of their position in the Legislative Council to secure the resumption of transportation. The threatened breakdown of the penal system in over-crowded Van Diemen's Land prompted Gladstone, then secretary of state for the colonies, to ask the New South Wales government late in 1846 if it would accept convicts under carefully controlled conditions. The squatters, who had opposed the ending of transportation, welcomed the prospect of its revival. A committee composed of pastoralists was appointed by the Legislative Council to examine Gladstone's proposal and pre-dictably prepared a case in its favour. This prompted an outcry among the colonists outside the council which subsequently narrowly rejected the report while some pastoralists were absent. By the time news of this development reached London, the new secretary of state, Earl Grey, had sent a fresh offer under which, if the colony would accept ticket-of-leave or conditionally pardoned convicts, the British government would despatch at its own expense an equal number of emigrants. Attracted by this offer the Legislative Council reversed its earlier decision. Earl Grey then revoked the Order in Council abolishing transportation and in 1849 the first convicts arrived aboard the *Hashemy*.

These events provoked an outcry in Melbourne and Sydney where angry crowds prevented the convicts landing. Faced with this opposition the Legislative Council changed its attitude, the squatter component having been reduced by the elections of June 1848. Subsequently Earl Grey dropped the matter after unsuccess-fully attempting to send convicts to Moreton Bay. Already, however, the issue had antagonised the colonists and increased the demand for self-government. At the same time, it strengthened the hand of those who wished to curb the power of the squatters in the Legislative Council. Amongst those wishing to achieve both ends was Robert

Lowe who had been returned to the council at the election of June 1848 as one of Sydney's two representatives. He had supported the squatters in their opposition to Gipps's regulations of 1844 but was repelled by their evident desire to monopolise the lands which they occupied. In the council he spoke out strongly against transportation which he saw as bolstering their power and as an example of British injustice.

Lowe was a liberal rather than a democrat. His lack of genuine sympathy for the workers as well as his opposition to manhood suffrage had lost him much support by the time he returned to England in January 1850 to regain his always precarious health. The men who had backed his election campaign and who supported his stand on transportation, however, included representatives of more radical hue. Amongst the migrants of the 1840s were former chartists who brought with them a belief in universal franchise and a legislature which should be representative of, and firmly controlled by, the people. Such people who included the young Henry Parkes, then a small-business man in Sydney, played an important role in the events of 1849. Already they were organised and they also had their own newspaper, the *Peoples' Advocate* which first appeared on 2 December 1848 under the editorship of E.J. Hawkesley, a former Roman Catholic school teacher. During the ensuing decade they were to emerge as a major political force in opposition to the squatters. While for the most part prepared to accept the British connection, they sought to gain for the masses control over their own affairs.

Political Agitation in the Other Colonies

In Van Diemen's Land during the 1840s the transportation question overshadowed other subjects of public interest. A substantial body of pastoralists and their associates, supported by some government officials and by Lieutenant-Governor Denison, still believed that cheap convict labour was essential. They found themselves increasingly on the defensive after 1840 as their opponents became more numerous and vocal. Since 1836 the colonial government had borne the cost of the police force and gaols. At first the burden was not onerous, but it became so once the probation system was introduced. Convicts served the first part of their sentences in large, poorly supervised gangs which acted as breeding grounds for crime and vice. Many escaped and became bushrangers. Additional money was needed for law enforcement and this had to be raised locally.

The situation became worse in the first half of the decade due to the depression which reduced the settlers' ability to pay for such charges. The switch from assignment to probation temporarily cut the supply of convict labour and forced the government to spend money on importing free labour. By the time fresh convicts were available the demand for labour had fallen and large numbers remained in government hands, increasing the problem of supervision. Now that settlers had to pay convicts a wage, some began to ask whether it was not better to rely on migration. Free workers had no doubts; like their counterparts in New South Wales they saw convicts as a threat to employment and wages.

The British government was aware of these problems. In April 1846 Gladstone promised to suspend transportation for two years and his successor, Earl Grey, implied that it would not be resumed at the end of that period. The absence of an alternative outlet, however, prevented him pursuing this course. On the other hand, the probation system was modified, the Treasury renewed its financial contributions to the police and gaol establishments after 1846 and it agreed to pay for the upkeep of convicts employed on public works. Administration was improved and became more effective.

None of these developments restored faith in the penal system. Growing numbers of colonists believed that they could manage without convicts now that some 4000 migrants were arriving annually. Moreover, although crime had been reduced, the convicts were a blight on the community. Clergy, magistrates and settlers showed increasing concern with the moral and social consequences of transportation. Prominent among those to engage in what became a virtual crusade was the congregational minister and journalist, John West, who used not only the press and public meetings, but also his *History of Tasmania* to express his conviction that transportation was a moral evil and an obstacle to the development of a free society. Although coloured by the author's political ideas this book remains one of the most important accounts of the island's history. In common with others he feared that the introduction of representative government would be delayed unless steps were taken to stop convicts coming.

The transportation question rallied opinion and gave birth to what has been described as 'the first party in Tasmanian politics'. It also had constitutional implications which complicated the task of Lieutenant-Governors Franklin and Eardley-Wilmot. Each was fortunate to have a nominated legislature whose members were normally co-operative. Times, however, were abnormal and between 1840 and 1846 the executive and legislature had their first serious clashes.

The promise of Franklin's early months in office after February 1837 was dissipated by his failure to dispense with the colonial secretary, John Montagu, and the head of the convict establishment, Matthew Forster, both of whom had been appointed by Arthur. The anti-Arthur group had hoped that the influence of these and other officials would be destroyed and was resentful when Franklin continued to employ them. This was a double mistake on his part because the Arthur faction far from being grateful treated him with scorn. After dismissing his private secretary, Alexander Maconochie, in 1838 Franklin found himself isolated and turned to his wife for assistance, which exposed him to further criticism, most of which was unjustified. To make matters worse the onset of economic depression reduced government revenues and led to a demand that the British government pay for the police and gaol establishments. Franklin was unable either to persuade his superiors to assume this responsibility, or to find a solution to the colony's difficulties. By the time he was recalled in 1843, after the government had refused to uphold his dismissal of Montagu for behaving offensively, discontent was strong, although the colonists conceded that in the field of education he had achieved much.

His successor, Sir John Eardley-Wilmot, arrived in August 1843 to face a deteriorating economic situation. Revenue continued to shrink and the British government refused to contribute more to the upkeep of the penal system. Attempts to balance the budget by retrenchment and borrowing from the commissariat failed. In desperation the lieutenant-governor in 1845 secured a bank loan and introduced a customs bill increasing ad valorem duties on foreign imports from 5 to 15 per cent. This last measure amounted to a tax on the colonists and, when attempts were made to raise revenue by such means as turnpike duties on roads, the council, sensitive to public opposition, rejected them. A major constitutional crisis ensued and the council refused to pass further financial measures until the British government agreed to pay for the police and gaols. Public meetings were held throughout the colony and the nominated members of the council, the 'patriotic six', first disrupted its proceedings and then resigned *en masse* in October 1845. Six new members were appointed and relations with the executive improved until September 1846 when half of their number opposed a new customs bill. This crisis was ended with the recall of Eardley-Wilmot by Gladstone who unjustly accused him of immoral behaviour. Thereafter, economic conditions improved and the British government increased its financial contribution to the colony.

These developments failed to allay the growing opposition of colonists to a system of government which denied them the right to elect representatives. At the height of the conflict with Eardley-Wilmot placards insisting on 'No Taxation without Representation' had been erected in Hobart. The issue was kept at the forefront by Lieutenant-Governor Sir William Denison, who ruled without a council in 1847 while awaiting advice from London as to whether he could reinstate the 'patriotic six'. By that stage majority opinion was against transportation and on the 'glorious sixth of May' 1847 a meeting demanded that that system be terminated. Thereafter, the movement for constitutional reform became even more closely linked with that for the cessation of transportation. The fact that Denison believed the government should continue sending convicts and that Earl Grey was considered to have gone back on his promise to end the system increased the colonists' desire to curb the powers of the executive and of the Colonial Office.

While the settlers of Van Diemen's Land were becoming increasingly sensitive about their political and social status, those on the opposite side of Bass Strait faced problems of a different kind. From the time when settlement in the Port Phillip region was officially sanctioned the district had come under the government of New South Wales. Bourke had entrusted Captain Lonsdale with responsibility for day-to-day affairs and he served there, first as police magistrate in charge of the residents then as treasurer until 1854. In September 1839, however, control was given to Superintendent Charles Joseph La Trobe, a man of wide accomplishments but no experience of command. This last shortcoming was of limited consequence because there was little scope for him to exercise initiative. No decision could be taken without reference to officials in Sydney who had control of the purse. This suited La Trobe who co-operated fully with his superiors and became a close friend and confidante of Governor Gipps.

The colonists were less than happy with an arrangement under which decisions affecting their welfare were made by a government located a thousand kilometres away. The members of the nominated council at Sydney had little knowledge of Port Phillip and, in common with other officials, placed its needs low on their list of priorities. They allocated too little money for public works and used the proceeds of land sold at Port Phillip for purposes not directly connected with its development. Concerned at this situation and at the delays necessarily incurred in referring every issue to Sydney, the colonists in 1840 formed a Separation Association whose object was to obtain an independent government for Port Phillip. The British authorities were not prepared to dismember New South Wales but from the outset they had recognised that the southern region had interests of its own. In the Constitution Act of 1842 provision was made for its inhabitants to choose six representatives to sit in the Legislative Council of New South Wales.

This concession was inadequate. The members for Port Phillip formed only a minority. What the colonists sought was not a voice in the running of New South Wales but a separate administration. None of the disadvantages of government from afar had been removed and hostility continued to mount as it became evident that local issues were still ignored in Sydney. In 1844 a further petition was sent to London, this time by the district's elected representatives, and the issue was given wide publicity in newspapers such as the *Port Phillip Gazette*, the *Port Phillip Herald* and the *Port Phillip Patriot*, all of which had been founded in the late 1830s. The lack of immediate concessions resulted in growing frustration culminating in the election in 1848 of Earl Grey himself as one of the Port Phillip representatives in the Legislative Council. Designed partly to attract publicity this move also demonstrated the antipathy of the colonists to absentee rule and their desire for control over their own affairs.

Similar ideas were current in South Australia. Sir George Grey, who was in office when the 1842 Act was passed, continued to govern until October 1845. He had no intention of sharing power and by skilful, if somewhat devious methods, preserved his autocracy until he was transferred to New Zealand to avoid conflict with the Legislative Council arising from charges of corruption levelled against him by Jacob Hagen, a landowner and non-official council member. Grey's successor, Major Frederick Robe, who arrived in November 1845, was ill-equipped for a post which he had been instructed to occupy. Autocratic by training and temperament, he was an extreme Tory and a high churchman who lacked sympathy with dissent and was opposed to 'popular tendencies'. He had no experience of civilian life, was a poor public speaker and a bachelor whose inappropriate choice of hostesses on official occasions upset society. An honest, cultured man he found himself in a situation where his undeniable talents could never be put to use. Against his will he was obliged to remain in the colony until August 1848 and during that period he faced constant opposition from his council. Much of the trouble arose because his superiors decided to take advantage of the mining discoveries by charging a royalty on minerals found on Crown land sold after March 1846. A measure designed to give effect to his instructions passed the Legislative Council on 2 October 1846, but only after Robe had used his casting vote. Proceedings were thereafter disrupted by the non-official members and the bill had eventually to be withdrawn.

These conflicts reminded South Australians of their subordinate position. Relations with the British government, however, were less troubled than was the case with some of the other colonies. There was no separatist issue and no convict problem to stir public feeling. Moreover, as far back as 1842 South Australians had been promised representative government once they could provide a civil list and once the Colonial Office considered the time appropriate. The knowledge that it was only a matter of time before this concession was implemented took some of the edge off political debate. The replacement of Robe by a civilian, Sir Henry Fox Young, improved relations between executive and legislative. As a result South Australia by the late 1840s was more quiescent than its eastern neighbours. Even the internal divisions between conservatives and radicals did not cause serious trouble partly because established settlers were dominant, partly because no public issues arose to bring latent tensions into the open.

The same was true of Western Australia whose colonists were preoccupied with the problem of survival. They were too heavily dependent on Colonial Office goodwill to worry unduly about their subordinate position. They recognised that by accepting convicts they would remain a Crown colony and be unable to benefit from constitutional changes being considered elsewhere.

The Australian Colonies Government Act

In Britain there was growing recognition of the need to settle the constitutional problems of southern and eastern Australia. Developments in other parts of the empire, particularly Canada, had helped change attitudes towards colonial government. It was now widely recognised that colonists would have to be given greater control over their own affairs if the empire was to survive and prosper. Lord John Russell had come to office in 1846 pledged to such a programme and his secretary of state for the colonies, Earl Grey, did much to implement it. New South Wales could expect no further concessions for the time being, but it was now considered feasible for the institutions which had existed there since 1842 to be established in other colonies and for the demands of the residents of Port Phillip, now a flourishing and securely established settlement, to be accepted.

The first intimation of change was made in a despatch of August 1847 in which Grey also put forward proposals for a constitution that would unite the Australian colonies under a federal government and give each a new set of municipal councils and a bicameral legislature. An upper house would curb the lower, while district councils would increase regional autonomy and provide civic training. A federal body would check separatist tendencies and above all remove the threat of tariff rivalries between colonies which Grey as an ardent free trader was anxious to avoid. His scheme, modelled on one that had been drafted by James Stephen for use in New Zealand, aroused little enthusiasm among the colonists. In New South Wales it was seen as irrelevant to the main issues of the day and as another example of Colonial Office interference. Elsewhere, there were fears that federation might impede the development of full self-government and make the other colonies subordinate to New South Wales. Despite this Grey embodied the broad features of his plan in a bill which was framed for submission to parliament in 1850 after the whole subject had been considered by the Privy Council Committee for Trade and Plantations which met under his chairmanship in 1849. In the light of experiences in New Zealand, however, he no longer insisted that municipal councils and bicameral legislatures should be established and he also withdrew his federation proposals after speakers in the House of Commons debate had exposed weaknesses.

The Australian Colonies Government Act which became law in June 1850, therefore, differed from Grey's original intentions. Instead of introducing a comprehensive reorganisation of governmental institutions it did little more than bring all the colonies, with the exception of Western Australia, into line with New South Wales. Representative government was established in South Australia, Van Diemen's Land and the Port Phillip district which was renamed Victoria and given its independence. Everywhere the franchise was widened and legislatures were empowered to make further changes in their constitutions subject to their being approved in London. In an attempt to keep the federal idea alive

Grey made provision for the governor of New South Wales to become Australia's first governor-general, but no other changes affecting that colony were introduced. The same applied in the case of Western Australia which, as a penal colony, could not be granted an elective council. Not until 1870 were the terms of the Act applied there.

seven: Society

Social Groups

The economic and political advances which occurred between 1830 and 1850 were paralleled by developments in other spheres. The existing societies of New South Wales and Van Diemen's Land grew larger and more complex and new communities were founded in Western and South Australia. The last two had in common the fact that they were inhabited almost exclusively by middle and working-class migrants. Few settlers of aristocratic birth arrived and those who did were younger sons whose futures at home were uncertain. By the same token, while the lowest elements of British society could not secure passages, distance from the eastern colonies prevented any influx of former convicts. The Irish, too, came to the Swan River in small numbers and formed only about 10 per cent of the population in South Australia. By 1850 there were also some local-born residents, but these formed a small and insignificant group, most of whose members had barely passed their teens.

The circumstances of these last colonies produced some divergences. The Swan River settlers were intent on material gain. The same was true of South Australia. Yet there the emphasis placed on political liberty and religious freedom appealed to a more idealistic kind of migrant. Most came from Britain but the colony also drew to its shores the only significant group of Europeans to arrive on the continent before 1850. These were 6 271 German Lutherans who came from Silesia over a period of some twelve years after 1838 to escape persecution by the Prussian government. The first arrivals had been told of the colony by compatriots in the employ of the South Australian Company. News of its potential quickly spread and pastors such as the Reverend Augustus Kavel of Zullichau and G.D. Fritsche of Posen persuaded whole congregations to follow them to the region. They were encouraged by George Fife Angas, founder of the South Australian Company who saw that their sober, diligent habits and high standards of morality would benefit the settlement. A man of deep religious conviction, he shared their desire for civil and religious liberty and used the resources of the company to assist them.

Once in the colony they congregated first at Klemzig on the banks of the Torrens River and later around Hahndorf and Tanunda. They lived in compact communities which enabled them to preserve their language, customs and style of building. Agriculture was their main occupation and they played a major part in founding the South Australian wine industry. They impressed contemporaries, one of whom described how in 1839,

> There are now at least three villages consisting of German families besides a number of individuals of both sexes who are working as servants among the colonists. We have heard only one report of their conduct and that is as favourable as it is possible to be. They are peaceful and able to turn their hands to a variety of work. The women are experienced in almost all kinds of domestic and farm work.

Governor Gawler praised their 'religious, moral, loyal and industrious behaviour' and stated that he would 'be delighted to see 100,000 of them between the Gulf and the Murray'. The presence of such people contributed to the high moral tone upon which South Australians prided themselves. All the colonists had arrived free and this, in their own eyes, made the settlement superior to New South Wales and Van Diemen's Land, both of which had long associations with the English penal system.

In 1847 convicts formed only 3·2 per cent of the population of New South Wales, but a sizeable proportion of the remaining colonists had originally been transported. This in itself may appear of little consequence if one accepts the romanticised view of the convicts presented by early twentieth-century writers such as G.A. Wood and Frederick Watson. These historians depicted the convicts not as vicious criminals but as the unfortunate casualties of rapid economic change and an unjust penal code. A more plausible interpretation, based on recent investigation of records, is that the

Klemzig, a village of German settlers near Adelaide. Prussian Lutherans played a major part in the development of agriculture and wine growing and contributed to the high moral tone on which the South Australian free population prided itself.

convicts were less the victims of society than its sweepings. Far from being political offenders or starving poor who had been driven by desperation to commit minor offences in an effort to survive, they were mostly urban ne'er-do-wells who chose crime in preference to any other occupation.

The penal system was also responsible for introducing into New South Wales substantial numbers of rural Irish. Nearly one third of the convicts came from southern Ireland bringing with them the hatreds and bitterness engendered by centuries of British rule. In the colony they found themselves once again living under an alien Protestant government and in a community whose values and prejudices were those of the men whom they regarded as oppressors. Forcibly wrenched from families and friends and condemned by their lack of skills and education to a menial existence, it was little wonder that they should sometimes have proved troublesome. In March 1804 they were responsible for an abortive uprising at Castle

Hill the objective of which was to join forces with convicts in other parts and seize power. Thereafter a close watch was kept on their activities. Their experiences while under sentence gave them little chance to improve their position and after being freed they continued to occupy a lowly place in society. Much the same was true of a large proportion of the convicts from other parts of the British Isles. Once pardoned they mostly found employment in unskilled occupations. In the bush they were known as 'old hands' and according to the Port Phillip squatter, Charles Griffith, enjoyed a reputation for being 'a daring energetic, hard working class of men, with a considerable fear of infringing the law, or at least of the consequences of being made amenable to it, but at the same time requiring a strict hand to keep them in order'. They had a 'strong esprit de corps, which is kept up by their speaking a language so full of cant expressions as to become almost a separate dialect'. Although their standard of morality was low they were not without principles. At the same time they were noted for their improvidence and heavy drinking.

Not all fell into this category. Historians have long recognised that among the convicts were men and women who fit the favourable description once applied to all. Many had no desire to repeat the experience of serving a sentence and rehabilitated themselves. A number acquired great wealth and rose to the fore in every branch of industry. Others without reaching such heights led useful and respectable lives as small farmers, innkeepers, traders and tradesmen. The few who had professional backgrounds resumed their careers as lawyers, teachers, clergymen and doctors. Together they made an important contribution to the development of a community into which they were now more fully accepted. The view of the French visitor, A.S. de Goncourt, who wrote in 1850 of the 'separating wall' that was still raised 'between the convict, whose brow bore the mark of infamy, and the merchant, workman or farm labourer who had arrived as a free man with his family' was an exaggeration. Now that convicts were ceasing to arrive the old lines of division were fading and the term emancipist had lost its old significance.

This was a matter of importance to the local-born colonists commonly referred to as the 'currency' lads and lasses. According to Surgeon Peter Cunningham, author of *Two Years in New South Wales,* the label was originally coined 'by a facetious paymaster of the seventy-third regiment quartered here—the pound currency being at that time inferior to the pound sterling'. By 1846 colonial-born formed roughly a third of the population of New South Wales. They included politicians and landowners such as William Charles Wentworth and James Macarthur; the poet, Charles Harpur; the explorer, Hamilton Hume; John Batman, pioneer of Melbourne; and Phillip Parker King, the Norfolk Islander, who became one of Britain's leading hydrographers and commissioner of the Australian Agricultural Company. Such people were far from typical of the first generation of currency lads. Most were the progeny of convicts some of whom remained unmarried. From an early stage they possessed characteristics which distinguished them from their parents. Nutritious food, a healthy climate and an active outdoor life enabled them to develop physiques superior to those of the typical convict. The latter never fully recovered from the cold and misery of urban England or the grinding poverty of rural Ireland. To contemporaries they looked a breed apart. One traveller described them, no doubt in exaggerated terms, as having, 'A peculiarity of visage, different from all other men ... their countenances are of a dark brown hue, parched and dried up, muscles and all, as if they had been baked in one mass'. The currency youths, in contrast, were depicted as forming,

> A remarkable exception to the moral and physical character of their parents: they are generally tall in person and slender in their limbs, of fair complexion and small features. They are capable of undergoing more fatigue and are less exhausted by labour than native Europeans; they are active in their habits but remarkably awkward in their movements.

This description, penned by Commissioner Bigge in 1820, was confirmed by Surgeon Cunningham and later observers. Recent research has shown that not only were the physical attributes of the native-born superior to those of the convicts, but they were also less prone to drunkenness, immorality and crime. To some extent this was a reaction against the ways of those who brought them up, but it also reflected the advantages of an environment free of many of the social problems and tensions that helped generate crime in England. If transportation did not necessarily reform the convicts, it at least gave their children an opportunity to become respectable citizens.

There were, therefore, wholesome elements in New South Wales and these became more noticeable after the end of transportation in 1840. Each year saw the arrival of more migrants whose calibre was high and whose impact was felt in important areas of life.

This was particularly true of the Scots who were much valued from the earliest days. They were frugal, hard working and dedicated, and their determination to make good was reinforced by the Calvinist doctrine of their Presbyterian church which saw in success a sign of divine grace. Since the arrival in 1798 of Robert Campbell, Australia's first free merchant, Scots were prominent as business and professional men, merchants and graziers. They were among the pioneers of the New England and Moreton Bay districts and spearheaded the opening of Port Phillip. They formed the dominant group in the Western District of Victoria and there, as in other parts, played a role out of all proportion to their numerical strength.

In Van Diemen's Land the Scots had also provided a dynamic element for long past and it was indeed from there that they first moved to Port Phillip. The Irish, in contrast, were less important than they were in New South Wales. No Irish convicts were sent directly to Van Diemen's Land before 1839 and most of the men and women who migrated from Ireland in the 1830s and 1840s went to New South Wales where employment prospects were better and where many of their compatriots were already settled. Convicts remained a numerically and proportionately larger element than was the case on the mainland. They formed 41·6 per cent of the population in 1830, 38·4 per cent in 1840 and 38·1 per cent in 1848. In absolute terms their total increased from 10 195 in 1830 to 28 459 by the middle of the nineteenth century when the population was 69 187. One consequence of having so many convicts was that by 1850 there were also large numbers of emancipists in the colony. Mostly they occupied the lower rungs of society, although some rose higher. For the rest the population was composed of currency lads and free migrants with the latter predominating.

The presence of substantial numbers of emancipists and local-born residents helped to distinguish the eastern colonies from the other Australian settlements. It also contributed to the emergence, particularly in New South Wales, of a strong patriotism. 'The currency youths', wrote Cunningham, 'are warmly attached to their country, which they deem unsurpassable'. While these people knew no other land the emancipists saw Britain as the country that had made them outcasts. Not only had they been banished for the duration of their sentences, but it was made clear that their return, even after they had been pardoned, would not be welcomed. At first their view of their new land was equally jaundiced. This was, after all, a place of punishment whose harsh physical environment brought hardship and suffering. Gradually, however, they accustomed themselves to their new life and began to appreciate the advantages of its healthier climate and blue skies. Lacking any alternative emotional focus they formed an attachment to a colony which was in process of becoming their permanent home. Commissioner Bigge perceived such a sentiment emerging as early as 1820. In the following decades it continued to grow as additional opportunities for permanent settlement were made available. According to one view it was most pronounced among the bushworkers of the outback. Many of these people had been convicts and their life at once isolated them from what was peculiarly English and brought them into contact with what was distinctive in their antipodean environment. It was in the bush that, it has been claimed, there gradually took shape a stereotype of the typical Australian which eventually became a focus for nationalist sentiment.

There is no reason to suppose that patriotic sentiment was confined to the currency lads and to former convicts. Judging by their correspondence and printed writings many of the migrants also developed feelings of affection towards their adopted land. On the other hand, they were not cut off emotionally from Britain in the way that was true of other sections of the community. They adjusted to life in the antipodes and were conscious of its attractiveness, but at the same time they retained a pride in the mother country as the land where they had been born and which had shaped their earlier existence. There was in their outlook a dualism, the twin elements of which varied in proportion to the length of time they had been in the colonies. In eastern Australia the older established migrants were more fully acclimatised than the more recent arrivals of Southern and Western Australia. Even so, the attachment to Britain was strong and since migrants formed a dominant group they coloured the tone of society. Not until later was the feeling of such people for the mother country to be submerged in a locally oriented sentiment.

Social Conditions

Such were the principal groups that formed colonial society. These divisions into emancipist and free, colonial-born, English, Irish and Scottish, were cut by vertical lines that were of considerable significance. There was no traditional aristocracy to dominate politics and determine manners. When William Charles Wentworth urged in the 1850s that one should be established the notion was ridiculed and scorn was poured on the 'bunyip aristocracy'. Nevertheless class distinctions were by no means lacking. The landed interest necessarily predominated in communities that drew their wealth mainly from primary production. Yet within the ranks of propertied men were gradations of wealth and standing. The small to middling farmers lived an often precarious existence which prevented them accumulating any great substance. Their houses ranged from comfortable to primitive and their possessions and life styles varied accordingly. Much the same was true of the pastoralists whose level of attainment, however, was generally higher than that of farmers. The wealthiest graziers were situated at the very apex of society. Amongst their number were the established families who, like the exclusives of New South Wales, saw themselves as distinct from and superior to the rest of the community. Every colony had its share of these people who modelled their lives on the English gentry, furnished their spacious houses with costly imports, employed servants and governesses, kept stables of thoroughbred horses and entertained on a lavish scale. They dominated society both in the capital cities and in the country districts where their properties were located, served as magistrates, and played an active part in civic affairs.

At the base of the social pyramid in town and country were property-less workers who formed the largest single class. In the bush employment was available for workers of all kinds. Before the invention of wire fencing in the second half of the century stock roamed over vast acreages and there was a constant demand for men to tend them. On cattle stations the stockman, sometimes an Aboriginal but more often white, became a characteristic figure. Venturesome and daring, he regarded himself as pre-eminent among the rural work force. He spent much of his time in the saddle and developed a great pride in his equestrian skill as well as in his ability to handle danger and hardship. More numerous were the shepherds whose occupation was less demanding. Generally, a single person tended a whole flock and in the outback this meant spending long periods cut off from human contact. There was little to do during the day while the sheep were feeding and even at night the task of warding off the occasional dingo presented few problems. Marauding natives could be dangerous, but as settlement spread they were driven back. Lonely and isolated, the shepherd followed an existence that sometimes produced insanity or, more often, a mild eccentricity.

By 1846 there were some 6000 stockmen on the mainland and 15000 shepherds as well as a diversity of other workers. Some remained for long periods with a single employer while others were itinerants. A number, like the shearers whose skills were highly valued, engaged in seasonal occupations but others were simply men of independent mind who preferred a nomadic existence. They included sawyers, splitters, fencers, carpenters, blacksmiths and masons—men who placed a premium on their labour and took a pride in their work. Amongst the most remarkable bush men were the overlanders who drove stock from one market, or one colony to another in the hope of making a profit. Often from good English families and well-educated, they were adventurers of great personal courage who had developed a love for the roving life. Rivalling them in toughness and endurance were the teamsters, or bullock drivers, who took wool over long distances to the nearest port, negotiating barely marked bush tracks that often passed through wild and precipitous country. They were described by the writer, G.C. Mundy, as,

> A strange wild looking sunburnt race, strong, rough and taciturn, they appear as though they have never lived in crowds and have lost the desire and even the power to converse. So deeply embrowned were the faces, naked breasts and arms of these men, and so shaggy the crops of hair and beard that a stranger had to look twice to be certain they were not Aborigines.

Picturesque characters such as these were less common in the towns where a large proportion of the workers were located. Most found their occupation in small concerns in which the gap between employer and employee was narrow. The owner often worked alongside his men and there was no managerial staff to separate the two. Small manufactories producing consumer goods for local use and generally employing less than ten men predominated. They included printers' shops, tailors' workshops, tanneries, foundries, cloth factories, breweries and soap factories. Retail shops provided work for substantial numbers but more important at a time of marked urban growth was the building industry. Stone-masons, bricklayers and carpenters were in constant demand. Together they formed a significant proportion of the urban proletariat.

As was to be expected of a society whose leaders derived their values from Victorian England, the workers whether rural or urban were kept in a subordinate position. Improvements did, however, occur partly in response to local circumstances and partly as a result of changes in England. The Masters and Servants Acts which governed the relationship between employer and employee were weighted in favour of the former, but their conditions did become more moderate. In New South Wales, for example, penalties imposed under the 1828 'Act for the better regulation of Servants, Labourers and Workpeople' were halved by an Act of 1840. Hitherto, employees who abused their masters' property or who refused to work could be sentenced to six months in gaol. In 1840 the maximum was reduced to three months. Trade unions which had been banned up to 1825 were thereafter permitted subject to safeguards aimed at protecting employers. Workers in some trades took advantage of the relaxation of the law. During the prosperous 1830s unions were formed in eastern Australia by printers, tailors and tradesmen in the building industry. Their object was not only to obtain better working conditions but also to provide the needy with assistance. Some of these organisations combined the function of a Friendly Society with that of a union. There were also indications of a working-class interest in political matters in New South Wales. In 1843 a 'Trade Protection Society' was formed to improve the conditions of labour and secure direct representation for workers in the Legislative Council. This, however, came to little and in general the early trade unions remained small. In the bush labourers were too dispersed for organisation to be practicable. In the towns a sense of working-class solidarity and distinctiveness had not yet developed. Only the skilled tradesmen formed unions and in some occupations this move was opposed by men who had formed a close relationship with their employers. The growth of unionism as a vital force in Australian life did not occur until later.

The weak bargaining position of labour does something to explain the harsh conditions under which many workers operated. It has been estimated that real wages rose slightly between 1830 and 1850, but monetary wages fluctuated considerably and varied from one trade and one colony to another. The skilled consistently received more than the unskilled, but all suffered during the economic depression of the early 1840s when wages fell and there was considerable unemployment. Efforts were made to alleviate suffering. In New South Wales, for example, privately run benevolent societies had long existed to assist the aged, the sick and the unemployed. These increased their assistance and the Legislative Council took limited steps to provide relief works. Such measures, together with the dedicated work of Caroline Chisholm and her assistants touched only the surface of the problem. During the 1840s as in preceding decades society did little to assist those who were unable to fend for themselves. The idea that the state had a responsibility for its weaker members had not yet developed. It was widely believed that the poor were to blame for their plight and that any attempt to assist them would encourage improvidence and undermine the basis of society. The prevailing government attitude was similar to that of mid-Victorian England where the emphasis was on thrift and self-help. Workers were expected to labour for long hours; there were no guaranteed holidays and little leisure time.

If working conditions were severe, living conditions were little better. Rural labourers in each of the colonies experienced some benefit from the spread of amenities in the settled districts, but over much of the colony housing remained primitive. As late as 1850 workers' houses were often made of little more than rough timber with thatched roofs and the bare earth for a floor. Often there were no more than two rooms furnished with rough articles made from bush timber. Amusements were few and apart from reading and gambling, drink offered the main escape from a reality that was tough and forbidding. Small wonder that many workers preferred the towns where they could enjoy a gregarious existence and a wider range of entertainments. Drinking in the public houses that abounded in all of the capital cities, including sedate Adelaide, was a favoured occupation. Gambling of various forms, horse racing and prize fighting were all common pastimes. Yet despite its variety, town life had drawbacks. In the poorer parts slums and over-crowding were common. Sewage facilities were lacking and many houses were not connected to the water supply. Rentals could also eat heavily into wages, creating for the town dweller a problem greater than existed in the bush.

Yet, in general, it seems likely that in coming to Australia the convicts and poorer migrants had improved their situation. The pace of life in the colonies was more casual and the pressures fewer. The climate was healthier and so too was the diet which already included substantial quantities of meat. The ration issued to rural workers during the 1840s, for example, normally comprised between 7 and 10 lbs of flour, beef, or mutton, together with 2 oz tea, 1 lb sugar, 2 oz salt and some soap and tobacco. This was more than most could have hoped to obtain in Britain.

Above the workers on the social scale was the urban middle class which, given the minor role occupied by secondary industry and commerce, necessarily remained small. Less than 10 per cent of the population could be described as bourgeois and in the newer colonies the proportion was even lower. This element included government officials, professional people, manufacturers, traders and shopkeepers. Their occupations and life style varied but they could enjoy an existence comparable to that of their counterparts in Britain. Admittedly, the country towns were provincial in outlook and narrow in their range of activities. But the cosmopolitan cities had much to offer. Sydney, Hobart and even the more recently established Melbourne and Adelaide had theatres where local and overseas actors performed Shakespearian plays as well as modern works. Opera also became popular and orchestral concerts were common. It was possible to attend lectures and discussions arranged by societies such as the exclusive Philosophical Society in Sydney that enjoyed vice-regal patronage under the scientifically minded Governors Brisbane and Denison. Subscription libraries existed as did clubs, the first of which, the Australian Club, opened in Bent Street, Sydney, in 1838. Sport was also growing in popularity. People went boating and yachting in every colony and cricket was assuming importance. What has been referred to somewhat loosely as the first Test Match was held in Sydney in 1832 between a team of New South Wales youths and eleven Englishmen. Six years later the Melbourne Cricket Club was established and shortly afterwards Adelaide followed suit. Horse racing had a large following and there were also numerous festive occasions which were celebrated publicly.

Literature and Art

Although life in the colonies had its rigours and hardships, therefore, it did possess other dimensions. By 1850 the pioneering days had ended in much of eastern Australia and were receding elsewhere. Once the foundations for economic growth had been laid, greater attention could be devoted to non-material ends. A sprinkling of the migrants and convicts who came to the colonies had artistic and literary talent. Three of the leading artists had been transported for forgery. First was Thomas Watling who drew illustrations for his employers, Surgeon John White and Judge-Advocate David Collins. Before leaving the colony in 1800 he painted on his own behalf. One of his pictures, 'A Direct North View of Sydney Cove', hangs in the Dixson Gallery, Sydney. Second was Joseph Lycett, a Staffordshire portrait painter and miniaturist who reached Sydney in early 1814 and was sent to Newcastle a year later after a second conviction for forgery. The commandant, Captain James Wallis, used his services to design Christ Church and paint its altarpiece. Subsequently he was pardoned by Macquarie who commissioned

'A Direct North View of Sydney Cove' by Thomas Watling, who was transported for forgery but arrived in New South Wales to find employment as
an illustrator of scenic views, flora and fauna. He later painted for himself
and was one of the leading colonial artists.

him to produce landscapes of New South Wales and Van Diemen's
Land. A third forger, Thomas Wainewright, was sent to Hobart in
November 1837 where he established a reputation for his portraits.
   Most artists, however, had arrived free. They included part-time
amateurs such as Surgeon John White, Governor P.G. King and
Captain Wallis, all of whom were stationed here. In addition, there
were visitors like William Westall who accompanied Lieutenant
Matthew Flinders, the navigator and hydrographer. While aboard
the *Investigator* between 1803 and 1805 he made many sketches
which formed the basis for his later paintings. Others settled
permanently, amongst them John William Lewin who arrived as a
settler in January 1800, John Glover who migrated to Van Diemen's
Land in 1832, Samuel Thomas Gill of South Australia and above all
Conrad Martens, the son of a German merchant. An accomplished
artist, Martens came to Sydney in 1835 after a period of voyaging
and opened a studio in the Rocks area of Sydney. He and some of his

contemporaries had a local following, but in general the demand for art among the colonists was only limited. The principal market was overseas where illustrated books of travel and of natural history were much in vogue. Many of the local paintings and drawings were produced for such works, a fact which affected their subject matter. Scenic views of Sydney and its environs, meticulous sketches of flora and fauna and pictures of Aboriginal customs predominated. As settlement spread into the interior new themes encompassing the activities of squatters, explorers and bushrangers emerged. No original native style developed because all the early artists had been trained overseas and their approach was strongly influenced by fashions which derived from Europe. Some of the first painters, indeed, distorted the local scene by depicting it in English terms. Trees and shrubs were made to resemble those at home, the bush was given the appearance of English parkland and the Aboriginals the physique and bearing of Europeans. Later artists accepted the environment and introduced more realism into their work. No really great art was produced, but much was memorable and of more than passing interest.

The same was true of literature. Many books were written about each of the colonies by overseas visitors and local residents. The first were in the tradition of the eighteenth-century journal and combined factual reporting with reflection and discussion. Examples included the annals of the first fleet officers. Those of Tench, Phillip, Hunter, White and Collins were published, while the ones written by Bowes, Bradley and Clark existed only as manuscripts. From the 1820s a range of books appeared designed to provide information for prospective migrants and during the next two decades several works of fiction were also produced. The undistinguished *Quintus Servinton*, written by the forger Henry Savery and printed in Hobart in 1830–1, was the first novel published in Australia. Part fiction, part autobiographical, it was followed by others including Charles Rowcroft's *Tales of the Colonies* (London, 1843) which also had its setting in Van Diemen's Land, Mary Theresa Vidal's *Tales for the Bush* (Sydney, 1845) and Alexander Harris's *The Emigrant Family* (London, 1849) which followed the same author's *Settlers and Convicts* (London, 1847), a fascinating and well-substantiated account of his experiences in New South Wales.

Poetry in Australia had a longer history than fiction but was also largely derivative in form and theme. The first verse published in Australia was written by Michael Massey Robinson who between

1810 and 1821 annually produced odes for the *Sydney Gazette* to celebrate the king's and the queen's birthdays. Others had earlier written verse without printing it. Amongst them was the Irish convict attorney, Laurence Davoren, whose 'A New Song made in New South Wales' satirised the Rum Rebellion. Such works, lampooning those in authority were common and amongst their authors was William Charles Wentworth who in 1816 anonymously attacked Colonel Molle, lieutenant-governor and commandant of the 46th Regiment. Later, while a student at Cambridge, Wentworth won second prize for his patriotic poem 'Australasia' and in 1823 he published a book of verse under the same title. Another prominent versifier was Judge Barron Field whose *First Fruits of Australian Poetry* (Sydney, 1819) contained an engaging account of the kangaroo, formed by nature from 'the squirrel fragile' and the 'bounding hart'. Overshadowing all the early poets was Charles Harpur who was born at Windsor, New South Wales on 23 January 1813. Under the influence of English contemporaries such as Byron, Harpur became one of the leading representatives of the Romantic movement in Australia. He was much admired by the literary men of his day, particularly for his poem 'The Creek of the Four Graves' with its evocative descriptions like that of the creek which was,

> ... shaded o'er
> With boughs of the wild willow, hanging mixed
> From either bank, or duskily befringed
> With upward tapering feathery swamp-oaks.

Religion

The inspiration for Australian literature and art was largely secular, a fact that was true in other fields of intellectual endeavour. Nevertheless, organised Christianity played an important part in shaping the ethos. By 1830 each of the principal denominations was represented, the largest being the Anglican. Whether the Church of England was 'established' is a question that has been debated among historians. Certainly it was seen by the government as the official church. This was only to be expected given its privileged position in England and the fact that at home there were missionary bodies, prominent public figures and a powerful hierarchy, with seats in the House of Lords, anxious to safeguard its interests. Anglican clergymen were present from the outset in eastern Australia. At first they alone were appointed to minister to the convicts, their stipends were partly financed from public funds and land was set aside for their use. In 1826 Earl Bathurst approved a charter for the Anglican-controlled Church and Schools Corporation which was given control over one seventh of the lands of New South Wales. This, in the opinion of one historian, represented a definite attempt 'to endow the Church of England permanently and finally as the established Church in the Australian colonies'.

Despite government assistance the Church of England made only limited headway before the 1830s. The amount of public aid and the number of clergy was only small. Much depended on the voluntary effort of organisations such as the London Missionary Society and the dedication of individual clergymen. Australia's first incumbent, the Reverend Richard Johnson who arrived in 1788, and his successor, the Reverend Samuel Marsden who reached Port Jackson in 1794 and assumed charge of the church in 1801, were confronted by widespread indifference and hostility. The convicts who formed the bulk of the population either did not belong to the Anglican communion or came from urban regions over which it had never gained a hold. Anglicanism was the creed of the men who had sentenced the convicts to transportation and kept them in subjection. The fact that the local clergy also often acted as magistrates made matters worse because in this latter capacity they sat in judgement on convicts and often punished them severely. In addition prominent clergy such as Marsden and the ex-Tahitian missionary, Rowland Hassall who fled to Port Jackson in 1798 with some of his fellows, engaged in material pursuits.

Again, the organisation of the church left much to be desired. Matters improved after 1824 when eastern Australia was brought within the diocese of Calcutta and an archdeacon was given local charge. Thomas Hobbes Scott, who had been ordained after returning to England with Commissioner Bigge, filled this position until September 1829. He proved a sound administrator and tireless worker who travelled widely and extended the influence of the church in New South Wales and Van Diemen's Land. Yet there were limits to what he could accomplish at a time when settlement was rapidly expanding and his association with the Macarthurs cost him the sympathy of press and public.

This disadvantage did not affect the remaining denominations which received only limited state assistance. Nevertheless, Roman Catholics and protestants also faced problems that impeded their work. The Presbyterians, who built their first church at Ebenezer in 1809 and maintained a regular clergyman from 1823 when John

Dunmore Lang arrived, remained few in number. So too did the Wesleyans whose first missionary clergyman, the Reverend Samuel Leigh, came in 1815. The Roman Catholic church, in contrast, had a substantial following, principally among the Irish convicts, but its activities were slow in starting. Two attempts were made to establish a priesthood, the first by Father James Harold and Father James Dixon who were transported from Ireland in 1800 for taking part in the 1798 uprising. Dixon was allowed to celebrate mass from 15 May 1803, but the concession was withdrawn after disturbances among the Irish made the authorities wary of permitting them to congregate. The second initiative came from Father Jeremiah O'Flynn whose missionary zeal brought him to Port Jackson in 1817. He was deported by Macquarie who feared that 'he would do a great deal of mischief among the lower order of Catholics'. At first the British authorities were not prepared to accept the establishment in Australia of a faith that had been banned in England since Elizabethan days. During the early nineteenth century attitudes began to change. Representations from O'Flynn and his Irish supporters persuaded Earl Bathurst that it was unjust to bar Catholicism from colonies in which so many worshippers lived. In 1820 two priests, Father John Therry and Father Phillip Conolly, were permitted to sail, the one to Sydney and the other to Hobart. Both laboured unremittingly, but it was impossible to compensate for thirty years of neglect in a single decade.

After 1830 organised Christianity spread more rapidly in eastern Australia due partly to Governor Bourke's decision to distribute financial aid among the various denominations on a more equitable basis. A tolerant Anglican, whose Irish connections gave him Roman Catholic relatives and friends, Bourke recognised the needs of churches other than his own. In England the notion of allowing exclusive rights to the Church of England was under question. The Church and Schools Corporation had been attacked within the colony, particularly by J.D. Lang and Father Therry. It had not proved a success and in 1833 was dissolved, creating a vacuum which Bourke filled with his Church Act of 1836. This named the churches of England, Scotland and Rome as recipients of government aid and invited others to apply for assistance. The Act was accepted in England and its principles were extended to Van Diemen's Land in 1837. The churches still had to raise money privately, but henceforth they received an annual subsidy proportionate to their size which helped finance buildings and clerical stipends.

As the largest denomination the Anglicans of New South Wales received most money but in general they were disappointed by Bourke's Act. It repudiated the concept of an Anglican establishment, ended hopes of the church securing a status analogous to that which it occupied in England and opened a new phase in church-state relations. The state which had given Anglicans a privileged position now placed their finances on the same footing as those of the remaining churches. Even the right of their leading cleric to sit ex officio on the Legislative and Executive Councils was to be dispensed with. In September 1837 the church's constitutional basis was altered by Bourke's English Church Temporalities Act which established the legal conditions under which it could own land. Earlier, on the governor's recommendation its organisation was improved by the British government's decision to create a bishopric for New South Wales.

The first Anglican bishop, W.G. Broughton, had succeeded Scott as archdeacon in 1829 and retained control of the church until his death in 1853. A firm believer in establishment he was forced to watch other denominations grow while the standing of his own was reduced. He also faced internal dissension. In England the emergence of the Tractarian movement which stressed the Catholic rather than the Protestant traditions of the church aroused a controversy that was heightened when leaders of the movement, including John Henry Newman, were converted to Rome. The dispute had repercussions in New South Wales where there was a strong evangelical tradition dating from the days of Johnson and Marsden. Some clergy were Tractarian sympathisers and two, the Reverends R.K. Sconce and T.C. Mackinnon, became Roman Catholics in 1848. Their opponents used the issue to attack Broughton whose authoritarianism, high churchmanship and sympathy for the Tractarians aroused discontent.

Despite these conflicts Broughton accomplished much. His attempt to establish a theological college had less success than he hoped but the number of clergy and parishes expanded unprecedentedly. At first Broughton had responsibilities for the whole of eastern Australia which involved him in much travelling. In 1842, however, Francis Russell Nixon, a Tractarian sympathiser, was consecrated bishop of Van Diemen's Land. He carried out his task vigorously despite opposition from clergy who did not share his doctrinal position and conflict with the civil authorities over the disciplining of clergymen. By 1850 he had placed the church on a sound footing. Meanwhile, in 1847, bishoprics had been created at Newcastle and Melbourne, the latter being filled by Charles Perry, an evangelical of scholarly attainments. These developments and the establishment of a new diocese at Adelaide created the need for a machinery of consultation. The first step was taken in 1850 under the inspiration of Broughton who in October presided over a conference of bishops at Sydney. Although its discussions aroused controversy it laid the basis for inter-colonial co-operation in the religious sphere.

If the Anglicans of eastern Australia lost their exclusive rights during the 1830s, the Roman Catholics were treated better than before, thanks initially to Bourke. The government provided financial aid and allowed a hierarchy with territorial jurisdiction to be established some nine years before one was permitted in Britain. In April 1842 John Bede Polding, who had served in New South Wales since June 1834 as Australia's first bishop, was appointed 'Archbishop of Sydney and Metropolitan of Australia'. For the next thirty years he dominated the affairs of his church. An English Benedictine he sought to preserve New South Wales for his Order but failed to win the support of Rome or attract his fellows to the colony. He established Benedictine Orders of Nuns at Subiaco and Lyndhurst but in general his efforts were resisted by the predominantly Irish priesthood which objected to the Benedictines as being too intellectual, too English and too upper class. Irish priests like the popular Father John McEncroe vigorously opposed Polding whose dreams were already fading by 1850.

During the Polding era, therefore, the church, far from being monolithic was split on political, social and religious issues. Nevertheless, the period was one of substantial growth and by 1850 the number of priests, churches and parishes had multiplied more than threefold. Much was due to Polding who travelled widely and established friendly connections with his flock. No administrator, he left organisation to others. The priest upon whom he first relied was W.B. Ullathorne, one of his former pupils at Downside whom he had persuaded to enter the Benedictine Order. Ullathorne had come to Sydney in September 1832 under instructions from W.P. Morris, Vicar-Apostolic of Mauritius, and had taken over from Therry who had alienated fellow Catholics and government. Thoroughgoing and businesslike, Ullathorne served Polding loyally until 1840 when, recognising that his Order would never become dominant, he returned to England. His replacement, Henry Gregory, who became vicar general in 1844, took charge while Polding was in England from 1846 until 1848 but caused much trouble by his insensitive treatment of the Irish.

Meanwhile, reforms had been introduced in Hobart. The first priest, Father Conolly, who had arrived in 1821 eventually succumbed to the loneliness of his duties in so brutal a community and until Therry was sent to the colony as vicar general in 1838 the church languished. Therry placed it on its feet but his factious, quarrelsome behaviour created problems both for the church and for the first bishop, R.W. Willson, a secular priest from Nottingham. Willson accomplished much, particularly among the convicts, but his conflict with Therry who refused to submit to his authority divided the church and embittered relations with Polding.

Anglicanism and Catholicism were not the only branches of Christianity to expand in eastern Australia after 1830. Of the two principal denominations, Presbyterian and Methodist, the former, which had a tradition in Scotland of close association with the state, found it easiest to accept financial aid. The decision troubled some consciences, however, and became an issue in conflicts which impeded the growth of Presbyterianism after 1837. First, the aggressively individualistic John Dunmore Lang formed his own Synod to further that brand of independent, evangelistic Presbyterianism for which he stood. Then in 1846, three years after the Scottish schism of 1843, a group of rigorous Calvinists led by the Reverend William McIntyre formed the Free Church Synod when the rest of the church stood by the Established Church of Scotland. Underlying these developments were clashes of personality, a struggle for power and disputes about doctrine. Important too was the question of whether the church should exist independently of the state or maintain closer relations with it. This problem did not arise in Van Diemen's Land where the church was dominated by the Reverend John Lillie, son of a Glasgow merchant, former tutor to the family of the Duke of Argyll and a man of considerable learning and administrative ability. Under his guidance Presbyterians remained united and active. By 1850 they totalled 4 485 compared to 18 156 in New South Wales and 11 608 at Port Phillip.

The Methodist church had been divided since the death of Wesley in 1791 had removed its founder and the only man capable of holding it together. In eastern Australia there were to be found each of the main forms of Methodism: Primitive, Welsh and Wesleyan, the latter being the largest. The existence of divisions did not seriously interfere with the spread of a decentralised movement which depended on its emotional appeal. It won increasing support among the middle class and expanded more rapidly than any other church. By 1851 it had 10 008 worshippers in New South Wales and 4 988 in Port Phillip.

The denominations thus far mentioned were present in Western and South Australia. In the first their growth was hindered by the harsh conditions which served to intensify the materialist outlook of many colonists. Symptomatic of this attitude was the failure to include a clergyman among the first pioneers. Not until Christmas Day 1829 was communion celebrated and then only as a result of the presence of Archdeacon Scott who spent a year there awaiting repairs to his England-bound ship that had been wrecked off Fremantle. Thereafter, the Church of England made slow progress. Its claim to establishment was rejected and its only assistance was under an Act passed by Governor Hutt who distributed a meagre sum among the various denominations between 1839 and 1843, when money ran out. Until 1848 Broughton in far-off Sydney bore responsibility for the church but the appointment of J.R. Wollaston as archdeacon and the later improvement in economic conditions opened the way to more rapid development after 1850.

Serious problems also confronted the Roman Catholic mission despatched by Polding in 1843 under the Irish priest John Brady who became Bishop of Perth in May 1845. There were few Catholics in the colony and the mission's main purpose was to convert the Aboriginals. By 1850 it had made little impact and in addition to heavy indebtedness Brady was engaged in a dispute with his recently appointed coadjutor, Bishop Serra, over possession of the diocese. This conflict split the Catholic community.

In South Australia with its small, dispersed Catholic population the Roman Church, headed by Bishop Murphy who was appointed to Adelaide in 1844, remained weak. More than half of the population was Anglican but the distinctive feature was the strength of 'non-conformity'. The founders had insisted that there be no established church and although an Anglican chaplain was appointed and paid from government funds the principle of religious freedom was recognised. The result was a proliferation of sects prominent among which were the Wesleyan Methodists, followed by the Presbyterians. Most Protestants, including an important section of the Church of England, sought to preserve their independence. Just as the self-supporting mechanism broke down in colonial affairs, so the voluntary principle proved impossible to sustain in the religious field. In 1847 Governor Robe extended state aid to religion and although this was rejected by Bishop Murphy who feared government interference, it was temporarily accepted by most protestant groups although only after much controversy.

Education

The divisions within and between churches lessened their impact on colonial society. Another source of weakness arose from the rapid dispersal of settlement. It was beyond the capacity of any denomination to keep pace with the outward movement and as a result large areas of the inland had little contact with organised Christianity. Within the settled areas indifference and materialism created obstacles that were only partly overcome. Substantial numbers of colonists in the towns, particularly among the workers, remained out of touch with the churches just as they did in England.

Much the same held true in the field of education. The first university, that of Sydney, was not established until 1850, but secondary schooling expanded. In 1831 the Australian College was founded by the Presbyterian, Dr J.D. Lang, and a year later two King's schools were created by the Anglican Archdeacon Broughton at Sydney and Parramatta. The first failed due to lack of support and a weak headmaster, but the second flourished. The non-denominational Sydney College opened its doors in 1835 and two years later Saint Mary's seminary, staffed by Benedictines, became Australia's first Roman Catholic secondary school. By 1847 there were in New South Wales some 250 private schools, mostly very small, but offering advanced education. No other colony could rival this achievement but most contained some secondary establishments to cater for those wishing to enter the professions or the business world. All were fee paying and privately owned; most were run under religious auspices.

The fact that it cost money to send children to these schools meant that they were accessible only to parents of means. Nevertheless, attempts were made to ensure that children of all classes received some elementary instruction. The state showed an interest in promoting education long before it did so in England. Concerned lest the convicts contaminate their children and produce a race of potential criminals the British authorities had from the earliest days urged governors to 'interfere on behalf of the rising generation, and by the exertion of authority as well as of encouragement to educate them in religious as well as industrious habits'.

Phillip and Hunter were too preoccupied with other issues to pay much attention to this order but it was taken seriously by later governors. Some schools, such as the Orphan Schools for Girls and a similar institution for boys, established successively by King and Macquarie, were founded under government auspices. For the most part, however, governors gave assistance to church schools of which those run by the Anglicans were the most numerous. This policy culminated in the creation of the Church and Schools Corporation which embodied an attempt to create a co-ordinated system under Anglican control. It functioned too briefly to accomplish much and by 1833 when it was dissolved most colonial children were still receiving no education.

To cope with this situation Bourke in 1833 put forward proposals for a government system of elementary instruction. He was aware that there were many, particularly among the Anglican and Catholic clergy, who believed that education and religion were indissolubly linked and that to separate them was to make education worthless. To counter this argument and to meet the different requirements of Protestant and Catholic, Bourke based his plan on the Stanley or National system that had operated successfully in Ireland since 1831. It provided for religious instruction and included guarantees designed to meet the doctrinal requirements of the various denominations. The fact that it had proved acceptable in Ireland predisposed the Roman Catholic Church in favour of it. The scheme, however, foundered on the rock of Protestant opposition. Led by Bishop Broughton who considered that the position of his own church was threatened, the Protestants bitterly attacked the measure which they considered subversive of their doctrines and unduly favourable to the Catholics. A divided Legislative Council, some of whose members believed it dangerous to educate the masses, reluctantly voted money to finance the scheme, but in view of the strong opposition Bourke wisely left it in abeyance.

Three years later, his successor, Sir George Gipps, made new proposals for government schools in which religious instruction would be given in accordance with the practices followed by the British and Foreign School Society. Although acceptable to nonconformists the scheme failed to win Anglican and Roman Catholic support and had to be dropped. A similar fate met the recommendations of a committee headed by Robert Lowe which urged the establishment of a state-supported, non-denominational system based on the Irish model. Although accepted by the Legislative Council in 1844 this was shelved by Gipps after it had met widespread opposition outside the council. The report of the committee, however, showed that more than half of the colony's children were receiving no education. Clearly steps needed to be taken. Anglican opposition to state schools was weakening in the face of a deterioration in the church's finances which had been affected by the depression. In 1847 Broughton accepted a compromise devised by Governor FitzRoy under which a dual system of church and 'national' schools each under a separate board was established.

The first 'national' schools came into existence too late to have exerted much influence by 1850. Meanwhile the denominational system had expanded. Governor Bourke made public funds available for school buildings and teachers' salaries. His policy was followed by Governor Gipps and given further standing by the Constitution of 1842 which provided for an annual grant of £30 000 to be divided among the churches according to the number of worshippers as recorded in the 1841 census. Even before a government system had been introduced, the Anglican church had lost its monopoly over elementary education. By 1847 it controlled seventy-seven schools compared to the sixty-eight run by the remaining Protestant churches and the thirty-nine conducted by Roman Catholics. This represented a considerable expansion since the 1830s, but the task of financing it was considered by the government to be too costly. Moreover, there had been a concentration of effort and some duplication in the towns, leaving country areas, particularly those on the fringe of settlement, short of facilities. State education was introduced to counter these deficiencies. Liberals saw this reform as a means of bridging the gap between children of different denominations and spreading their own beliefs which had a secular basis. It was partly fear of liberalism that had prompted Bishop Broughton to resist the actions of Bourke and Gipps and it was this which also aroused apprehensions among the Roman Catholics. Conflicting views of man and of the role which religion should play in society underlay much of the dissension between liberals and Christians.

Similar issues were also at stake in Van Diemen's Land where, at the end of 1839, a public system of elementary schools was established. This step was the outcome of growing government concern about the existing schools, all of which were Anglican. Arthur had considered them exclusive and inefficient but was recalled before any decision had been taken on his own recommendations. His successor, Sir John Franklin, took the management of schools away from the Anglican church and established a lay board of education which consulted ministers from every denomination and permitted them to visit schools as often as they wished in order to give religious instruction. Lay teachers were to read biblical extracts daily but could not impart dogma.

This scheme was accepted by Roman Catholics, non-conformists and an important section of Anglican opinion. It was rejected by Church of England clergy under the leadership of Bishop Nixon who refused to co-operate with the board and attacked its schools as inefficient, backward and subversive of Anglican doctrine. Opposed equally to Roman Catholics and to other Protestants he refused to share facilities with either and urged the government to assist each denomination to establish its own schools. His demands, although opposed by Lieutenant-Governor Eardley-Wilmot, won sympathy in London after W.E. Gladstone, a staunch high churchman, became secretary of state for the colonies. Gladstone, whom Nixon prejudiced against Eardley-Wilmot, recalled the lieutenant-governor and ordered his successor Sir William Denison to reform the board system and extend financial assistance to church schools. By 1850 government and denominational schools operated side by side as in New South Wales but the state system had been seriously weakened by Anglican opposition. Only eight schools operated and the board had resigned in protest against Gladstone's change of policy. Of the remaining sixty-three schools, fifty-nine were Anglican which meant that the church monopolised the scene to an extent that was no longer true on the mainland. Although there had been some expansion the general standard of instruction was low and organisation was wanting.

In Western Australia by 1850 schools were also few and were attended by less than half of the children. Funds were scarce and struggling settlers needed their offspring to assist on their farms. Not until the 1840s was a serious attempt made to establish an educational system. In 1847 Acting Governor Frederick Irwin, a staunch Anglican, established an education committee whose first task was to draw up plans for elementary instruction. The outcome was a scheme which provided for religious instruction in a form that was acceptable to Protestants but not to Roman Catholics who already had their own schools. No solution could be found until 1849 when the new governor, Captain Charles Fitzgerald, gave a separate grant to the Roman Catholic church, thereby perpetuating a dual system similar to that which later became a feature of other parts of Australia.

South Australia followed a somewhat different course. The various proposals for colonisation had all stressed the need to instruct the young but the ideas of George Fife Angas for a non-sectarian educational system, supported by voluntary contribution, triumphed initially. His South Australian School Society had plans for a two-tiered system founded on religious principles to offer elementary instruction for the masses and proprietary school education for the 'better classes of colonists'. Only one school was established, however, and this was forced to close as a result of the depression of the 1840s. Meanwhile the churches had also established schools of which twenty-six, catering for 700 of the colony's 2100 children, existed by 1844. Standards, however, were low and funds scarce. In 1847 Governor Robe made the first grants of public money to aid denominational schools and established a board of education to supervise the distribution of funds. This action although accepted by the various churches split their followers many of whom believed deeply in the voluntary principle. In the event this principle triumphed. After the introduction of representative government in 1851 the state dissociated itself from religion and denominational education, making South Australia temporarily unique among the Australian colonies.

Relations with the Aboriginals

The growth of educational and other facilities brought little benefit to the Aboriginal Australians. Far from sharing the advantages of western civilisation their way of life was disrupted and their standing debased. Tribal rights to land were swept away under a legal system which recognised as landowners only the Crown and those to whom it sold or allotted grants. The Aboriginals were treated as mere intruders whose claims to the regions which they had occupied since time immemorial were invalid. A peaceable race, they lacked the weapons, the organisation and the determination to counter the white advance and, although individual tribes resisted, the outcome was always defeat. In each of the colonies the pattern was broadly the same. The frontier regions were the scene of incidents that were provoked by a variety of causes including the theft of livestock and other possessions, resistance to white invasion of sacred areas or mutual retaliation for acts of aggression. The outward movement of settlers, however, proved irresistible. Those who tried to stem it were killed. The rest either fled further into the interior, or remained within the settled districts eking out a miserable existence around the towns and on diminishing areas of vacant land.

Some settlers, particularly those with a Christian conscience, were concerned at this situation, but others proved indifferent. The convicts were notorious for taking out their own frustrations on the Aboriginals who responded in like measure. Yet free persons were often little better and the non-penal colonies witnessed incidents no less deplorable than those which occurred in eastern Australia.

Many viewed the Aboriginals as a subhuman race whose level was little higher than that of wild animals. Respect for the 'noble savage' whose ways had aroused the curiosity of first fleet officers such as David Collins was soon replaced by the conviction that the natives were capable of nothing more than idle, dissolute and drunken behaviour. Racial prejudice, as has recently been shown, was strongly marked among the colonists, regardless of whether they had arrived free or under sentence.

All this confronted governors both at home and in the colonies with a difficult problem. The British authorities had from the outset ordered their representatives 'to open an intercourse with the natives and to conciliate their goodwill, requiring all to live in amity and kindness with them'. Yet settlers had to be protected. Although the early governors of New South Wales and Van Diemen's Land encouraged missionary activities among the Aboriginals and established schools to educate their children, they were also obliged to organise punitive expeditions when farmers and graziers were attacked and robbed. The same was at first true in Western Australia where Governor Stirling actually led such an expedition that culminated in the Battle of Pinjarra of 28 March 1834 when forty members of the Murray River Tribe were killed. By this stage British policy was about to change. In 1836 pressure from evangelicals and humanitarians who had recently brought about the abolition of slavery in the British Empire resulted in the appointment of a House of Commons Select Committee to enquire into the plight of the native people in British settlements. Its report produced some positive action. Governors were reminded that the natives were British subjects and that as such they were entitled to equal treatment before the law. Protectorates were established in Western and South Australia and in the Port Phillip district. Their objectives were to reduce friction between black and white, to encourage the natives to abandon their wandering existence and to educate them so that they could be assimilated into colonial society.

These measures had to some extent been anticipated in Van Diemen's Land by Lieutenant-Governor Arthur. The restricted size of that island prevented the Aboriginals escaping from a white population which included large numbers of men who had been brutalised by the penal system. Earlier administrators had failed to control the situation and Arthur at first had no greater success. In October 1830 he organised his 'Black Line' of 2 000 troops and colonists who were to drive the natives into Tasman Peninsula. The campaign cost £30 000 and resulted in the capture of one woman and a boy. As a last resort Arthur encouraged George Augustus Robinson, a religiously inclined Hobart builder, to travel among the natives and by personal persuasion achieve what troops had failed to do. By 1835 some 200 Aboriginals had been moved to a reserve at Flinders Island where Robinson, until his appointment as protector at Port Phillip in 1839, unsuccessfully sought to educate and care for them.

On the mainland humanitarian governors made a sincere attempt to put the government's policy into effect. In New South Wales Gipps took the unprecedented step of allowing the hanging of seven white station-hands who in 1838 had been found guilty of the massacre of twenty-eight natives camped near Henry Dangar's Myall Creek Station on the Liverpool Plains. To bring order to outlying parts the governor established the border police in 1839 and he also tried unsuccessfully to secure the admissibility in court cases of evidence given by Aboriginals. In Western Australia Governor Hutt set up protectorates at Perth and York, encouraged settlers to employ and train natives, assisted the Wesleyans and Roman Catholics in their missionary work and established a penal station on Rottnest Island where Aboriginals who broke the law could learn new skills. In South Australia the chief work was done by Governor Grey. While resident magistrate in charge of King George's Sound between 1839 and 1840 he had published a book on Aboriginal dialects and a report recommending assimilation as the only means of preserving the natives. After becoming governor he appointed the explorer, Edward John Eyre, to take charge of the protectorate at Moorundie on the Murray River, established orphan schools near Adelaide and ensured that the law was administered justly.

These reforms were at best palliatives that could only marginally assist the Aboriginals. In Van Diemen's Land numbers continued to dwindle and by 1850 the Negritos were on the verge of extinction. On the mainland the position was less critical, but the spread of settlement made further inroads into tribal territory, and dislodged increasing numbers of Aboriginals. Governors necessarily found themselves devoting more attention to maintaining order than to civilising the natives who in any case showed little desire to accept western ways. Settlers for their part continued to assert their own interests and obstructed the work of protectors. By 1849 the Port Phillip protectorate, one of the most ambitious schemes, had failed. It had been given too little financial support, its officers were untrained and overworked and there was much opposition from local graziers and the press in Sydney and Melbourne. Much the same occurred in other colonies.

Race relations, therefore, created perennial problems whose solution was nowhere in sight by the middle of the nineteenth century. Yet in other spheres much had been accomplished. In the space of little more than seventy years white colonists had established themselves permanently in the habitable regions of Australia and had converted vast areas to productive use. Four of the five colonies had placed their economies on a sound footing and were laying the basis for sophisticated, complex social systems that catered for a divergence of interests. All this says much for the dynamic qualities of the colonists but it also reflected the willingness of the British government to create conditions in which expansion could take place. By 1850 there was every indication that progress would continue, but what could not have been foreseen was that gold was shortly to be discovered and that this was to give the ensuing decade a distinctive character. Political institutions, economic structures and social patterns were to undergo change. A new phase of development was about to open and some of the familiar landmarks were soon to disappear.

TABLE 10
Colonial Governors before 1850

New South Wales	Van Diemen's Land — Hobart	Van Diemen's Land — Port Dalrymple	Western Australia	South Australia
1788–92 Capt. A. Phillip, RN				
1792–4 Major F. Grose[1]				
1795 Capt. W. Paterson[2]				
1795–1800 Capt. J. Hunter, RN				
1800–6 Capt. P.G. King, RN	1803–4 Lt J. Bowen, RN	1804–8 Capt. W. Paterson		
1806–8 Capt. W. Bligh, RN	1804–10 Col D. Collins			
1808 Col G. Johnston[3]	1810 Lt E. Lord	1808–10 Capt. J. Brabyn		
1808–9 Maj. J. Foveaux[3]	1810–12 Capt. J. Murray	1810–12 Maj. G.A. Gordon		
1809 Lt Col W. Paterson[3]	1812–13 Maj. A. Geils	On 30 June 1812 Port Dalrymple was made a dependency of Hobart and the whole island came under a succession of Lieutenant-governors:		
1810–21 Maj. Gen. L. Macquarie	1813–16 Col T. Davey			
1821–5 Maj. Gen. Sir T. Brisbane				
1825 Lt Col W. Stewart[1]	1816–24 Col W. Sorrell			
1825–31 Lt Gen. R. Darling	1824–37 Lt Col G. Arthur		1828–32 Capt. J. Stirling, RN[6]	
1831 Col P. Lindesay[4]			1832–3 Capt. F. C. Irwin[7]	
1831–7 Maj. Gen. Sir R. Bourke			1833–4 Capt. R. Daniell[7]	
1837–8 Lt Col K. Snodgrass[4]	1837–43 Sir John Franklin		1834–8 Capt. J. Stirling, RN	1836–8 Sir John Hindmarsh[8]
1838–46 Maj. Sir George Gipps	1843–6 Sir John Eardley-Wilmot		1839–46 J. Hutt	1838–41 Lt Col G. Gawler
1846–55 Sir Charles FitzRoy	1846–7 C.J. La Trobe[5]		1846–7 Lt Col A. Clarke	1841–5 Capt. G. Grey
	1847–55 Sir Wm Denison		1848–55 Capt. C. Fitzgerald, RN	1845–8 Maj. F.H. Robe
				1848–54 Sir Henry Fox Young

[1] Lieutenant-governor (this position was abolished in 1827)
[2] Administrator
[3] These men ruled after the Rum Rebellion. None was appointed by the British government.
[4] Acting governor
[5] Acting Lieutenant-governor
[6] Stirling was at first a Lieutenant-governor
[7] Administered the colony while Stirling was in England
[8] Shared power with Commissioner J.H. Fisher

TABLE 11
Secretaries and Under-secretaries of State
for Colonial Affairs

Prime Minister	Home Secretary	Under-secretary	
1783–1801 William Pitt (Tory)	Lord Sydney (1783–9) Lord Grenville (1789–91) Henry Dundas (1791–4) Duke of Portland (1794–1801)	Evan Nepean (1782–95) William Huskisson (1795–1801)	
1801–4 H. Addington (Tory)	*Secretary of War* (with responsibility for colonies) Lord Hobart	John Sullivan	
1804–6 William Pitt (Tory)	*Secretary for War and Colonies* Lord Camden	Edward Cooke	
1806–7 Lord (Whig) Grenville	William Windham	Sir George Shee	
1807–9 Duke of (Tory) Portland	Viscount Castlereagh	Edward Cooke	
1809–12 Spencer (Tory) Perceval	Lord Liverpool	C. Jenkinson (1809–10) R. Peel (1810–12)	
1812–27 Lord (Tory) Liverpool	Lord Bathurst	*Political* H. Goulburn (1812–21) R.J. Wilmot Horton (from 1822)	*Permanent* R.W. Hay (from 1825)

Prime Minister	Secretary for War and Colonies	Under-secretary Political	Permanent
1827 Apr. George to Sept. Canning (Tory)	Viscount Goderich	R.J. Wilmot Horton	R.W. Hay
1827–8 Viscount (Tory) Goderich	William Huskisson	R.J. Wilmot Horton E.G. Stanley (3rd Under-sec.)	R.W. Hay
1828–30 Duke of (Tory) Wellington	William Huskisson (1828 Jan.–May) Sir George Murray	Lord Francis Leveson Gower (to May 1828) Horace Twiss (from May 1828)	R.W. Hay
1830–4 Earl Grey (Whig)	Viscount Goderich (Nov. 1830– Mar. 1833) E.G. Stanley (Mar. 1833– June 1834) Thomas Spring-Rice (June 1834)	Lord Howick (later 3rd Earl Grey; Nov. 1830 –Apr. 1833) J.G.S. Lefevre	R.W. Hay James Stephen (Asst Under-sec. Sept. 1834)
1834 Lord (Whig) Melbourne	Thomas Spring-Rice	J.G.S. Lefevre (to Aug. 1834) Sir Geo. Grey	R.W. Hay
1834 Duke of (Tory) Wellington	Duke of Wellington	—	R.W. Hay
1834–5 Sir Robert (Tory) Peel	Earl of Aberdeen	W.E. Gladstone (Jan.–Apr. 1835)	R.W. Hay
1835–41 Lord (Whig) Melbourne	Lord Glenelg (Apr. 1835– Feb. 1839) Lord Normanby (Feb.–Sept. 1839) Lord John Russell (from Sept. 1839)	Sir George Grey (Apr. 1835– Feb. 1839) H. Labouchere (Feb.–Aug. 1839) R. Vernon Smith (from Sept. 1839)	R.W. Hay (resigned Feb. 1836) James Stephen (from Feb. 1836)
1841–6 Sir Robert (Tory) Peel	Lord Stanley (1841–5) W.E. Gladstone (Dec. 1845– July 1846)	G.W. Hope (Sept. 1841– Dec. 1845) Lord Lyttleton (Dec. 1845)	James Stephen
1846–52 Lord John (Whig) Russell	Earl Grey	Ben. Hawes (July 1846– Oct. 1851)	James Stephen (resigned Oct. 1847) Herman Merivale

Sources: D.M. Young, *The Colonial Office in the Early 19th Century*, London, 1961.
H. King, 'Pulling Strings at the Colonial Office', *Journal of the Royal Australian Historical Society*, Vol. 61, Pt. 3, Sept. 1975.

Further Reading

General Histories

Australian Dictionary of Biography, Vols 1 and 2, 1788–1850, Melbourne, 1966, 1967.

Birch, A., and Macmillan, D.S., *The Sydney Scene 1788–1960*, Melbourne, 1962.

Blainey, G., *The Tyranny of Distance: How Distance Shaped Australia's History*, Melbourne, 1966.

Butlin, S.J., *Foundations of the Australian Monetary System 1788–1851*, Cambridge, 1953.

Clark, C.M.H., *Select Documents in Australian History: 1788–1850*, Sydney, 1950, reprinted 1965.

Clark, C.M.H., *A History of Australia*, Vol. 1, Melbourne, 1962; Vol. 2, Melbourne, 1968; Vol. 3, Melbourne, 1973.

Coghlan, T.A., *Labour and Industry in Australia . . .*, London, 4 Vols, 1918, reprinted Melbourne, 1969.

Crowley, F. (ed.), *A New History of Australia*, Melbourne, 1974.

Fitzpatrick, B., *British Imperialism and Australia 1783–1833: An Economic History of Australasia*, London, 1939, reprinted Sydney, 1971.

Fitzpatrick, B., *The British Empire in Australia: An Economic History; 1834–1939*, Melbourne, 1941, 1949.

Giblin, R.W., *The Early History of Tasmania*, Vol. 1, 1642–1804, Melbourne, 1928; Vol. 2, 1804–1828, Melbourne, 1939.

Grant, J., and Serle, G., *The Melbourne Scene 1803–1956*, Melbourne, 1957.

Greenwood, G. (ed.), *Australia, A Social and Political History*, Sydney, 1955.

Griffin, J. (ed.), *Essays in Economic History of Australia*, Brisbane, 1967.

Jeans, D.N., *An Historical Geography of New South Wales to 1901*, Sydney, 1972.

McLeod, A.L. (ed.), *The Pattern of Australian Culture*, New York, 1963.

193

Madgwick, R.B., *Immigration into Eastern Australia 1788–1851*, London, 1937; Sydney, 1969.

Melbourne, A.C.V., *Early Constitutional Development in Australia*, 2nd ed., Brisbane, 1963.

Pike, D., *Australia, the Quiet Continent*, Cambridge, 1970.

Roberts, S.H., *History of Australian Land Settlement 1788–1920*, Melbourne, 1924, reissued, 1968.

Shaw, A.G.L., *The Story of Australia*, London, 1962.

Ward, J.M., *Empire in the Antipodes: The British in Australasia: 1840–1860*, London, 1966.

Ward, R., *Australia*, Sydney, 1965.

Ward, R., *The Australian Legend*, Melbourne, 1958, 2nd edn, 1965.

Contemporary Accounts

Atkinson, J., *An Account of the State of Agriculture and Grazing in New South Wales*, London, 1826; facsimile edn, Sydney, 1975.

Backhouse, J., *A Narrative of a Visit to the Australian Colonies*, London, 1843.

Bradley, W., *A Voyage to New South Wales 1786–92*, facsimile edn, Sydney, 1969.

Collins, D., *An Account of the English Colony in New South Wales*, London, 1798, 1802, facsimile edn, Adelaide, 1971; new edn with notes and introduction by B.H. Fletcher, Sydney, 1975.

Cunningham, P., *Two Years in New South Wales*, London, 1827, reprinted Sydney, 1966.

Curr, E., *An Account of the Colony of Van Diemen's Land*, London, 1824.

Curr, E.M., *Recollections of Squatting in Victoria*, London, 1883.

Harris, A., *Settlers and Convicts*, London, 1852, reprinted 1953.

Holt, J., *Memoirs of Joseph Holt*, T.C. Croker (ed.), 2 vols, London, 1838.

Joyce A., *A Homestead History*, G.F. James (ed.), Melbourne, 1942.

Macarthur, J., *New South Wales, Its Present State and Future Prospects*, London, 1837.

Macarthur-Onslow S. (ed.), *Some Early Records of the Macarthurs of Camden*, Sydney, 1914, reprinted 1973.

Maconochie, A., *Thoughts on Convict Management*, Hobart, 1838.

Mudie, J., *The Felonry of New South Wales*, London, 1837.

Mundy, G.C., *Our Antipodes*, London, 1855.

Tench, W., *Sydney's First Four Years*, L.F. Fitzhardinge (ed.), Sydney, 1961.

Therry, R., *Reminiscences of Thirty Years' Residence in New South Wales and Victoria*, London, 1863, reprinted Sydney, 1974.

Wakefield, E.G., *A Letter from Sydney*, London, 1829; *England and America*, London, 1833; *A View of the Art of Colonisation*, London, 1849.

Wentworth, W.C., *A Statistical, Historical and Political Description of the Colony of New South Wales*, London, 1819.

West J., *The History of Tasmania*, 1852, reprinted, A.G.L. Shaw (ed.), Sydney, 1971.

Historical Records of New South Wales, Vols I–VII, Sydney, 1892–1901.
Historical Records of Australia, published by the Library Committee of the Commonwealth of Australia in four series, 1914–25.

1 Discovery

The Aboriginals and Prehistory

Abbie, A.A., *The Original Australians*, Wellington, 1969.

Berndt, R.M. and C.H., *The First Australians*, Sydney, 1952.

Berndt, R.M. and C.H., *The World of the First Australians*, Sydney, 1964.

Berndt, R.M. and C.H. (eds), *Aboriginal Man in Australia*, Sydney, 1965.

Blainey, G., *Triumph of the Nomads: A History of Ancient Australia*, Melbourne, 1975.

Elkin, A.P., *The Australian Aborigines*, Sydney, 4th edn, 1964.

Lindsay, H.A., 'The First Australians', *Science News*, Vol. 43, 1957.

Mulvaney, D.J., *The Pre-History of Australia*, London, 1969.

Discovery

Beaglehole, J.C., *The Exploration of the Pacific*, London, 1947.

Beaglehole, J.C. (ed.), *The Journals of Captain James Cook* (C.U.P. for the Hakluyt Society), 3 vols, 1955–67.

Dunmore, J., *French Explorers in the Pacific*, 2 Vols, Oxford, 1965, 1969.

Major, R.H. (ed.), *Early Voyages to Terra Australis Now called Australia*, Adelaide, 1963.

Sharp, A., *The Discovery of Australia*, Oxford, 1963.

Wood, G.A., *The Discovery of Australia*, new edn, revised by J.C. Beaglehole, Melbourne, 1969.

Fitzgerald, C.P., 'A Chinese Discovery of Australia?' in T. Inglis Moore (ed.), *Australia Writes*, Melbourne, 1953.

Kelly, C., 'Geographical Knowledge and Speculation in regard to Spanish Pacific Voyages', *Historical Studies*, Vol. 9, No. 33, November 1959.

Leggett, G.R., 'The Great South Land, Evidence of Early Visits by Explorers of European Nations', *Victorian Historical Magazine*, Vol. 29, No. I, February 1959.

Spate, O.H.K., 'Terra Australis—Cognita?', *Historical Studies*, No. 29, Vol. 8, 1957.

Ward, J.M., 'British Policy in the Exploration of the South Pacific', *Journal of the Royal Australian Historical Society (JRAHS)*, Vol. 33, Part I, 1947.

Worsley, P.M., 'Early Asian Contacts with Australia', *Past and Present*, No. 7, April 1955.

The Controversy over the Reasons for Settlement

Atkinson, A., 'Whigs and Tories and Botany Bay', *JRAHS*, Vol. 61, Part 5, March 1976.

Blainey, G., 'Botany Bay or Gotham City', *Australian Economic History Review*, Vol. 8, September 1968.

Bolton, G.C., 'The Hollow Conqueror: Flax and the Foundation of Australia',

Australian Economic History Review, Vol. 9, March 1969.

Bolton, G.C., 'Broken Reeds and Smoking Flax', *Australian Economic History Review*, Vol. 9, March 1969.

Clark, C.M.H., 'The Choice of Botany Bay', *Historical Studies*, Vol. 35, November 1960.

Dallas, K.M., 'First Settlements in Australia: Considered in relation to Sea-Power in World Politics', *Tasmanian Historical Research Association Proceedings*, Vol. 3, 1952.

Dallas, K.M., 'Commercial Influences on the First Settlements in Australia', *Tasmanian Historical Research Association Proceedings*, Vol. 16, September 1968.

Dallas, K.M., *Trading Posts or Penal Colonies: The Commercial Significance of Cook's New Holland Route to the Pacific*, Hobart, 1969.

Frost, A., 'The Choice of Botany Bay: The Scheme to Supply the East Indies with Naval Stores', *Australian Economic History Review*, Vol. XV, No. 1, March 1975.

Frost, A., 'The East India Company and the Choice of Botany Bay', *Historical Studies*, Vol. 16, No. 65. 1975.

Fry, H.T., 'Cathay and the way thither: the background to Botany Bay', *Historical Studies*, Vol. 56, April 1971.

Mackay, D., 'British Interest in the Southern Oceans, 1782–1794', *New Zealand Journal of History*, Vol. 3, No. 2, October 1969.

Mackay, D., 'Direction and Purpose in British Imperial Policy 1783–1801', *Historical Journal*, Vol. 17, No. 3, 1974.

Martin, G., 'The Alternatives to Botany Bay', *University of Newcastle Historical Journal*, Vol. 3, 1975.

Martin, G., 'A London Newspaper on the Founding of Botany Bay, August 1786–May 1787', *JRAHS*, Vol. 61, Part 2, June 1975.

Reese, T.R., 'The Origins of Colonial America and New South Wales: An Essay on British Imperial Policy in the Eighteenth Century', *Australian Journal of Politics and History*, Vol. 7, November 1961.

Remyi, J., 'Botany Bay Revisited', *Melbourne Historical Journal*, Vol. 10, 1971.

Roe, M., 'Australia's Place in the Swing to the East, 1788–1810', *Historical Studies*, Vol. 8, 1958.

Shaw, A.G.L., 'The Hollow Conqueror and the Tyranny of Distance', *Historical Studies*, Vol. 13, 1968.

Swan, R.A., *To Botany Bay*, Canberra, 1973.

2 Settlement

A detailed survey of the main works dealing with the period before 1821 is B.H. Fletcher, 'New South Wales: 1788–1821: An Appraisal of recent historical writing', *Teaching History*, Sydney, Vol. 7, No. 2, July 1973. For the years up to 1810 see D.M. MacCallum, 'Empty Historical Boxes of the Early Days: Laying Clio's Ghosts on the Shores of New Holland', *Arts* (Journal of the Sydney University Arts Association), No. 6, 1969.

The Convict System

Cobley, J., The Convicts 1788–1792, A Study of a one-in-twenty sample, Sydney, 1965: 'The Crimes of the First Fleeters', *JRAHS*, Vol. 52, Part 2, June 1966.

Clark, M., 'The Origins of the Convicts Transported to Eastern Australia, 1787–1852' *Historical Studies*, Vol. 7, No. 26, May 1956; Vol. 7, No. 27, November 1956.

Kiernan, T.J., *Transportation from Ireland to Sydney 1791–1816*, Canberra, 1954.

O'Brien, E., *The Foundation of Australia, 1786–1800, A Study in English Criminal Practice and Penal Colonisation in the Eighteenth Century*, Sydney, 1937, 2nd edn, 1950.

Robson, L.L., *The Convict Settlers of Australia: An Enquiry into the Origins and Character of the Convicts transported to New South Wales and Van Diemen's Land 1787–1852*, Melbourne, 1965, reprinted 1970.

Shaw, A.G.L., *Convicts and the Colonies, A Study of Penal Transportation from Great Britain and Ireland to Australia and other parts of the British Empire*, London, 1966.

Smith, A.E., *Colonists in Bondage, White Servitude and Convict Labor in America, 1607–1776*, California, 1947.

The Beginnings of Private Enterprise

Abbott, G.J., and Nairn, N.B. (eds), *Economic Growth of Australia, 1788–1821*, Melbourne, 1969.

Fletcher, B.H., 'Government Farming and Grazing in New South Wales, 1788–1810', *JRAHS*, Vol. 59, No. 3, September 1973.

Fletcher, B.H., *Landed Enterprise and Penal Society: A History of Farming and Grazing in N.S.W. 1788–1821*, Sydney, 1976.

Hainsworth, D.R., *Builders and Adventurers: The Traders and the Emergence of the Colony 1788–1821*, Melbourne, 1968.

Hainsworth, D.R., *The Sydney Traders, Simeon Lord and his Contemporaries 1788–1821*, Sydney, 1972.

McCarty, J.W., 'The Staple Approach in Australian Economic History', *Business Archives and History*, Vol. IV, No. I, February 1964.

Steven, M., *Merchant Campbell, 1769–1846, A Study of Colonial Trade*, Melbourne, 1965.

Steven, M., 'The Changing Pattern of Commerce in New South Wales 1810–1821', *Business Archives and History*, Vol. 3, August 1963.

Walsh, G.P., 'The Geography of Manufacturing in Sydney, 1788–1851', *Business Archives and History*, Vol. 3, No. I, 1963.

The Spread of Settlement

Perry, T.M., *Australia's First Frontier: The Spread of Settlement in New South Wales, 1788–1829*, Melbourne, 1963.

Robinson, K.W., 'Geographical Aspects of Land Settlement in the Sydney District, 1788–1821', *JRAHS*, Vol. 48, Part I, 1962.

The New South Wales Corps

Austin, M., 'Paint My Picture Truly', *JRAHS*, Vol. 51, No. 4, December 1965.

Parsons, T.G., 'The Social Composition of the Men of the New South Wales Corps', *JRAHS*, Vol. 50, No. 4, October 1964; also 'The New South Wales Corps–A rejoinder', *ibid.*, Vol. 52, No. 3, September 1966.

Shaw, A.G.L., 'Some Aspects of the History of New South Wales, 1788–1810', *JRAHS*, Vol. 57, Part 2, June 1971.

The Rum Rebellion

Evatt, H.V., *Rum Rebellion: a study of the overthrow of Governor Bligh by John Macarthur and the New South Wales Corps*, Sydney, 1938, reprinted London, 1968.

Fletcher, B.H., 'The Hawkesbury Settlers and the Rum Rebellion', *JRAHS*, Vol. 54, No. 3, September 1968.

McMinn, W.G., 'Explaining a Rebellion: An historiographical enquiry', *Teaching History*, Vol. 4, No. I, May 1970.

Shaw, A.G.L., 'Rum Corps and Rum Rebellion', *Melbourne Historical Journal*, Vol. 10, 1971.

Biographical Studies

Currey, C.H., *The Brothers Bent: Judge-Advocate Ellis Bent and Judge Jeffrey Hart Bent*, Sydney, 1968.

Dow, G., *Samuel Terry, The Botany Bay Rothschild*, Sydney, 1974.

Ellis, M.H., *Lachlan Macquarie: His Life, Adventures and Times*, Sydney, 1949, reprinted 1970.

Ellis, M.H., *Francis Greenway: His Life and Times*, Sydney, 1949, 2nd edn revised 1953.

Ellis, M.H., *John Macarthur*, Sydney, 1955, 2nd edn, 1967.

Mackaness, G., *Admiral Arthur Phillip*, Sydney, 1937.

Mackaness, G., *The Life of Vice-Admiral William Bligh*, Sydney, 2 vols, 1931, revised edn, Vol. I, 1951.

3 Convicts and Capitalists

The Bigge Enquiries

Eddy, J.J., *Britain and the Australian Colonies 1818–1831; The Technique of Government*, Oxford, 1969.

McLachlan, N., 'Bathurst at the Colonial Office, 1812–1827', *Historical Studies*, Vol. 13, No. 52, April 1969.

Manning, H.T., *British Colonial Government After the American Revolution, 1782–1820*, Yale University, 1935.

Parsons, T.G., 'Does the Bigge Report follow from the Evidence?' *Historical Studies*, Vol. 15, No. 58, April 1972.

Ritchie, J., *Punishment and Profit: The Reports of Commissioner John Bigge on the Colonies of New South Wales and Van Diemen's Land 1822–1823*, Melbourne, 1970.

Ritchie, J., *The Evidence to the Bigge Reports*, 2 vols, Melbourne, 1971.

A More Rigorous Penal System
(see the list for chapter 2, Settlement)

Growth of Private Enterprise

Hartwell, R.M., 'The Australian Depression of the Eighteen Twenties', *Historical Studies*, Vol. 3, No. II, November 1947.

Hartwell, R.M., 'Australia's First Trade Cycle', *JRAHS*, Vol. 42, Part 2, 1956.

Jeans, D.N., 'Crown Land Sales and the Accommodation of the Small Settler in New South Wales, 1825–1842', *Historical Studies*, Vol. 12, No. 46, April 1966.

Ker, J., 'The Wool Industry in New South Wales 1803–1830', *Business Archives and History*, Vol. I, No. 9, May 1956; Vol. 2, No. I.

Little, B., 'Sealing and Whaling in Australia before 1850', *Australian Economic History Review*, Vol. 9, No. 2, September 1969.

Political Issues in the 1820s

Currey, C.H., *Sir Francis Forbes: The First Chief Justice of the Supreme Court of New South Wales*, Sydney, 1968.

King, H., 'The Struggle for Freedom of the Press in New South Wales, 1825–1831', *Teaching History*, No. 13, May 1965.

McLachlan, N., 'Edward Eagar (1787–1866): A Colonial Spokesman in Sydney and London', *Historical Studies*, Vol. 10, No. 40, May 1963.

Melbourne, A.C.V., *William Charles Wentworth*, Brisbane, 1934, reprinted 1972.

Rose, L.N., 'The Administration of Governor Darling', *JRAHS*, Vol. 8, Part 2, 1922.

Shaw, A.G.L., *Ralph Darling*, Melbourne, 1971.

Shaw, A.G.L., *Heroes and Villains in History: Governors Darling and Bourke in New South Wales*, Sydney, 1966.

Shaw, A.G.L., 'Judge versus Viceroys' (Review Article), *Historical Studies*, Vol. 13, No. 52, April 1969.

Teale, R., *Thomas Brisbane*, Melbourne, 1971.

Tilley, A. G., 'Brave Men and Fit Governors: The Recall of Governor Darling from N.S.W.', *JRAHS*, Vol. 61, Part 4, December 1975.

Van Diemen's Land

Forsyth, W.D., *Governor Arthur's Convict System: Van Diemen's Land 1824–1836*, London, 1935, reprinted Sydney, 1970.

Hartwell, R.M., *The Economic Development of Van Diemen's Land 1820–1850*, Melbourne, 1954.

Levy, M.C.I., *Governor George Arthur, A Colonial Benevolent Despot*, Melbourne, 1953.

Shaw, A.G.L., 'A Colonial Ruler in Two Hemispheres: Sir George Arthur in Van Diemen's Land and Canada', *Tasmanian Historical Research Association. Papers and Proceedings*, Vol. 17, May 1970.

Shaw, A.G.L., 'Some Officials in Early Van Diemen's Land', *ibid.*, Vol. 14, No. 4, April 1967.

4 New Policies and Settlements

Wakefield and Imperial Policy

Bloomfield, P., *Edward Gibbon Wakefield: Builder of the British Commonwealth*, London, 1961.

Buckley, K., 'E.G. Wakefield and the Alienation of Crown Land in New South Wales to 1847', *Economic Record*, Vol. 33, 1957.

Burroughs, P., *Britain and Australia, 1831–1855: A Study in Imperial Relations and Crown Lands Administration*, Oxford, 1967.

Burroughs, P., 'Wakefield and the Ripon Regulations of 1831', *Historical Studies*, Vol. 11, No. 44, April 1965.

Mills, R.C., *The Colonisation of Australia, 1829–1842*, London, 1915, reprinted, Sydney, 1974.

Phillip, J., *A Great View of Things; Edward Gibbon Wakefield*, Melbourne, 1971.

Phillip, J., 'Wakefieldian Influence and New South Wales 1830–1832'. *Historical Studies*, Vol. 9, No. 34, May 1960.

Pike, D.H., 'Wakefield, Waste Land and Empire', *Tasmanian Historical Research Association. Papers and Proceedings*, Vol. 12, No. 3, March 1965.

Reform of the Penal System

Barry, J.V., *Alexander Maconochie of Norfolk Island: A Study of a Pioneer in Penal Reform*, Melbourne, 1958.

Barry, J.V., *The Life and Death of John Price: A Study of the Exercise of Naked Power*, Melbourne, 1964.

Bateson, C., *Patrick Logan, Tyrant of Brisbane Town*, Sydney, 1966.

Cranfield, L., 'Early Commandants of Moreton Bay', *Royal Historical Society of Queensland, Journal*, Vol. 7 No. 2, 1963–4.

McCulloch, S.C., 'Sir George Gipps and Captain Alexander Maconochie: The Attempted Penal Reforms at Norfolk Island, 1840–44', *Historical Studies*, Vol. 7, No. 28, May 1957.

Shaw, A.G.L., 'The Origins of the Probation System in Van Diemen's Land', *Historical Studies*, Vol. 6, No. 21, November 1953.

Shaw, A.G.L., 'Sir John Eardley-Wilmot and the Probation System in Tasmania', *Tasmanian Historical Research Association. Papers and Proceedings*, Vol. 11, No. I, September 1963.

Settlements on the Northern Coast

Allen, J., 'Port Essington: a successful limpet port?', *Historical Studies*, Vol. 15, No. 59, October 1972.

Bach, J., 'Melville Island and Raffles Bay, 1824–1829. An Unsuccessful Settlement', *JRAHS*, Vol. 44, 1958, Part 4.

Graham, G.S., *Great Britain in the Indian Ocean, a study of Maritime Enterprise, 1810–1850*, Oxford, 1967.

Howard, D., 'English Activities in the North Coast of Australia during the first half of the nineteenth century', *Proceedings of the Royal Geographical Society of Australasia*, Vol. 33, 1932.

Macknight, C.C. (ed.), *The Farthest Coast*, Melbourne, 1969.

Spillett, P.G., *Forsaken Settlement. An Illustrated History of the Settlement of Victoria, Port Essington, North Australia 1838–1849*, Melbourne, 1972.

Western Australia, South Australia and Port Phillip

Anderson, H., *Out of the Shadow, the career of John Pascoe Fawkner*, Melbourne, 1962.

Bassett, M., *The Hentys: An Australian Colonial Tapestry*, London, 1954.

Battye, J.S., *Western Australia: a history from its discovery to the inauguration of the Commonwealth*, London, 1924.

Crowley, F.K., *Australia's Western Third*, London, 1960.

Hasluck, A., *Portrait with Background, A Life of Georgiana Molloy*, Sydney, 1960.

Hasluck, A., *Thomas Peel of Swan River*, Melbourne, 1965.

Hodder, E., *The Founding of South Australia*, London, 1898.

Hodder, E., *George Fife Angas, father and founder of South Australia*, London, 1891.

Kiddle, M., 'Vandiemonian Colonists in Port Phillip 1834–1850', *Tasmanian Historical Research Association. Papers and Proceedings*, Vol. 3, No. 3, May 1954.

Mills, R.C., *The Colonisation of Australia 1829–1842*, reprinted Sydney, 1974.

Peel, L.J., *Rural Industry in Port Phillip Region, 1835–1880*, Melbourne, 1974.

Pike, D., *Paradise of Dissent: South Australia, 1829–1857*, 2nd edn, Melbourne, 1967.

Price, A.G., *The Foundation and Settlement of South Australia, 1829–1845*, Adelaide, 1924.

Stephens, R., 'Possessory Lien: The First European Settlement, King George's Sound, New Holland, 1826–31', *W.A. Historical Journal*, Part 1, 1962.

Turner, H.G., *A History of the Colony of Victoria*, Vol. 1, 1797–1854, London, 1904.

5 Economic Development

Squatting

Buckley, K., 'Gipps and the Graziers of New South Wales, 1841–1846', *Historical Studies*, Vol. 6, No. 24, May 1955; Vol. 7, No. 26, May 1956.

Burroughs, P., *Britain and Australia, 1831–1855: A Study in Imperial Relations and Crown Lands Administration*, Oxford, 1967.

Dyster, B., 'Support for the Squatters', *JRAHS*, Vol. 51, Part I, 1965.

Jay, L.J., 'Pioneer Settlement on the Darling Downs. A Scottish Contribution to Australian Colonisation', *Scottish Geographical Magazine*, Vol. 73, No. 1, April 1957.

Kiddle, M., *Men of Yesterday: A Social History of the Western District of Victoria, 1834–1890*, Melbourne, 1963.

Roberts, S.H., *The Squatting Age in Australia, 1835–1847*, Melbourne, 1935, reprinted Melbourne, 1964.

The Pastoral Age in New South Wales

Abbott, G.J., *The Pastoral Age, A Re-examination*, Hong Kong, 1971.
Birch, A., 'The Origins of the Colonial Sugar Refining Company 1841–1855', *Business Archives and History*, Vol. 5, No. 1, February 1965.
Dunsdorffs, E., *The Australian Wheat Growing Industry 1788–1948*, Melbourne, 1956.
Hoban, M., *Fifty-One Pieces of Wedding Cake: a biography of Caroline Chisholm*, Kilmore, 1973.
Kiddle, M., *Caroline Chisholm*, Melbourne, 1950.
(see also general economic histories listed earlier)

Economic Development in Van Diemen's Land

Butlin, S.J., 'The Van Diemen's Land Slump of the Forties: A Reply to Professor R.M. Hartwell', *Historical Studies*, Vol. 5, No. 17, November 1951.
Butlin, S.J., 'The Van Diemen's Land Slump of the Forties: A Further Comment', *ibid.*, Vol. 5, No. 18, May 1952.
Hartwell, R.M., 'The Van Diemen's Land Government and the Depression of the Eighteen Forties', *ibid.*, Vol. 4, No. 5, November 1950.
Hartwell, R.M., 'The Van Diemen's Land Slump of the Forties: A Rejoinder', *ibid.*, Vol. 5, Nos 17 and 18.

The Economic Problems of Western and South Australia

(see list for chapter 4, New Policies and Settlements)
Charlton, R., *The History of Kapunda*, Melbourne, 1971.
Oldham, W., *The Land Policy of South Australia from 1830 to 1842*, Adelaide, 1917.
Uren, M.J.L., *Land Looking West, the Story of Governor James Stirling in Western Australia*, London, 1948.

6 Government and Politics

New South Wales

Cross, A., *Charles Joseph La Trobe, Superintendent of the Port Phillip District 1839–51, Lieutenant-Governor of Victoria 1851–4*, Melbourne, 1956.
Dyster, B., 'The Fate of Colonial Conservatism on the Eve of Goldrush', *JRAHS*, Vol. 54, No. 4, December 1968.
Forrest, J., 'Political Divisions in the New South Wales Legislative Council, 1847–1853', *JRAHS*, Vol. 50, No. 6, December 1964.
Hume, L.J., 'Working Class Movements in Sydney before the Gold Rushes', *Historical Studies*, No. 35, November 1960.
Irving, T.H., 'Some Aspects of the Study of Radical Politics in New South Wales before 1856', *Labour History*, Vol. 5, November 1963.
King, H., *Richard Bourke*, Melbourne, 1971.

Knight, R., *Illiberal Liberal: Robert Lowe in New South Wales: 1842–1850*, Melbourne, 1966.

McCulloch, S.C., 'Unguarded Comments on the Administration of New South Wales, 1839–1846: The Gipps-La Trobe Private Correspondence', *Historical Studies*, Vol. 9, No. 33, November 1959.

McCulloch, S.C., *George Gipps*, Melbourne, 1966.

Molony, J.N., *An Architect of Freedom: John Hubert Plunkett in New South Wales 1832–1869*, Canberra, 1973.

Roe, M., *Quest for Authority in Eastern Australia, 1835–1851*, Melbourne, 1965.

Ward, J.M., *Earl Grey and the Australian Colonies, 1846–1857; A Study of Self-Government and Self-Interest*, Melbourne, 1958.

Van Diemen's Land

Fitzpatrick, K.E., *Sir John Franklin in Tasmania, 1837–1843*, Melbourne, 1949.

Townsley, W.A., *The Struggle for Self Government in Tasmania, 1842–1856*, Hobart, 1951.

Western and South Australia

(see earlier lists for general works)

Borrow, T.C., *Lieutenant-Colonel George Gawler*, Adelaide, 1955.

Morphett, G.C., *Sir James Hurtle Fisher*, Adelaide, 1955.

Pitt, G.H., *The Press in South Australia 1836–1850*, Adelaide, 1946.

7 Society

Social Groups

Coughlan, N., 'The Coming of the Irish to Victoria', *Historical Studies*, Vol. 12, No. 45, October 1965.

Connell, R.W., 'The Convict Rebellion of 1804', *Melbourne Historical Journal*, Vol. 5, 1965.

Gollan, R., 'Nationalism and Politics in Australia Before 1855', *Australian Journal of Politics and History*, Vol. I, No. I, November 1955.

Ingham, S.M., 'A Footnote to Transportation to New South Wales: James Ingham, 1824–1848', *Historical Studies*, Vol. 12, No. 48, April 1967.

Kiernan, T.J., *The Irish Exiles in Australia*, Dublin, 1954.

Macmillan, D.S., *Scotland and Australia 1788–1850: Emigration, Commerce and Investment*, Oxford, 1967.

Macnab, K., and Ward, R., 'The Nature and Nurture of the First Generation of Native-born Australians', *Historical Studies*, Vol. 10, No. 33, November 1962.

Price, C.A., 'German Settlers in South Australia, 1838–1900', *Historical Studies*, Vol. 7, No. 28, May 1957.

Price, C.A., *German Settlers in South Australia*, Melbourne, 1945.

Rimmer, G., 'The Convict Settlers of Australia' (Review Article), *Tasmanian Historical Research Association. Journal and Proceedings*, Vol. 13, No. 3, May 1966.

Triebel, L.A., 'The Early South Australian German Settlers', *Tasmanian Historical Research Assoc. Journal and Proc.*, Vol. 8, No. 3, May 1960.
Wood, G.A., 'Convicts', *JRAHS*, Vol. 8 Part 4, 1922.
Ward, R., 'Social Roots of Australian Nationalism', *Australian Journal of Politics and History*, Vol. I, No. 2, May 1956.

Social Conditions

Inglis, K.S., *The Australian Colonists: An Exploration of Social History 1788–1870*, Clayton, 1974.
Nadel, G., *Australia's Colonial Culture: Ideas, Men and Institutions in Mid-Nineteenth Century Eastern Australia*, Sydney, 1957.
Ward, R., and Robertson, J., *Such was Life: Select Documents in Australian Social History 1788–1850*, Sydney, 1969.

Literature and Art

Dutton, G. (ed.), *The Literature of Australia*, Melbourne, 1964.
Green, H.M., *A History of Australian Literature*, 2 vols, Sydney, 1961.
Miller, E. Morris, *Australian Literature from its Beginnings to 1935*, 2 vols, Melbourne, 1940.
Serle, G., *From Deserts the Prophets Come: The Creative Spirit in Australia, 1788–1972*, Melbourne, 1973.
Smith, B., *European Vision and the South Pacific 1768–1850*, Oxford, 1960, 1969.
Smith, B., *Australian Painting, 1788–1970*, Melbourne, 1971.
Smith, B.J., 'Early Western Australian Literature, a Guide to Colonial Life', *University Studies*, Vol. 4, No. 1, 1961–2.
Wilkes, G.A., and Reid, J.C., *The Literatures of the British Commonwealth. Australia and New Zealand*, Pennsylvania, 1970.

Religion

Barrett, J., *That Better Country: the religious aspect of life in eastern Australia, 1835–1850*, Melbourne, 1966.
Bollen, J.D., 'A Time of Small Things—The Methodist Mission in New South Wales 1815–1836', *Journal of Religious History*, Vol. 7, No. 3, June 1973.
Border, R., *Church and State in Australia, 1788–1872: A Constitutional Study of the Church of England in Australia*, London, 1962.
Campbell, K.R., 'Presbyterian Conflicts in New South Wales 1837–1865', *Journal of Religious History*, Vol. 5, No. 3, June 1969.
Molony, J.N., *The Roman Mould of the Australian Catholic Church*, Melbourne, 1969.
O'Farrell, P.J., *The Catholic Church in Australia: 1788–1967*, Melbourne, 1968.
Suttor, T.L., *Hierarchy and Democracy in Australia, 1788–1870: The Formation of Australian Catholicism*, Melbourne, 1965.
Waldersee, J., *Catholic Society in New South Wales 1788–1860*, Sydney, 1974.

Education

Austin, A.G., *Australian Education 1788–1900; Church, State and Public Education in Colonial Australia*, Melbourne, 1961.

Barcan, A., *A Short History of Education in New South Wales*, Sydney, 1965.

Cleverley, J., *The First Generation: school and society in early Australia*, Sydney, 1971.

Fogarty, R., *Catholic Education in Australia 1806–1950*, Melbourne, 2 vols, 1959.

Goodin, V.W.W., 'Public Education in New South Wales before 1848'. *JRAHS*, Vol. 36, 1950, Parts 1–4.

Gregory, J.S., *Church and State, Changing Government Policies towards Religion in Australia; with particular reference to Victoria since Separation*, Melbourne, 1973.

Grose, K., '1847: The Educational Compromise of the Lord Bishop of Australia', *Journal of Religious History*, Vol. 1, No. 2, December 1961.

Pike, D., 'Founding a Utopia', in E.L. French (ed.), *Melbourne Studies in Education*, Melbourne, 1959.

Saunders, G.E., 'The State and Education in South Australia, 1836–1875', in *Melbourne Studies in Education*, E.L. French (ed.), Melbourne, 1966.

Turney, C. (ed.), *Pioneers of Australian Education*, 2 vols, Sydney, 1969, 1972.

Relations with the Aboriginals

Corris P., *Aborigines and Europeans in Western Victoria*, Canberra, 1963.

Foxcroft, E.J.B., 'The New South Wales Aborigines' Protectorate, Port Phillip District, 1838–1850', *Historical Studies*, Vol. 1, No. 2, October 1940; Vol. 1, No. 3, April 1941.

Hasluck, P., *Black Australians*, Melbourne, 1942.

Hassell, K., *The Relations Between the Settlers and Aborigines in South Australia, 1836–1860*, Adelaide, 1966.

Plomley, N.J.B. (ed.), *Friendly Mission: The Tasmanian Journals and Papers of George Augustus Robinson 1829–1834*, Hobart, 1966.

Reece, R.M.W., *Aborigines and Colonial Society in New South Wales Before 1850*, Sydney, 1974.

Reynolds, H. (ed.), *Aborigines and Settlers, The Australian Experience 1788–1939*, Melbourne, 1972.

Reynolds, H., 'Racial Thought in Early Colonial Australia', *Australian Journal of Politics and History*, Vol. 20, No. 1, April 1974.

Rowley, C.D., *The Destruction of Aboriginal Society*, Sydney, 1970.

Travers, R., *The Tasmanians: the Story of a Doomed Race*, Melbourne, 1968.

Turnbull, C., *Black War. The Extermination of the Tasmanian Aborigines*, Melbourne, 1968.

Woolmington, J. (ed.), *Aborigines in Colonial Society 1788–1850, From 'Noble Savage' to 'Rural Pest'*, Melbourne, 1973.

Index

63, 67, 69, 74, 80; relations with
Macquarie, 56–7
Blainey, Professor G., 19–20, 21–2
Bland, Dr William, 148
Blaxland, Gregory and John, 33,
35, 39, 79
Bligh, Captain William, 189;
appointment of, 27–8; overthrow
of, 42–3; views of, 39, 48
Blue Mountains, crossing of, 39
Bolton, Professor G.C., 20
Bourke, Sir Richard, 189;
background of, 137–9; attitude
to settlement of Port Phillip,
106–7; establishment of bounty
system, 88; penal policy, 89;
policy towards education, 182–3;
policy towards squatting, 106,
110, 112; political views, 138;
quoted, 79; religious policy, 176
Bowen, Lieutenant John, 23–4, 189
Bremer, Captain James, 94, 95
Brisbane, Sir Thomas, 189;
achievements of, 75; appointment
of, 75; criticism of, 79; land
policy, 63, 67, 71, 110; recall of,
75–6; sympathy for emancipists,
81; treatment of convicts, 61–3
Britain, conditions in, 18–19, 25,
58–60, 65–66, 84–5; exploration
of Pacific, 7–8, 10–11, 16–17;
policy towards Australian
colonies, 65–6
Brosses, Charles de, 17
Broughton, William Grant, 139,
177, 181–3
bush workers, 167–8
Butlin, Professor S.J., 121

Campbell, Robert, 37, 165
Castle Hill uprising, 162–3
cattle industry, in New South
Wales, 30, 34–5, 44, 70, 120;
in South Australia, 131; in Van
Diemen's Land, 50, 52, 126; in
Western Australia, 128
Charter of Justice, 73

Childs, Lieutenant Joseph, 91
Chinese contacts with Australia,
3–4
Chisholm, Caroline, 122, 169
Church of England, 174–5, 176–7,
180, 182–4
Cook, Captain James, 14, 16–17, 22
Collins, Captain David, 23, 29, 48,
104, 105, 171, 186, 189
convicts, assignment of, 63;
character of, 161–3, 175; number
of, 25, 26, 60, 88, 125, 165 (*see
also* penal system, transportation,
emancipists)
Cox, Lieutenant William, 39
Cumberland Plain, 71, 110
Cunningham, Allan, 77
Curr, Edward, 67–8, 69
currency lads, 163–4, 166

Dallas, K.M., 19, 21–2
Dampier, William, 16
Darling, Lieutenant-General Ralph,
189; achievements, 77;
administrative reforms, 76–7;
attacks on press, 81–2;
background of, 76; encourages
exploration, 77, 99; land policy,
67, 71, 97–8, 110; political
attitude, 138; recall of, 82;
Sudds-Thompson case, 81
Darling Downs, discovery and
settlement, 108–9
Davey, Lieutenant-Governor
Thomas, 48–9, 189
Davidson, Walter, 36, 108
Denison, Sir William, 93, 152,
155, 184, 189
depression, of 1812–14, 45; of
1820s, 70; of 1840s, 120–2, 185
Dumaresq, Henry, 76
Dutch, exploration, 8, 10–15, 17;
rivalry with Britain, 11, 20, 94

Eardley-Wilmot, Sir John, 93,
153–5, 184, 189
Earl, George Windsor, 94